PSYCHO STEVE

PSYCHO STEVE

'I SWAM THE SOLENT TO FREEDOM.
NO JAIL CAN HOLD ME.'

STEVE MOYLE
WITH
STEPHEN RICHARDS

JB
JOHN BLAKE

Published by John Blake Publishing Ltd,
3 Bramber Court, 2 Bramber Road,
London W14 9PB, England

www.blake.co.uk

First published in hardback in 2006

ISBN 1 84454 251 3

British Library Cataloguing-in-Publication Data:

A catalogue record for this book is available from the British Library.

Design by www.envydesign.co.uk

Printed in Great Britain by Creative Print & Design, Ebbw Vale

1 3 5 7 9 10 8 6 4 2

Papers used by John Blake Publishing are natural, recyclable products made from wood grown in sustainable forests. The manufacturing processes conform to the environmental regulations of the country of origin.

All photographs from the author's collection.

Some names and locations have been changed for legal reasons.

For the devil, God almighty and the deep blue sea: a decent psychopath these days is hard to find.

CONTENTS

INTRODUCTION

Daring escapes don't come any more audacious than that of self-confessed and clinically diagnosed psychopath Stephen Moyle from a high-security prison on Hell Island ... the Isle of Wight.

What to some is a pleasant hovercraft or ferry journey across the Solent was, for Stephen, a mad and dangerous midnight swim across one of the most hazardous and unpredictable stretches of sea in England; the current and tides are so atrocious that nothing like this has ever been attempted before or since.

After doing the just about impossible, the escapee was caught in a blaze of publicity and returned to prison.

This extraordinary tale of madness, leading up to Stephen being sectioned off to the lunatic asylum at Broadmoor, also reveals Stephen's fight to win his freedom, which saw his legal team mount a successful challenge against the 'criminally insane' label that was keeping him there. Moyle's legal team argued that he was either a criminal or insane – he could not be both.

This successful challenge of the law resulted in Stephen being freed from Broadmoor. Currently, he is still a free man although, when it comes to standing his ground, he is still highly dangerous.

Violence was second nature to the psychopathic and ultraviolent Stephen Moyle, who was already a seasoned street fighter, after having half his face torn off in a street fight with three other men.

This book reveals how Stephen, working in West Sussex, soon becomes involved with the wide-boys and gangsters. A £1million deal that Moyle is involved in is threatened and starts to go pear shaped when London sub-contractors try to muscle in with a heavy mob.

Soon, sawn-offs are blasted in public and the unmistakable rage of Stephen sees him on a journey of madness that takes him to the very brink of murder when he seeks vengeance for his girlfriend's stress-induced miscarriage ... his only aim is to maim and murder those responsible.

Moyle had been in and out of trouble since he was 14, and had already served a three and a half-year prison sentence for firearms offences, so he knew the ropes of police interrogation. His time on bail was used to find and assault each of the four henchmen that attacked him. He also needed time to try and beat the charge or, at worst, receive a lesser prison sentence, by intimidating the witnesses.

Soon, Moyle revenges himself against one of the subby's thugs when he spots him in the street ... one down, three to go. Searching for the next two thugs, Moyle decides he will either blow their heads off, or shoot them in the legs.

Family flashbacks to his younger days and gang fights build up the bigger picture when Moyle takes his girlfriend and their daughter to visit family 'up north' to escape the problems 'down south'. More drug-fuelled violence soon follows.

Moyle makes the decision to abscond to Toronto, Canada, knowing that he could walk across the border into the USA from there, then make his way down to Florida and disappear.

The story picks up in Canada, where Moyle starts making arrangements to cross the border, but sexual conquests are on his mind and the narrative action hots up. Soon, the immigration services are on his back and he develops a wacky plan to swim across the Niagara River!

Ending up in Hamilton, Moyle becomes involved in a fight with some bikers and is arrested. He ends up in Toronto Detention Centre and is deported back to an English prison.

After being sentenced to a lengthy spell of imprisonment for gun charges, Moyle starts to lose his mind and has numerous violent encounters with the MUFTI squad. In some fine narrative, Moyle describes how he hears the voices of God and the devil. He is eventually sectioned off to Broadmoor Special Hospital. In Stephen's own words, herein he tells his unmatched story of pure psychopathic madness.

1
QUE SERA SERA

The Railway pub was situated at the corner of the shopping boulevard that served the council estates. They were notorious hives of trouble: a definite knocking shop for all that lived in the area. For those who risked association with the numerous single mothers housed in that part of town, it was an outstanding, natural location for love and free sex.

The estates were in a new town in West Sussex, and the Railway's estate was the newest in the township, its houses being less than 20 years old. Building work, for those that wanted it, was always available and paid good wages. Many of the locals had been there from the beginning, and their various characters had developed and matured along with the towns.

The estate, though, was by no means all sin, sex and punch-ups – it had its 'stockbroker belt' of plush roads and cul-de-sacs on the edge of the estate, lived in by those that were quite well-to-do: small-time businessmen who had made the price of an eighty-grand mortgage and who could handle the hire purchase on a middle-of-the-range car. They were proud to live in that part of the country.

And on the weekend, wallowing in the underbelly of the local mafia, they would enjoy an early evening pint in the Railway pub. This association with the criminal world seemed to give them a much-needed ego boost.

The thieves and villains had adopted the pub as their den of iniquity and given it, over the years, a reputation as a 'rough house'. Walking into the place, you could be forgiven for thinking you had just walked into the local rogues' gallery. Mind, not all the locals drank there; many shied away from its troubled reputation and preferred to use more sedate pubs, either in the main town or one of the more upmarket estates. The locals – grafters, villains, thieves and the young single mothers, who outnumbered the young single men by a ratio of three to one – thrived in and around the pub and shopping boulevard.

The pub was a regular meeting ground for those seeking salacious gossip, the place awash with talk of the punters' latest conquests and who was shagging who, or who was next to break up. The manner in which these subjects were discussed was one of intense jealousy, craziness and bitchiness from the women, which overflowed into outright confrontation by both sexes. Women who had lost their latest romance to a close friend or neighbour commonly used broken bottles and glasses to bolster their fractured urban lives.

At times, the fights escalated to the supporters of either side and the violence would spill out onto the boulevard where Stanley knives and hatches were used. The police would throw the injured and battered into hastily arriving police vans. These conflicts would be the talking point of the town for weeks on end, particularly around the estate.

Suffice to say, the picture of the dodgy dealings in the pub should be firmly embedded in your mind's eye: where to buy or sell; who was selling the best and cheapest dope, heroin or speed that week. There was always someone who could fix you up, or knew someone who could.

As sad testimony to what was going on, it was not unusual to see the huge glass windows in and around the pub premises broken and boarded up. Further support to this was the way kids in their early teens hung around the opposite end of the boulevard and casually sauntered past the pub after closing time. The gang, sensing when trouble had been about, would jeer and provoke the landlord as he swept up the remnants of decaying life. Once the meleé was over, the gang would slink off home to sleep off the six or seven cans of lager they'd each guzzled on the seats at the end of the boulevard.

Brian Leigham was landlord of the Railway for years. He took over the reins of this Wild West pub from a decent and law-abiding old Scottish bloke whose resolve to run such a pub just seemed to be whittled down by the trouble.

Brian had had a reasonably quiet life for a long time. No major disasters, and damages were nil. The punch-ups were no longer a common occurrence and only went off when Brian returned to his hometown for a holiday, and relief management stood in. Most of the troublemakers had been sorted out and barred.

Now the locals – the old locals – were up in arms about losing their old stomping ground and wanted to oust Brian ... they tried all sorts, but all were rejected: a petition and complaints to remove him as landlord headlined the local newspapers.

Looking as sharp as Sweeney Todd's razor, Brian struck a formidable figure as he donned his smart suit and tie. He was the ideal man for the job as landlord, and didn't the brewery know it ... complaints from the police were down, there were less damages and profits were up. No, the previous pub clientele would not regain their upper hand with this man in the driving seat.

The mandatory death threats were sent to Brian by those not brave enough to step out from behind their veil of secrecy, and the tried and trusted method of spraying graffiti on the premises extolled the virtues of why the landlord was a 'piece of shit'. This sort of behaviour didn't even make him blink from his position of power; after all, the brewery and the local police were firmly on his side.

Although Brian had ten years' experience of pub management with his wife, he fully understood that it would only be a matter of time before he required some help to sort out the troublemakers and set his scams into action.

In order to establish where I come into this little scenario, we need to go back a bit. Only weeks after Brian came into town, I entered the bar at 6.10pm. There was only one customer at the bar, and Brian was chatting to him. Back then I had muscles on my muscles, I was tattooed and tanned, wore the tightest of jeans to accentuate my snakelike waist, and the whitest of tight vests to accentuate my muscle-packed torso. To top it all off, I had the nicest piece of eye candy on my arm in the form of a stunning, long-legged, mini-skirted blonde.

Three years after that, on the evening of 28 April 1987, something would happen that would leave its mark of pain, love and grief on the pub and most of the people on the estate.

My mood was one of lingering, deep thoughtfulness that flickered on the edge of despair. I hated thinking so fucking hard and despised the problems that made me feel as I did. I was 26 years old and throughout my life I had always jumped in at the deep end of everything, and the result was always to lose a pound of flesh – from my soul.

I wondered where the present disasters would lead to, but I knew the problems were not going to go away. I recall staring across the table at my mate Eddie, and listening to him mouth non-stop verbal diarrhoea that only ceased between him taking gulps of lager or a puff on his cigarette. Obviously Eddie, even in his own drunken world, knew I was not on form to his incoherent babbling. He was completely engrossed in the surrounding atmosphere and the conversation he was having with Chris.

Chris Hawley, who lived in the area, quietly let Eddie's drunken babble go in one ear and out the other. He wasn't interested other than to make prompting one-liners, which Eddie would digest in his immature wisdom, and, for a second or two, he would shut up and think about Chris's comments. Then Eddie, to his amazement, would come out with some idea that would be delivered in his drunken, garbled Geordie dialect, to which Chris would respond to with a mild smirk.

By nature, Chris was suspicious and sly, and believed that he had to be hard with a violent streak. And in his case, he acquired this with only six or seven pints of lager or a snort of speed.

One or the other of these would put Chris in a fighting mood, and he made sure everyone around him was aware of this by mouthing off. He didn't enjoy getting pissed because he chanced being arrested for public-order offences – a constant result of not being able to handle his drink. He didn't really like socialising and preferred to spend his time indoors with one of the single mothers he had recently pulled, whom at the age of thirty-two was eight years his senior and just wanted to screw.

In particular, he didn't like the some of the new arrivals he'd befriended either. He envied the way that they'd moved in on the estate and commandeered the Railway as their second home. He was always jealous at the way they seemed to get the best jobs on the building sites, the way they stuck together and always had money in their pockets.

As the jukebox played a Bruce Springsteen tune, I noticed that Chris kept one eye on me. He decided not to go home but to stay and wind up the blond man later in the evening. He swigged his pint, seeming to relish the alcoholic buzz that fuelled his arrogance. At the thought of my devastating circumstances, Chris allowed himself a little wry smile of pleasure.

I tried to forget my depression; I drank deeply from my pint of Hölsten lager and fought my simmering mood, searching for the level in my mentality that didn't care about the gang of thugs that had attacked and smashed up my family home. Inside, I cringed at the thought of what the outcome may have been if they had managed to get my fiancee and four-year-old daughter.

I badly wanted the revenge I was due, but I pondered on the probability of arrest and conviction for a very long time. Regardless of the cajoling and prompting from my friends, I knew I had to bide my time.

I looked at Eddie and Chris, and felt better about Eddie, dealing with the feeling that he would do anything to avoid an outbreak of violence that would upset his quiet life in the pub.

As I absorbed these bitter inner feelings, I had a fleeting flashback and remembered Eddie as a younger man back up north. Then he'd been a laugh, fun to be with, but now the sight of him made me sick to the stomach. Somehow he had lost his appeal. I took a long, slow breath. Thankfully the last five pints had relaxed me enough to forget about it.

Then I glanced at Chris and, as Eurythmics' 'Sweet Dreams (Are Made of This)' rained from the jukebox, I became acutely aware of what had been occurring. Lately, Chris had been drinking in places where any of the crowd or I could easily lay eyes on him. I mean, usually he would disappear for three or four months at a time unless on occasion he needed money, then there would be a knock on my door and he would ask for a day's work labouring with the work gang, which he got ... cash in hand. These were the only times anyone laid eyes on Chris.

This is when it dawned on me like being hit on the head with a brick. He only came to watch me sweat at not having retaliated against the thugs that had smashed up my home and threatened to kill my family.

My chaotic predicament was even more distasteful to me as I dealt with the thought of the cowards who had hid behind my reputation as a fighter and a hard man, and that Chris was only in my company to gloat. Only a rat could do that. The thoughts made me imagine, for the hundredth time since the attack, the way in which I so wanted to maim, torture and kill the men involved.

I quickly regained my composure as visions of me being arrested made my stomach churn. I sat up straight, swigged my lager and lit a cigarette, which I inhaled unusually deeply. It all helped to repress my feelings of insanity.

My sullen gaze shifted to the pool game and my two friends, Harry and Steve. I noticed Steve's style. The confidence and arrogance with which he watched Harry make his shot, as if he knew Harry would miss and that he was just toying with his opponent until he felt like potting the black.

Steve was tall and broad, with the beginnings of a beer belly. His face was slightly chubby. He thought he had seen and done it all. Steve and his brother Arthur were in the building trade.

He had followed his brother Arthur from the north to London. One morning he got up and simply got pissed off looking at his wife Tina and the dismal streets around them. He told her he was going to the corner shop for the proverbial pint of milk and a paper. Needless to say – but I will – that was the last anyone heard of him in there. Six months later Steve wrote to tell Tina he was living with Arthur and his wife in London.

In somewhat extenuating circumstances, she caught up with her estranged husband. Steve had caught Hepatitis B from sharing a needle with a known addict, or so he claimed to Tina. She, of course, believed her husband's story, but Arthur, knowing his brother to be a lowlife lying rat, suspected it could have come from any one of a dozen women. Steve wasn't sure from whom he had caught the disease, but he wasn't about to admit to Tina about his affairs. He really thought he wasn't lying to her by putting the disease down to a dirty needle. He had tried mainlining heroin a couple of times and on his numerous days off work he was on a constant drinking bender.

When Steve became bed-ridden with the disease he asked his

brother Arthur to contact Tina. He felt so ill that he thought he was about to die. Tina arrived at Arthur's house with suitcases in hand and Steve let forth with his usual routine of lies about how he left without telling as he was going to get steady work and build a new life for them both in London. Of course he was going to have a new house to start their new life. She was completely in his power, näive to the point of being dumb. She believed Steve and threw herself into nursing him back to health.

They lived in London until 1980, when Arthur and his family had to move due to a fraud case. Arthur received a suspended sentence and Steve had managed, as he so often did, to fade into the background and no charges were brought against him.

However, the brothers had upset some of the boys who had been operatives of a sub-contracting company. They were the type of people who broke bones as a part-time job. So Arthur moved out of London, and Steve and Tina soon followed.

Steve had relied on his brother all of his life and, as he had grown, the relationship hadn't changed. He still abused and cashed in on his brother's superior knowledge, and he preyed on his weaknesses when they were drunk and in good-time moods. Steve would have been a master manipulator if he could get away with it, but he preferred using his tactics on women, treating his wife like shit then being the prefect boyfriend to his latest conquest. He had a name for his extramarital activities, which involved young and old alike; in fact, anyone who would open their legs – it was called 'slut fucking'.

The affairs he preferred were the most dangerous, next-door neighbour or Tina's friends around the area. He loved it when one of his sluts called on Tina. She would leave the room to make the coffee and he would quickly slip his hand down his slut's knickers and give her a quick fingering, then sit back and continue the conversation. Tina was never any the wiser when she came in with the coffee. Whether his adulterous ways were down to his misplaced mentality or due to the shortfall of eligible males on the estate, only Steve would know.

Where violence was concerned, Steve was last in line fighting his way out of an argument. For him, fucking the other bloke's wife then boasting about it the next day down the pub was the way. That's why he was scared shitless of me, a guy whom Steve had seen knock out blokes weighing six stone more than himself, and start fighting with three or four blokes at once and come out on top.

He made it a point to give me the respect I was due, and made sure that when talk at work or in the pub turned to taking the piss out of each other, I was not misinterpreting Steve's meaning, and that it was only a laugh he was having.

He'd have one over on anyone if he could, but he was very careful where money-men and violent men were concerned, and I came into this category. Until lately, I had being a worthwhile mate as well as a good worker. Without wanting to sound too pompous, my reputation had rubbed off on Steve and the other mates.

Of course, Steve took advantage of this; he knew he would be given that extra respect as a mate of mine. When drinking on an estate across town where the locals were fussy concerning who drank in their pubs and enjoyed the company of their women, Steve would stand out with loud laughter and Geordie wit, attracting the attention of the women and sending the message, hard, to the southern blokes in the pub that he was my mate.

However, with the attack and its disastrous consequences, things had rapidly gone downhill. Steve was playing the part of a caring mate and gave assurance to my suspicious questioning that he'd be the first to sort out any reprisals. And yet, at the same time he was frightened of taking on the gang that I was at war with.

Steve thought he could play it both ways, looking for a way out and at the same time being fully on my side. He was in no doubt that there was a way to avoid the coming clash, and had stressed the point to me of waiting for the right moment, and warning me of the prison sentence I would face if I was caught. In reality, though, I could see he was trying to evade any future hassle, whilst still giving it the large.

Anything that threatened to alter his way of life he viewed as aggravation; he could do without it and would distance himself from the point it originated. Appropriately, at that time, 'Suspicious Minds' by the Fine Young Cannibals sprang forth from the jukebox, and Steve grinned at Harry's missed shot that left the last of his balls over the corner pocket.

Steve placed his smouldering cigarette in the ashtray on the windowsill and strutted cockily round the table to take his shot, while Harry cursed and drank from his pint glass. He lit a Marlboro and mentally ticked the balls off the table the way he thought Steve would play them, game on, and Harry cursed again in frustration.

I watched Steve grinning and laughing, and I understood Harry's feeling of suspicion towards him. It had always been difficult to fathom Steve's real meaning and I struggled with my gut feeling in trying to pin-point and nail down the man's character.

I kept dealing with the gestures that Steve had made for me, and I weighed these off against the good turns Harry had done for Steve. Nothing wrong in that; it was what made the world go round, mates helping mates out.

But I was bothered over the feeling left by Steve after he'd made one of his gestures, like he owed me. Like he was indebted to me. When the house had been attacked and it had been Steve and Harry that helped repair the damage, these vibes of owing had been at their strongest, and although I had been grateful to my two mates who had worked all day fixing windows, doors, cupboards, knocking out dents and filling holes throughout the downstairs of the property, Steve had, I felt, shied away from the reality of how big the crime was.

The facts of the situation were that there was a gang of men running around ready to smash my skull in, not caring whether my family were in the way or not. I felt that Steve didn't have the bottle to sort this out with violence, and it angered me because of this that Steve had the nerve to make light of the feud.

I admitted to myself that the womaniser was not much of a mate and even less of a man. I toyed with the pros and cons of having Steve as a mate and it angered me even more. I seemed to be in the position that meant I was on my own, surrounded by so-called mates that were completely hopeless and did nothing but aggravate me. I sat there mentally breaking their characters down and making excuses for their inadequacies.

Then there was Donna, my four-year-old daughter whom I had left with Tina one Friday evening after returning from the hospital. I felt waves of guilt for my fiancée Judith, who had miscarried a child. And what made the loss of the baby even worse was that I convinced myself it was the fault of the men who had smashed our home up. The worry that I knew Judith had been coping with because of the attack would surely have contributed to the miscarriage.

In my mind I saw vengeance as the only answer, but I had to look after my family first. They must not be put through added pain by losing me to years in prison. Tina was the only one doing Judith and me a favour, not Steve. I relaxed myself with the thought of the domestic scenario that was happening just around the corner in Steve and Tina's house: Donna happily playing with Steve's daughter Lisa, who was the same age as Donna, and Tina sat drinking tea like she did most nights, pleased that Lisa had someone to play with who kept her quiet and left Tina in peace and able to watch the television. This cosy family scene made me smile to myself, and the guilt of not being with my daughter at such a disturbing time faded.

I jumped into the new van, which Arthur and I had leased for work, and headed up to Tina's, leaving my mates to guzzle more alcohol. I had had a bad shock having seen Judith earlier that afternoon in hospital. My heart was heavy for my kid. Donna was a beautiful blonde with brown eyes, like her mother, but it was a very sad and bitter thought that a four-year-old kid had to go through what she had.

I thanked Tina for minding Donna and they both jumped in Dad's new van. I felt a pang of guilt when I looked at my daughter; there was so much she deserved that I had failed to provide.

Donna was excited that Daddy was taking her to see her mam in hospital and her first question was, 'When's Mammy coming home?' I pulled the new van outside the newsagent's hoping there would be something I could buy as a present for Donna. Luckily they had a doll and cosmetic set. I bought them both.

Now she was in the hospital showing off her new toy to her mam. It was not a nice experience watching Judith put on a brave face for her daughter. She had lost a baby. Only the grown-ups understand, while the young keep wondering.

I left the hospital with Donna in tow. I was even more determined to sort out the thugs that I held responsible for my woman's condition and the loss of our child. I wished for a moment that I was single and that Donna wasn't around, just so I could pin all my attention on the business in hand, which was to maim and kill my enemies without the fear of doing life in jail.

I remembered only minutes before how Judith and I had kissed and cuddled, telling each other of the love we felt, while Donna looked on and then joined in the cuddles. Tears sprang to my eyes as I helped Donna jump in the van. She crawled across the driver's seat, presents held tight, and I felt grateful to have such a wonderful and beautiful gift from God. It was time to drop Donna back off at Tina's, then pick up the gun from the family's flat. Then, *que sera sera*, what ever will be, will be.

2
VENGEANCE IS MINE

I dwelled on the last few weeks and I felt sick because none of it should have happened. The light was fading when I dropped Donna off at Tina's. She ran in to show Lisa, Tina's daughter, the new toy that Daddy had bought her.

I left Donna with cuddles and kisses, feeling that my daughter was in good hands, and handling the guilt with the intensity of revenge at being in a position that controlled me, not the other way round. That's why I bought a sawn-off shotgun. Donna watched me chop the barrels off to make it more lethal; a weapon despised by the courts and feared by the police. I would use it. It was not just for the protection of my family; I'd bought it to blow away my enemies.

I drove past the Railway pub. It was dark now and the welcome lights of the open sign blazed out onto the boulevard. The time was 8.45pm and the pub was buzzing with punters, many of them my friends and associates.

Paula Jones and her friend walked into the pub. I had been having an affair with Paula for the past eight weeks. The women, both tarted up, walked into the public bar and had a good look around. Finding that I was not there, they headed for the lounge. Paula hoped that, as she was carrying our child, she would have some say in my life.

I picked up the weapon of death and a dozen heavy shot cartridges from the darkened flat. The feel of the gun when it was loaded gave me a feeling of power and confidence. My mind set, I placed the sawn-off in a sports bag and headed off to look for the gang of thugs that had wrecked the lives of my family. I could think of nothing else as I drove towards the pub where the gang drank. I convinced myself that I had all the backup I needed with the shotgun. As I went over the attack in my mind, a cold shiver ran down my spine.

How close the gang had come to physically harming my woman and child left a bitter taste in my mouth. I wished I was drunk and devoid of all reason, like a machine that acts without thought.

I recalled how the trouble had come about. Work had been going well when Arthur and I had won a million-pound contract to lay the brickwork on an office block that was being built in town, next to the railway station. Arthur had used his experience as a quantity surveyor to measure up and price the job and, along with my 715 tax exemption, it sealed the deal with the main contractor's grouches. With Arthur's experience and keenness we could make the deal work. With a struggle, we thought we would be out of the woods in three months and the cash would start rolling in.

Several years previously, Arthur had done business with a sub-contractor who had been involved in a million-pound fraud that had included the IRA. Arthur had walked free from court while the others he dealt with had been found guilty.

This sub-contractor had priced the same job that Arthur and I had. He was outpriced, but inside information had told him who by, and when the contractor heard the name Arthur he decided to steal the contract from us.

I had big ideas and believed we had a stroke of luck in netting the contract. I had never given thought to another sub-contractor trying to take over. The contractors from London scared the shit out of Arthur; he was more than surprised. He was frightened out of his wits and came straight to me and told me he wanted to pull out. Arthur was an opportunist who tried to go for the big one whenever the chance arose. But his past experience with the fraud, London sub-contractors and the IRA made him nervous. Violence had never been his strong point: that's why he relied on me. Arthur thought of me as a psychopath: violence and standing my ground was second nature. The building trade was full of wide boys and gangsters, so my natural abilities allowed Arthur a free hand when doing business deals. Muscle was Arthur's partner.

When I heard Arthur's suggestion that we should pull out of the contract and give it to that sub-contractor for a few grand, I blew my top and refused to budge. I wanted the first crack on my way to a million pounds to be a success, and the threat of London sub-contractors meant nothing to me. Basically, if they faced me with violence then violence is what the London sub-contractors would get in return. Deals were offered from London over the period of a month, leading up to when the job started. I told them all, 'No deal!'

Then the London gang attacked one sunny Sunday afternoon, in the third week of August. The gang of thugs, with total disregard, smashed through my house, causing thousands of pounds' worth of damage. By the grace of God my woman, Judith, and child, Donna, were not in the house; they were out visiting Judith's sister.

I had jumped out of bed and fought with the thugs, slinging 20-kilo weights at the gang as they tried to scale the stairway. Totally naked I hurled the weights at the heads of my attackers; the thugs backed off and ran out to a waiting getaway car.

I was so incensed that I was oblivious to all as I ran over broken glass, holding a five-foot weightlifting bar. The glass tore the soles of my feet as I chased the gang's car up the street. I remember breathing heavily as I cursed, failing to catch my enemies.

The sub-contractor had done his worst. Now it was payback time. I wanted vengeance. I had asked around and questioned various associates, gradually putting the pieces together in order to find out who had been involved in the attack and where they were to be found.

I decided to leave the head man until later. I wanted the thugs that tore my house apart and destroyed my family home. This gang had caused my woman to have a miscarriage and caused my daughter to face a life interlaced with violence and fear.

I would let the ringleader see that I meant business by maiming and killing his henchmen, before confronting the top man himself.

I walked into the pub with the sawn-off tucked under my sheepskin coat. I was alert and noticed the sly looks and whispers from the locals that had heard what was going down. I would have pulled the sawn-off out and used it if the people I was looking for had been there. As I drove my van back to the Railway pub, I was angry at not locating the thugs in their own local.

I was now in two minds whether to call the retaliation off. When I walked through the doors of my own local I had a face like thunder. There were more of my mates in, all immediately aware of my presence and mood. Each in their own way was sapping my nervous energy and using it for their own awareness, in a way that kept them feeling good and important.

Fuelled by my aroma, Eddie immediately got loud. He was a mate and would stand by any decision his mate made. Eddie was loud and straight to the point on many occasions, and often blurted out the truth that only he knew about, and often against the wishes of my associates. Basically they were all cowards that deep down felt hatred towards me.

Two things happened that night. The time was 10.00pm. I decided that I would leave the debt that came in the shape of a shotgun cartridge for my enemies ... for now. Time and experience made me patient, waiting for the right moment. I would not use the shooter that night.

Paula and her mate saw me. Briefly, the friends exchanged words then quickly got to their feet and came to talk to me. Paula was not in a good mood. She loved me but feared rejection. The thought of bringing my baby up on her own was a problem that definitely scared Paula.

I could tell that she wondered if I thought more of her than Judith and my kid. I loved to party, and Paula feared that it would be my choice to continue living that sort of life, with her pushed into the background and coming second to my genuine family.

To me, Paula was like a dozen other women I had been with, while my wife stayed in the house and minded our child. I could not give a toss about Paula. It was just a way of venting my aggression, going with women that didn't give me hassle, but that was soon to change.

The atmosphere changed in the bar and I made a less than pleasant remark that the child she was carrying was not mine. Paula slung her vodka straight in my face and I moaned in pain as the spirit stung my eyeballs. As my eyes struggled to focus, I felt my way to the toilets to wash the alcohol from my eyes. As I doused my eyes with tap water, I cursed at the latest turn of events. Why was all the shit and bad luck directed at me? I felt like running to the van to get the sawn-off and blowing someone away.

Steve came into the toilets asking how I was after hearing about my bastard child from Paula. This amused Steve and he sensed divorce and scandal of the sort that suited his twisted sense of humour. Followed by Steve, I came out of the toilets. My eyes were red and flaming as I screamed at the punters in the bar, enquiring where Paula was. She left the pub knowing what the consequences of her actions would be at a later date.

The group of people in the public bar that night were my mates of one sort or another. Those that did not know me personally knew of my reputation. Chris Hawley approached me as I stood at the bar, counting his lack of blessings. Chris could not miss this opportunity to push me that bit extra, so I cracked and went wild, and a major incident was about to come about.

I listened as Chris firmly stated that I had to act and do the thugs that had attacked my home. If I did not then I would lose more than my reputation; maybe my family. The more that Chris went on droning in my ears, the more and more I was wound up: tarts, a pregnant woman in hospital, little Donna having to be lied to.

When Chris told me he knew where one of the thugs lived, it was more than I could have dreamed of. Even more exciting was when Chris offered to take me there. I downed my pint and headed for my van, Chris in tow. When I opened the van door and grabbed the sawn-off, it left Chris Hawley in awe.

Besides the sub-contractor there were four people that I wanted to kill. The London firm had been cautioned that a dispute was going on, and the men that worked for him had been warned to take precautions. He had about 25 people that regularly worked for him and he had done business regularly with the thug in the house that Chris Hawley and I were heading to. This was one of his henchmen.

I parked the van at the bottom of the housing estate street. The cul-de-sac had a dozen houses. I held the sawn-off to my side … I was determined to kill. Confidence was my biggest feeling.

Chris banged on the door. The downstairs lights were out, but the upstairs light went on and then the staircase light. I levelled the shotgun as a silhouette reached and unlocked the door.

I did not recognise the man at the door and, in split-second time, I pointed the barrel of the fearsome looking weapon at the downstairs living-room window, blew that out and then levelled it at the bedroom window above, and blew that out. The owner of the property literally shit his pants and slammed the door. As I casually walked down the road and jumped back in the van, I felt as though the whole street could hear the pounding of my heart, and what made it worse was that I had shot the windows out of a house of someone I did not know. I cursed myself for listening to Chris, whom, it turned out, had known vaguely the man who I had just threatened with the sawn-off shotgun!

I was drunk. Just drunk enough to kill my enemies with the sawn-off, but that heightened my nerve. But as to shooting the right men ... I would not make the same mistake that Chris had led me to. I was alert enough to recognise the consequences of what could have occurred, but luckily only it was only the property that had been damaged.

3
PUMPING OUT THE AGGRESSION

I dropped Chris off at the pub and dumped the van in the housing estate, away from the main route where cruising police cars could not spot it. I had been seeing a Mediterranean girl, who had the looks of a page-three girl. I knocked on the door. The lights were out but an upstairs window opened and the young, exotic woman came to the window. She saw it was me and ran downstairs to let me in.

I ravished the woman, my tongue slavering over her hard nipples and ample breasts. She comforted me sexually and we both relished the hot sex. My thoughts were of mixed feelings: about performing exceptionally with such a good-looking woman; about what I had just done with the sawn-off shotgun. I tried to forget the latter as I kissed and tongued my way round the girl. But my mind was only partly on the job of sex in hand.

Soon, any shying away was gone. I studied the beautiful woman lying beside me and wondered how much prison time I'd get, but that wasn't important. What was important was protecting my kid and my woman. I had decided that nothing else mattered except their safety. I did feel guilty that I'd always fuck a decent-looking bird, and the one lying next to me sleeping was no exception.

How could I love Judith and then shag other women? I still could not fathom that one out. There was nothing that I would not do or give for my woman and child. Yet, with little or no interest, I'd fuck anything that came my way.

Some nosey bastard had taken the registration of the van. The police were out in force looking for it. They knew it was mine and there was a warrant out for my immediate arrest, and they, the police, all carried guns, side arms and high-powered rifles.

I woke to the smell of garlic toast and bacon that the svelte, big-breasted love machine downstairs, had cooked. I called down to her, feeling the nerves in my stomach tighten at the thought of the attack with the sawn-off shotgun. I felt a serious doze of craziness as I realised the offence I had committed. She came in the bedroom carrying my breakfast, but on seeing her large-nippled, ample-sized breasts, like two melons in a hammock, burst forth as her dressing gown swung open, I immediately became hard and grabbed hold of her as she placed the breakfast tray on the bedside table.

I slipped inside her and began to fuck her hard and fast, taking out my aggression on her as my thoughts moved to the law and arrest. As the creative juices flowed from my hard penis, spasms of pleasure racked my muscled torso. For a moment I basked in the pleasure, wrapped in the woman's arms.

I took what comfort I could and shrugged off the affections of the bird. I needed a drink and was going to get one, oblivious to the danger of being arrested. I worried about Judith and how she was, and Donna. I'd go and see Donna later and both of us would go to the hospital to see how Judith was.

By 11.00am prompt I was at the doors of the Railway public house and was the first one through the doors. The second man through the doors was Frank Hayes, a mate of mine. I immediately spoke to Frank and I told him where the van was parked and asked him to pick up the sawn-off from under the seat and hide it somewhere safe.

As I downed my first pint in record time, and looked through the bottom of the glass at the ceiling, time seemed to stand still. I followed this up with a double-whisky chaser and knocked that back. Brian the landlord came into the bar from his flat above. I listened as Brian told me that the police had been looking for me the previous night. I wanted to know why the police had told the landlord that I was wanted for a firearms offence.

The police, however, were not my first priority. I knocked back the next two drinks in succession. In my mind it was Judith and Donna who were my first priority. Looking back on it, and given what you will read later on, you might accuse me of having double standards, but I swear ... they were always in my mind. I was deciding when it would be best to pick Donna up and take her to see her mum.

The pub was filling up faster than a holed boat, and Brian and I still conversed deeply. The locals had heard of the shotgun offence and how the police were searching the neighbourhood for me – this was their cabaret show.

At first, I did not see the plain-clothes CID come into the bar through the lounge. They stood at the bar and asked the landlord if I was in the pub. One of the CID had photos of me, which he flashed at Brian. Protecting me, Brian lied and stated that he had not seen me. They came into the public bar end and scanned the room. I was playing pool and my heartbeat began to increase as the copper and I recognised each other.

With firearms being involved, the CID were visibly very wary. Thinking that I had a gun, they silently patted their side arms. The guns were comfortably tucked under their armpits. They were policemen with a grave, important task to complete. The elder of the two coppers locked eyes with me and held my gaze with the unflinching look of a seasoned pro as he walked over to where I was playing pool.

'Stephen Moyle, known as Geordie Steve, you're under arrest for possession of a firearm,' the copper said.

I confronted him with a look of nonchalance about me, stating that I wasn't (in possession of a firearm). Although the pub was busy, an uneasy silence pervaded the place. The streetwise locals concentrated on the confrontation. The hate could be clearly felt in the atmosphere of the pub; no one liked the police, and the Jack Lemon punters were ready to jump on them.

On sensing the unease from the locals, the two police officers immediately called for backup on the radio.

'Come with us,' the older of the two coppers said to me as riot vans and police cars pulled up outside the pub. Within minutes coppers were running in through both doors. There were now more coppers than locals.

I intended to make the police sweat and stated firmly that I was having a last drink before giving myself up. The police stared hard at me as I went to the bar and ordered a treble, single-malt whisky. There was silence as everyone in the pub watched the police with a cold loathing in their eyes. The police had stony hatred written all over their faces. I knocked the whisky back and stood bolt upright, ready for anything the police could throw at me.

At that exact moment, I knew that I was in control of the situation. I despised the police and made my move. I snatched a pint glass off the bar and slung it in the elder copper's face. The pub, with its villains and locals, went up, people throwing punches at the police. They kicked and bit at anything resembling a copper. Within a flash, the police had a mini-riot on their hands.

I ran from a standing start for the bar entrance, but was dived on by two CID and half a dozen uniformed coppers. Screaming with rage, I struggled with the police and, growing more frustrated with every second as my escape bid was foiled, my hands were cuffed behind my back. Brian jumped over the bar, stating that he would press charges if the police went beyond their job with violence.

Obscenities made the air turn blue as I was unceremoniously dragged through the door like a sack of spuds, out on to the boulevard. Passers-by stood and watched the chaos, shoppers standing in shocked silence as I unleashed a tirade of foul language in my Geordie accent. The police bundled me into a riot van and the free-for-all ended with threats from the locals of unfounded charges being brought for police brutality.

I was the only one arrested, the sergeant preferring to arrest the one they were after and not stir up hostilities by arresting drunks from the neighbourhood for disturbance of the peace.

Later that day, I sobered up and came to terms with this bad state of affairs. I sat in the police cell, counting the minutes until I would be interviewed. I knew that the police would let me sweat the drink off before they went ahead with their inquiries.

I later leaned that Judith had had a visit from Steve's wife, Tina. She had been told of the recent events. Donna was old enough to know something was seriously wrong. The thugs that attacked did not only hurt me, but were the cause of a breakdown in normality for my woman and child. By breaking their home up and destroying their sense of security, these thugs had gone way over the top and were out of order. They had no morals or principals; this behaviour had twisted my mind.

As I sat in the spartan police cell, I spat hatred for the people involved and swore vengeance once more. I wished I'd had the shotgun when the attack had happened. I would have been charged with murder but at least my mind would have been settled and at peace, knowing I had rid the world of these lowlife scum.

What filled me with anger was me being arrested when it was I who was in the right. No police had come to my family's needs, or mine, when our house was being attacked. Only hours ago I'd been in bed with a beautiful-looking woman, thinking about Judith and Donna. The only thing that had changed the way things were was being locked up. I knew that bail wasn't worth considering, as I knew that firearms offences were looked upon as very serious.

4
CUSTARD PIES AND SAWN-OFF FUN

The two CID policemen studied me from across the interrogation table. My expression was blank and defiant. I, in turn, studied the look of authority on the policemen's faces. I knew how to play the game and sat uninterested as they played bad cop, good cop. There was not even a clock on the wall, just three seats, a bare table and the bars on the window, high above on the back wall.

The police questioned where I had been the previous night when the offence had taken place. I said nothing, then waited, then on cue I requested my solicitor Simon Scamells & Co be present. That ended the interview, the police having gained nothing by interviewing a suspect before he'd had time to speak to his legal adviser.

The police informed me that more charges were being added to the list: discharging a firearm in a public place, possession of an illegal weapon, i.e. sawn-off shotgun, endangering life, criminal damage (the windows that I had shot out). After the charges had been read out by my solicitor, I was back in the interrogation room.

I was informed that the victim and other neighbours, who had come out of their houses at the sound of the shotgun, had identified me. The registration of my van had been written down. I had been seen carrying what the witnesses described as a gun that was about 18 inches in length. The solicitor reminded me that in court, if I were helpful towards the police, it would go well for me.

The only thing was the police did not have the gun; it had been buried and would stay there until a better hiding place could be found. The CID told my solicitor that if the gun were to be handed in, the gesture would be noted in court. As far as the police were concerned, they had the right man, but feared the fact that the weapon was still in the community; any nutter could be running around with the gun.

I knew that the police would want to get me to own up and make a statement. Confess to the sawn-off and turn the weapon over. It was a start. Not a very good one, but I could reach my freedom through not coming across with the gun. I knew that just by sawing the barrels off a shotgun you got an automatic five-year sentence in a crown court.

Thoughts of when Donna, my daughter, watched me saw the barrels off the shotgun flashed through my head. I thought of my toddler with a dozen questions as to what I was doing and asking me whether she could help. I had even given her the sawn-off barrel to play with.

I told my brief I intended to say 'no comment' to the charges and, in fact, would not answer any of the questions put to me by the police. The trick was not to answer anything at present and save my side, made up, or the truth, until a later date when applying for bail, or on the trial date.

Saying nothing meant I could get my head together over the forthcoming months and come up with the best story, as the police would have their case against me made up. This meant I could see exactly what evidence they had against me by virtue of advance disclosure and work my side of events around the prosecution evidence.

The courts hated this sort of behaviour and it did not go down well if the judge handed out a custodial sentence, as there had been no cooperation between me and the police. It's the type of behaviour that old lags play; prison was not that much of a problem and it gave a better chance of a not-guilty plea working.

My thinking was that the witnesses would grow less sure of the facts as the weeks and months passed by. Time was a great factor when waiting for a court case.

The police grew agitated as I remained insolently silent to their questions. The solicitor had the same expression as he had had when he had first met me in the interrogation room. The interview went on as the police fell back on their next approach, as all I had imparted to them was my name and address. They shifted into gear so that they could play my attitude of not helping the police, in fact impairing lines of questioning. It meant the CID, who began to furiously write down every question that was put to me, would use my reluctance to assist the police during the court case.

The prosecution in court would play on my refusal to help the police and, by doing so, would argue that I had admitted my guilt. The police tried to make me grass on the second man, but I met this line of questioning with a cold, icy stare. I reckoned it was time to request a cigarette. I knew the police would get my cigarettes out of my property to show the solicitor that they were being human.

They reacted by bringing two coffees, one for me, the other for my solicitor. The time was getting on. My stomach turned like a knot being tied. I figured that it was dinnertime, which meant I had to be put back in the cell to eat the slop supplied.

I puffed away on my second cigarette as I polished off my coffee, and still nothing had changed. The police had failed, so the cigarettes and coffee cost me nothing.

Back in the cell, the dinner plate remained untouched on the cell floor. I swigged the tea, which was in a disposable cup and tasted like diesel. It reminded me of what lay ahead in prison, and the fact that I'd shortly be on my way to HMP Lewes, which was the local catchment nick for prisoners in that area.

I toyed with the possibility of asking the police if I could make a phone call to my woman, then rejected the thought as I knew the police might refuse and take the micky about the circumstances of my request. I decided to get my solicitor to make the request for a call; the police would not ignore him.

I counted the number of cells I had been in since the age of 14, dismissing the thought they were all the same sweatboxes that stunk of dirty bodies and shit. I thought back to my release date of 2 June 1982, following a three-and-a-half year prison sentence. I had decided back then that I'd rather be out than in. I had proved that point the same day I was released. That was when I travelled south to start a new life away from the old reputation of the north.

I pondered that glorious day as I studied the four walls, wishing for the end before I'd even started the sentence. This was now the summer of 1987. I'd been out of trouble for almost four years. I'd been lucky to find a beautiful-looking woman who had given me a beautiful daughter. The very lives that I had revolved around, the two loves, had kept me from the long arm of the law. I decided that there were not many men that had been in my position, staring at the cell walls. I prayed that the thugs involved in destroying the world I'd built around my family would die or, at best, that their lives be shattered and shit on with a lengthy stay in hospital. Perhaps if they lived permanently crippled...

The copper that came to my cell broke my thoughts. I eyed him through the open hatch as he took the untouched meal away. I had smuggled three cigarettes and some matches from the last interrogation, and decided it was time to light up and enjoy a smoke. If the police saw me smoking in the cell they would come and search me.

Left alone, I was back to reflecting on my situation. So Stephen Moyle, convicted prisoner, was back in custody and looking at a possible five or six years behind bars. The life that I had built for my loved ones was torn to pieces, and the only thing I had was a bitter taste of hate and vengeance, the only comfort I had left.

I had a history of slinging food and drink in coppers' faces. I once shoved a custard pie in the face of Mayor Gallagher, back in my hometown in the north. There had been five or six of us school friends, and we had been drinking all day and decided to go to the Town Fair after the pubs had shut. We were all drunk and were standing talking between ourselves, watching kids pay 20p to hit a policeman in the face with a custard pipe. The field next to the park was packed with hundreds of people, kids and parents all playing on sideshows that were dotted around the field.

It was, we had been told, a twinning ceremony with another town from Germany, and the Mayor and VIPs that had come to the celebration were all mixing with their English counterparts and enjoying the sunny day in the middle of summer. The group of men and I joked and laughed between ourselves, enjoying the police being done with custard pies.

One of the officials close by walked over and told my friends and me to stop swearing. He was a nasty, pompous, jumped-up man in a grey suit who thought he was in charge of the Town Fair. His attitude stunk as he targeted me for the scolding. Mike, one of my friends, who had a skinhead haircut, watched me take the scolding and glared with hatred at the man in the suit.

Mike then smashed me in the face with a custard pie that had been meant for a policeman. I wiped the custard from my eyes and picked up the pie to hit Mike with, but Mike had run off. I focused on the man in the suit, the Mayor and, with hate-filled intentions, I pushed the pie in the man's face. He began to scream for the police to arrest me and grabbed hold of my arm. I snatched my arm back and decided not to stick around.

The man in the suit was the Mayor. He was entertaining the officials from Germany and his high-pitched squeals of anger were heard by everyone close by. The Mayor was shocked at the custard pie attack and wanted to vent his anger by having the perpetrator arrested and charged. What the charge was he was not quite sure yet.

I ran and a large group of people, that got bigger as the event went on, followed. I'd only been out of jail 12 months and was still on YP (Young Prisoner) sentence so if I was arrested I could be sent back to jail on what was called YP Recall.

Off-duty police gave chase. As I reached the burn – the stream which was covered in steel mesh and ran the full length of the field, under a bridge and into the River Wear – I jumped on to the mesh and walked along the middle towards the river. The crowd followed and walked on the footpath along the burn. I came to a hole in the mesh that had been put there by kids. I clawed back the mesh a bit further and I dropped the 15 feet into the stream below and walked in the water.

There were at least a hundred people that had run over to see what was going on. I remember my mate Bob Ashcroft jumped into the stream and spoke to me. Bob was worried and told me to have words with the old bill, who stared with blank expressions as the crowd became more and more rowdy.

Having warned him to watch his step, Bob somersaulted down the concrete slope of the stream, at which the crowd howled in hysterics as he ended up head first at the bottom of the ford. I pulled him up and convinced him to walk with me towards the river, only 100 metres away. Not having committed a criminal offence, I was mad because I knew I'd be charged and it made me sick inside.

My mate Bob, when I reached the bridge where the wire mesh ended, jumped down into the burn and plodded along in the water beside me. He talked sense and tried to get it through my head that I would not go back to jail for a custard pie offence.

I was not convinced, or why would the Mayor have made such a big thing out of the incident, which was a laugh, a bit of fun. I thought the police hated me and would have me arrested and charged.

We stepped down the small ford where the concrete was smooth and moss-covered just before the river. Again I told Bob to mind his step and this time he fell arse over tit and went into three feet of water. Everyone burst out laughing even more, and Bob surfaced frozen and pissed off. He decided to stop following me. He crawled up the bank towards five friends that were still in fits of laughter.

The police, half a dozen or so, had phoned for backup as they followed me from the path alongside my headed course. Where the burn met the river were fast flowing rapids that were chest height. Not caring how deep or strong the current was, I headed for the bank on the other side. The police and crowd stopped at the riverside and watched me, in T-shirt and jeans, cross over.

They watched amazed as I manipulated my way across the swiftly running rapids of the river, which came up to my waist. I was not washed away as I thought the police might have understandably hoped, but reached the safety of the other side.

I had swum in the river all my life; in fact most of my last year at school, when the weather permitted, was spent swimming in the river. The knowledge of a river that was unpredictable and fast flowing led me to think and know how to use it.

I crouched down behind some willow trees, lying on my back, in safety from the police. I stared at the blue sky; not a cloud in sight. I thought about what to do next, and in the distance heard the sound of police dogs that would cross over one of the two bridges with their handlers. Once again, I contemplated going back to jail, which was completely uncalled for.

After a four-hour chase by police and their dogs I was locked up in a police cell and charged with criminal damage to the Mayor's suit. I was released and bailed to attend Magistrates' Court.

My friends decided to write to the local papers and say that Mayor Gallagher could not take a joke on a fun day that the whole town had turned out for. When I got to court I had the papers there to hear the case, and I informed the local tabloids that I intended to badmouth the Mayor for not seeing the funny side of the event.

The Mayor, on hearing what I intended in court, did not want his name associated with being pompous and a self-righteous stick-in-the-mud. The prosecution spoke to me before I went into court and offered me a deal; they'd drop the charges if I agreed to be bound over to keep the peace for one year. I accepted the deal and went in and out of court in a matter of minutes. The magistrates accepted the prosecution's case and that was the end of that.

Just then, my thoughts vaporised as the door to my cell opened. The CID informed me that my solicitor was here to continue the interrogation. One of Simon Scamell's colleagues greeted me. He sat in same room and reminded the police of his client's innocence and denial of involvement in the charges.

The interrogation ended with the police informing me that I would be held in custody till the next morning, which was a Sunday, and that they had arranged a special hearing with the magistrate to remand me in to custody, although I would be making an application for bail ... a futile gesture of defiance on my part.

I was not happy being banged up in that place. Who would be? I hated the thought of my family visiting me in such a bad place. To think of something so true and beautiful as my daughter, and my woman Judith, I hoped my thoughts could not be taken as weakness and used against me by the police.

I'd been forensically examined: fingerprints taken, photos and swabs from my hands, which the police hoped would show powder flashes from the gun.

Judith had been told that she could go home from hospital the next day, and Donna was delighted that her mammy was coming home. She asked her, 'Will Daddy be coming home too?' Judith knew my passion for her and Donna. It made it so that we wanted to spend every single minute with each other. The craving of love shared between the family was like a drug. I was a real man and she respected this. I was nowhere near perfect, I drank and did not take her out as much as she'd like, but the love I had for her and Donna was unfathomable.

By late afternoon the change of clothes I sent out for had arrived. I had a shock as the CID interviewed Arthur, who had brought the clothes. They were trying to arrest the second man, and thought this could be Arthur.

Arthur panicked. He was frightened by the police and was shocked that they thought he had been the second man involved. He denied this emphatically and said that he was only delivering the clothes as asked for by Judith. The CID thought this may be a breakthrough and told Arthur that he would be watched, and that his movements would be recorded.

The police assured Arthur that the offence was extremely serious and that I would go to jail. The evidence the police had against me was unbeatable. They assured Arthur that if he helped them there was no hope that I would ever find out. Arthur considered the fact that he may be arrested and knew that the police would do their damndest to do so. The carrot they dangled was to be well in with the police if he did as they asked. It was too valuable to miss out on.

The CID informed me that my friend Arthur was here to see me and had clean clothes for me. I immediately became suspicious. The police hated visitors and unless they were family they were never let in to see the prisoner. And on top of that, I had not requested to see Arthur. Arthur sat in the interrogation room, puffing away on his liquorice-flavoured roll-up. There were no police there; Arthur passed the message on and strongly recommended I do as the police asked.

He encouraged me to confess to where the sawn-off was hidden. The police had played their card and hoped that Arthur could access the whereabouts of the gun. I was sickened at how easily Arthur had taken the side of the CID and immediately worked out that he, my partner, was scoring brownie points for himself in the attempt to get me to talk. I casually changed the subject and took one of Arthur's roll-ups. I asked about the welfare of my woman and child.

As far as I was concerned, Arthur was a coward. He'd figured that my predicament only meant a one-way ticket to the slammer, which would leave Arthur free from my friendship and allow him to double his profit in the building trade. It would be easier and cheaper to fill the position of his partner. This was, obviously, the answer to Arthur's prayers. It took an hour before the CID came into the interrogation room, and Arthur went as red as a beetroot.

I was escorted back to the cell, clutching my clean clothes, with Arthur's tobacco papers and lighter hidden in them. I spat bitterness at the cell floor. It was a big letdown for me to find out point blank that my friend and partner had tried to get me five years in the slammer for the sawn-off shotgun offence. There was not a chance in hell that I would confess. I tried in my mind to piece together my new state of affairs and realised that it was necessary to get bail to sort out my case. I decided to put my case together when I had access to pen and paper. I had to come up with something that was positive, something the prosecution did not expect.

Thoughts came and went, always returning to freedom and what was going down with my woman and child. You needed something extra, some sixth sense to put in perspective the wellbeing of being a prisoner or a convict. It's wasn't just the power of thought, but when and where you thought. To win your case in court you had to be very clever and sly. Things that were against you had to be interpreted by the prosecution in the manner that left room for the prisoner to react in a positive way. It was a skill you learned mostly by yourself, by many times facing a court and the police.

The police were vaguely aware of this method of facing the judge but were too pompous and sure of themselves to give it any full-time attention. When it came to their attention they believed in the system they worked in, and thought the defence was the way to defeat villains. The longer prison sentences handed down gave the police a lift in their righteous spirit, which was their shot in the arm from the community – the equivalent to a shot of speed.

I considered my next move. I checked out cases of villains and drug addicts who had done well in court, and decided that being a drug addict was the best bet, except I wasn't a drug addict so that door was closed, or was it? It would be possible to imitate a drug addict but I'd have to have an alibi for the judge to see that.

I thought back to the age of nine or ten and recalled my mother. Whenever I'd done wrong she would scold me and tell me that the men in white coats would come and take me away.

I recalled at the age of 15, I was up on a charge for malicious wounding and this put the men in white coats in to action, with my mother and then girlfriend backing me up too. My social worker had explained that blackouts happened when I could not remember my actions and that I'd blacked out while getting out of the bath. It had worked. I received a non-custodial sentence: one-year's psychiatric treatment and one year's probation.

The offence had been very serious. I had smashed a pool cue across the nose of a punk rocker and left a hole in the man's face. What used to be his nose was split in half like a burst balloon.

I was swiftly brought out of my reminiscences by the voice of the policeman as he informed me that my woman was coming to visit me after I'd been in front of the judge.

Judith had phoned the police station as soon as she'd got home from the hospital. The police had told her there was no visiting until I had been in front of the magistrates. Judith had contacted the solicitor and told him they were denying her visits. The solicitor rang the police and expressed the view that visits would be in order after I had been in front of the judge.

From a holding cell, along the corridor and up the locked stairwell, the police escorted me into the courtroom, where I faced a single magistrate. The prosecution, not surprisingly, opposed bail, and my solicitor, as agreed with me, made no application for it. I was immediately remanded into custody and was swiftly taken back to my cell.

I'd been remanded in custody for a week and hoped the next time I was up in front of the magistrate I'd be ready to request bail. I felt a great sense of vulnerability; it hurt in my heart. It was always hard to deal with police custody. It was no different than being in jail.

I cheered up slightly when I remembered walking in the woods and fishing. I climbed trees with my daughter, bunking her up to the branches because she was too small to reach, her mother half laughing and half concerned in case she lost her footing. A great sense of freedom for my child and her mother came to me. I wondered where life would take them together and I prayed.

In my mind I fought with conflicting thoughts, mad at myself for being nicked for my drunken warpath of revenge. Revenge is sweet, so they say, but my revenge was borne out of drunken madness. My mind was now back to its best. Revenge would be mine, and I would do it properly.

My woman and child came to visit me. The police stood by and supervised the visit. We cuddled each other, trying to ignore the copper stood in the corner, which made the situation worse. I was immediately aware of the sweet fragrance of my family. It made me think of what awaited me when I got back to the stinking cell. I did not want to let go of my family and tears from Judith made me hold her even tighter.

As her tears made the side of my face damp, I tried to assure my daughter that I'd be coming home, but I did not want to hurt her by telling the truth of what was about to happen. Even with my woman and child so close to me, I did not feel comforted. I was worried the thugs may attack my home while I was not there.

I told Judith to protect herself by changing houses. I urged her to go to the council straight away, and said that I was sure she'd be given a different house in an estate where the family was not known, somewhere quiet and secluded. For one thing, I was not going to tell Judith, yet, that I'd receive a big jail sentence ... if I were found guilty, that was.

Talking to Judith was hard because of the turmoil she'd been through with the loss of the baby. She broke down and cried as her miscarriage was discussed. Then Donna cried because her mother was crying. She asked when her new brother or sister was coming and was told, 'Not yet. It will be a while yet and you have to help by being good for mammy.'

Thirty minutes was all the police allowed for the visit, and we all cuddled and said our goodbyes. I returned to the stinking police cell and my thoughts immediately turned to revenge and to what I would do to the thugs who caused my grief. I'd make up my mind about what to do and how I'd defend my case when I applied for bail.

Nothing I could think of had an end to satisfy my anger and grief. It came in bursts of how I'd kill my enemies. I had to prepare alibis because the revenge attack would bring the police on to me. I would put my thoughts in motion once I got bail, but I knew that my case would have to be perfect for the magistrates to grant it.

Lying in the stinking police cell with the buzzing of the air conditioner annoyed me so much ... the constant buzzing affected your thinking. Sometimes I would jump up and punch the air, screaming at the top of my voice. Sometimes I was just vaguely aware of the noise in the back of my eardrum. Somehow, this constant ear bashing made me aware of all the little things that made up the stench of the cell.

Briefly I recalled being locked up and refused water for hours, and prisoners being forced to drink water from the toilet bowl. I felt I could still taste and smell the water, which tasted of bleach and other chemicals, and an underlining taste of piss and shit.

As I sat on the bench, vaguely it came to me. *Human rights*. I felt sure this was my answer. I thought that if I could appeal to the decency of the magistrate and show the abuse of my rights, I'd have a good chance of being granted bail.

I picked out the first thought and tried to apply it to my position. Breakdown of communication, refusal of visits by my family, refusal of stationery to write my case because the police would read anything and censor it.

At this particular time the prisons were full and few places were open for prisoners on remand. This meant that small, out-of-the-way police stations were being used to locate remand prisoners for weeks at a time. This meant the prisoners did not know where they were going until they got there. I was allocated to Bex Hill, which is a small town just off the coast. I and four other remand prisoners journeyed to the police station in a segregated police van.

One of the prisoners had a small radio. Rather than sit in the cells, the prisoners were allowed to sit in the locked corridor and listen to music. I muscled one of the prisoners who was in for fraud; he had a quarter of cannabis. Now let me tell you this:

doing time was made doubly easy when there was cannabis available. Needless to say, I associated with the other prisoners and shared a spliff.

The place smelled like junkies' paradise, the odour wafting down the corridor. I wondered whether the police would do a search. The possibility of being caught smoking cannabis played tricks with my mind, which was a familiar feeling. Smoking dope made you badly paranoid about being caught. As I dragged deeply on the spliff, I pushed aside this sense of paranoia.

I managed to speak to my woman over the phone, and the pain of talking was numbed by my infusion of cannabis. But still the tears came to my eyes as Judith sobbed on the phone. I asked how our toddler was doing, and was told that she was missing her dad.

Between the paranoia and the hallucinogenic feelings I kept my mind firmly together and handled the situation like a professional. To any outsider, I came across as cool, calm and collected, but I was buzzing from the fact that I was smoking cannabis in an old bill station, right under the noses of the enemy. I revelled in the fact that I was getting away with criminal activities.

The other prisoners sensed I was the alpha male amongst them. It was not just my physical build, but also the manner and the way in which I handled myself. They all knew I was not a man to be messed with, and treated me with the respect this sort of character demanded.

Moods changed and differed as hours ticked by. All the men were preoccupied with life in a small corridor and cell in jail. They would have stayed in their cells, probably asleep on their bunks. But the mood of local remand in a police station meant they were up and smoking. I quietly told the prisoner with the cannabis not to give it to the other prisoners, and that he should keep the small lump he had to share with me. I decided that the three prisoners that had no cannabis would have a smoke last thing at night.

I told the prisoners this, and the three men without drugs had a turn-on. This gesture was the old pal's act and gave the men something to look forward to after a hard day sweating. It gave me the boost that my ego needed. The prisoners were grateful and respected me more so.

After a while the prisoners became more accustomed to each other and opened up. Although I still retained my cool manner, I knew not to show any sign of friendship without a price. The old pal's act did not cover treachery, and in the minds of the prisoners was a desire instilled to climb the reputation ladder. They could not do that unless some form of weakness could be exploited. They would get well in with the Daddy, then set up a system to undermine him at the slightest opportunity.

If the prisoners saw any sort of deal, they would become jealous. I knew this, so whenever I did business I would do it away from the prying eyes of the other prisoners who weren't involved. This normally took place in a cell with the door half-open, or it could be done in a recess or shower house. Dealing in drugs was always done in a quiet manner, and respectfully.

Reputation counted on who got, or was turned away by, the dealer. I knew that if there were drugs about at the time, it meant there would be more on the way. So I dealt in a confident and quiet manner with the prisoner supplying me. Unspoken, the prisoner with the quarter made no attempt to hide the fact that he had drugs ready to be brought in, and that he planned to use me for muscle if it were necessary. I knew this and thought, if the prisoner had the drugs I would be happy to supply the muscle.

I did not usually bother with hard drugs like heroin; the junkies that craved it were nothing but trouble. They would constantly pester and annoy the dealers that sold and used the stuff. The screws and coppers would hassle the people who sold the stuff and I preferred not to get involved because of the attitudes of the enemy. However, all said and done, if the deal was a sound bet then I'd donate my skills as an animal to make money and get a piece of the action.

It was difficult to keep any sort of principals when you were locked up; the people around you were always trying to do you out of what was rightfully yours. Prison was a shithole and the people, cons and screws were all shit.

I decided I would get my own drug supply and then be able to distance myself from the rejects that I was dealing with. Only when necessary would I use the old pal's act and muscle to get by. This way I kept my head above water and some civilised principals that I put to use for relaxing in my cell when everyone was locked up.

The men were swapping stories of why they were banged up at that present moment. The conversation changed to villains they had known on earlier sentences. My ears pricked up as I weighed up the subject of the talk. It may help me in the future, I thought, to recognise some of the hard criminals with hard reputations.

5
TIME STANDS STILL

I had arranged for a visit with Judith that afternoon. Her father was going to bring her and our toddler.

I skinned up a joint, happy because I had beaten the police who may have made life difficult for me with the visit, but it was me and my ego that came out on top by smoking cannabis.

I hoped my visit was the only visit that afternoon because the police sometimes gave you a long visit if it was the only one. I was excited and at the same time sad. I felt sure there was a way out of this mess. My mind kicked in like it was on speed, thinking again about the answer to my predicament.

While I was locked in my own world, Judith had butterflies in her stomach and Donna was excited. The morning could not pass quick enough for them. Judith set to work getting our toddler ready for that afternoon. She finished dressing Donna and started on the child's long, blonde hair. She surveyed her handiwork and got Donna to do a little pose, showing her natural beauty. By the time Judith had finished, Donna's hair was perfect and she smelled of Dove soap.

Judith tried to dodge the bad thoughts that crossed her mind. She hated to think of me being locked up and occupied herself with making herself look beautiful for me. She knew what I would like her to dress like, but decided against it – black stockings weren't adequate for visiting in a police station. Jeans, sweatshirt and denim jacket were more appropriate, and she clipped her hair back with a silver pin that her mother had given her. She pinned the clip into place and, for a moment, thought of her mother and how she would have handled the present situation.

She guessed that if her mother were well and not dying of cancer, she would have thought of happier times, and those times would come again when today's saga was over and they were back together.

She held on to that thought. Judith knew me and felt my sadness inside her own heart. Silently she gave Donna a cup of orange pop. The child was sitting in front of the television watching *Thomas the Tank Engine*, which was her favourite programme.

Judith made a cup of tea and recalled when she first went out with me, how she took the rap for drunk driving to stop me being recalled on licence back into prison. She had switched seats with me when the police had pulled us over so that she was in the driving seat. The police had driven us back to the police station, where they breathalysed Judith. I told her to think of my cock when breathing into the machine. Judith could not bear the thought of losing her love, after finding the right one for her, so she had got herself charged for being a drunk driver.

She phoned her father to make sure he would be on time to pick her up. Once confirmed, she got Donna's coat and her own and they went to the shops to buy the stuff I had told her I needed: first-class stamps, A4 stationary and black biro pens. She wanted me back and was prepared to do anything to achieve this. She bought fruit and chocolate bars hoping I'd cheer up munching on some goodies.

The thought of the many times Donna and I had walked to the local shops brought tears to her eyes as she passed the familiar surroundings without me. It was weird the thought that came to her as she walked back home from the shops, and the thought frightened her.

Maybe the thugs that had smashed their house up were lying in wait for her. It made her stomach churn and replaced the excitement with worry and feared anticipation. She held on to Donna's hand tightly, and hoped her father would come soon. As she crossed the road and turned into the cul-de-sac she breathed a sigh of relief ... it was quiet and the only cars that were there were the ones parked outside of the neighbours' houses.

In contrast, my drinking mates thought the opposite to Judith and, at that moment were revelling in the attention they were receiving. There would be repercussions and that was big talk among the southerners.

After visiting me Judith was going to the council's housing department. She thought it would be best to go after the visit so that I could give her some more advice, or add to what I'd already said.

The house did not feel the same. Judith sensed this as she walked through the door. Donna was the same; the little girl became silent and munched on a Milky Way that her mother gave her.

Things could never be the same; nothing she did in the house – cook, clean, make dinner, none of it felt the same. Looking over her shoulder was a feeling she was not used to and it worried her. Could anything we'd shared ever be like it was?

But the power of the many precious moments we'd shared together would never leave her. The good, the bad and the ugly all smoothed out with the strength and power from the feelings of love that Judith, Donna and I felt for each other.

Judith checked herself in the mirror, feeling paranoid she may not look the same – blonde hair, brown eyes, five-foot seven, still the sexy looking woman that her man had fallen in love with, and still the lovely mother their daughter saw every morning, noon and night. She took some comfort from what she saw: a confident woman.

She was not going to back down from the situation and would follow her man to the ends of the earth; they would fight the enemies till the day they died.

But along with the good came the bad, as she recalled the last run-in with the southerners. Some thug had called her a slut because she was wearing a leopard-skin mini, with fishnets, as she walked hand in hand with me from the Commercial pub.

Of course, I immediately reacted and knocked the thug out, but then his two mates attacked and smashed a beer jug in my face. I had gone into a rage, fighting with three thugs. The left side of my face was torn open, my bottom lip split in half. The police were parked only a few yards away. They saw the whole thing and ran over, dragging me off one of the thugs. The crowd of drinkers that were standing outside the pub enjoying the late summer night became brazen and goaded the police. The copper that held me pinned to the taxi barrier let go and told me not to move.

As soon as the copper let go, I grabbed Judith's hand and hurried away from the commotion. We slipped up the back alley beside the bank. She'd inspected my face and told him me that I had to go to the hospital to have the four-inch gash and my bottom lip stitched.

I told her that I could not because the police would be waiting. They would assume I'd gone to the hospital and would leave word in the accident department to inform them if I had my injury seen to. When we reached home, Judith cried as she dressed my injuries as best she could. That was a bad time, she thought, and they'd survived that.

To Judith, her man had proved his love for her by fighting three men at once in her honour, and she loved him deeply for that. She felt safe in my company.

I liked her to wear sexy things, I enjoyed her beauty and sexuality, and Judith enjoyed dressing up for me. When we made love she had to be careful to mind my injury. She would lie there after we'd made love and run her finger over the scar, sad that her man's once-handsome face was scarred.

As she looked into the mirror she again ran her finger down her man's scar, but it was her own reflection and there was no vicious scar to be seen except in her mind. That's how she saw my scar, imprinted in her mind and soul, and she carried it in her heart because she loved me.

Judith was from a good home. Her father had a prominent job in a computer company, and he'd always worked and revelled in the responsibility the job gave him. They had, ever since Judith was a child, lived in the four-bedroom detached house in a secluded cul-de-sac. She had an elder sister and older brother, both of whom I considered snobs who lived constructive, everyday lives. None of her family had warmed to her choice of partner. Their introduction to me had been the morning after she had been charged with drunk driving. I had slept in the spare room, Judith being the only child left at home.

I was with her for support when we came down for breakfast. I felt guilty. Not many people would have taken the rap on a drink driving charge, It was partly naiveté and, mainly, love that had made Judith take the blame. There was no shouting match. Her mother and father took it quietly and did not confess their doubts about my true intentions towards their daughter.

Judith was a naturally quiet person; she would listen without argument to her parent's advice and opinions and usually take what they said as gospel. But she had a side to her that was stubborn and, if she knew she was right, what her parents said made little difference to her. Judith knew, although her mother and father had not said a great deal, that they would discuss with her the police episode that would leave her banned from driving, and more importantly their first impressions of her new boyfriend. But they would wait till she was alone.

I met Judith when she was 19 and I was 20. It was August 1992 when I had been working as a lifeguard at the local leisure centre. She'd been swimming with a friend and the handsome lifeguard – me – had seemed, so I found out from her later on, to be in a world of his own as the two friends swam and stopped at the side of the pool, where I lent on the safety rail surrounding the 12-foot end of the pool.

The two young women craned their necks as they tried to take a peep up the side of my shorts, trying to see if I was wearing underwear. As the two women laughed, I focused on them and struck up a sort of conversation, which was difficult over the noise of the people swimming as it echoed round the pool.

Partly through her persistence, Judith's character shone through and I was drawn to her, not her friend. Sensing this, the other girl wanted me for herself. The more I focused my attention on Judith, the more her friend became envious and put more effort into the chat-up lines. I just responded with more laughter at what Judith was saying.

The topic was: was I wearing underpants or did I prefer my cock to be unobstructed? We all laughed and I took the hint from the mischievous look in Judith's eyes that we would become lovers.

As Judith waited for her lift to the police station, she kept herself busy with Donna. She loved time spent with her daughter and as she sipped from her cup she remembered how she and I broke the news of Donna's pregnancy to Judith's mother and father.

Judith conceived three months after she first met me. We were living together, over her parents' objections. They had been sure that I was not the person for her and they expressed their concerns openly, but this made no difference to Judith. She was in love and determined to make the relationship work. Another couple shared the house with us: an ice-cream man and a secretary who were both single.

Sex between Judith and I was astounding, and the longer we were together the more we loved each other. Judith had a fetish about bananas and ever since she was a teenager she had wanted to use one as part of her love making, peeled of course. I obliged Judith with her fantasy and we had intercourse, after which I went down on her and had a desert of mashed bananas.

When relaxed, I decided that I wanted a baby with this beautiful woman. She was on the pill and I took them from the drawer and flushed them down the toilet. One month later she was pregnant and Judith wanted to tell her parents of the happy event, the birth of her first baby. Her mother had spoken to her daughter by herself. Judith's parents had not seen a lot of me and this new event made them even more anxious.

I had held a distance between myself and Judith's mother and father, sensing how unwelcome I was. Judith and I met her parents to discuss the pregnancy and my intentions. We sat around the dining-room table. I intended to get the meeting over as quickly as possible. I decided to agree to what her parents said as long as their plans did not affect ours.

They questioned me on how difficult it would be bringing up a child and whether we would be capable. As Judith listened to her mother, I could see that she felt sorry for me. I emphatically loved the woman and wanted to build my life around her and our unborn child.

While lying in the police cell, I wished I'd been faithful and worried that Judith would find out about my infidelity while I was locked up. It made me anxious because, if that happened, I'd be in the worst position locked behind cell doors, unable to do anything or defend myself.

I believed that having affairs was my decision and no one else's.

I thought that as long as Judith did not find out, it was all right to screw around. It was second nature for me to chat up and shag women, but at this particular moment the trouble that I was in made me feel guilty. I loved Judith and wanted her and her only.

My fear was well-grounded, considering the women I'd been with. I studied the possibility of this situation happening and thought that the longer there was no confrontation between Judith and one of my affairs the better; it would be the more likely that things would die down.

Of course, this is what I'd prefer to happen, but my name and reputation was big news, a talking point for the various women in the area. So maybe it was too much to hope for and, maybe, the situation would worsen if Judith found out. Maybe she would take our child and leave me. Might this be more of a possibility? If it was, I must be ready for the pain and expect the worst.

I felt my heart wrench, but maybe the pain in my heart and soul would not be as bad once I was with my family. I didn't think so, and prepared myself for some deep emotional feelings that I thought would result from the visit.

I wondered where and how far the family would move. I toyed with going back north and starting anew. It depended on how deep their love was, or if Judith still wanted to live in the area. She may think that a move from the estate, where the attack happened, was best.

As I recounted how one of my bits on the side had broken the news of her pregnancy, I decided to have a spliff. I cringed at the thought that she might have called on Judith, or would call on Judith. The pain of this thought plagued me to no ends as I rolled the spliff: if it got any heavier I thought my mind would shatter, or that my heart would be torn in half. I began to wonder if love was such a good thing after all, then cursed myself for the terrible thought of giving in.

I pulled heavily on the spliff and held my breath for a few

seconds, letting the cannabis fill my mind. My nerves felt relaxed but my paranoia continued.

In my mind I'd deliberately think about the spliff I'd just had and how good it felt to be able to smoke illegal substances under the nose of my enemies and get away with it.

Time ticked by for Judith. She decided to make some sandwiches for Donna and gave the toddler a plate of chocolate fingers while she put the sandwiches together. She made extra cheese and onion so that I, too, could have a bite to eat.

As she prepared the packed lunch she begun to despair at the thought that she may have many more similar visits to prepare for. She cursed the damned and prayed that this would not happen. The thought left her tearful and she wished me back and in her arms to comfort her. She looked at Donna sitting on the floor watching the TV and munching her biscuits. More sadness came to her. She hoped her child would understand and, at the same time, not feel the pain of loneliness because of her absent father.

Judith felt a wave of love; her man may not be there with her but his child was. Donna was the symbol of his love, something to cherish and watch grow. Donna would be there even if I wasn't, and when Judith looked at her child she would always see me and our love, which would go on forever.

She knew in her heart that the love between the three of them would get her through the tragic miscarriage and that they'd all come out better and wiser people.

It was all new to her – prison, police. That's where her man was heading. She wondered if she could forge an alliance with someone who was going the same way? Prison was always meant to be where the bad men and women went when they'd broken the law, that's what her mother had drummed into her when growing up. As she grew older, her mother was convinced I was one of the bad boys; an undesirable that was not good enough for their daughter.

Judith had listened to her parents and had made up her mind that her parents were wrong, and she intended to prove the point. Up till now we had been the victims and her man had only reacted to defend himself and his family. Judith was proud of me; I was right and I was being punished because of that.

The noise of a car pulling up outside was of a plush Mercedes, owned by Judith's father. He hooted the horn and waited. I often wondered if he contemplated the set of circumstances that had him waiting there. He was against the relationship that his daughter was caught up in, and not at all impressed by my plea of undying love.

As Judith got in the car with Donna, her father hardly acknowledged his daughter's welcome and his granddaughter's excitement at going to see her dad.

The journey to Bexhill Police Station was quiet between father and daughter. Judith was left with her own thoughts as her memory kicked in on the Brighton Road.

It was Cinderella Rockafella. I fastened up the rollerskates that seemed to have a mind of their own. The nightclub was dark and skaters were going at top speed. I held Judith's hand and she guided me on to the floor.

I got the feeling that when I wanted to go one way, the rollerskates tended to go the opposite. I was like a fish out of water. Never had I been on rollerskates, up north they weren't in fashion. On the other hand, Judith had had a lot of practice being a good skater in the south of England.

Judith was well known in the nightclub. That night was 'roller night' and she'd been coming to the event ever since she was 18 and old enough to get in the club. As a woman, young and full of mischief, she'd had a good look round to see if there was ever any new talent that she liked. That never was. She proudly showed off her new boyfriend and I returned affection as she taught me to skate.

As Judith sat in the back seat of her father's car, her toddler full of life beside her, she was now quite tearful. The memory of the nightclub and the great time together had happened before Donna was born. She wondered at the miscarriage and the thought of losing a child that would have been beautiful, like Donna. Quickly, she wiped the tears from her eyes. Donna saw Judith trying to hide her tears and straightaway asked her why she was crying; the toddler came to her mother and cuddled her.

Donna knew there was something wrong with her mother as Donna never cried 'cos her dad had told her not to let people see her cry, and to wait till she was alone in bed, maybe, before she should cry. He'd explained to his daughter that it was not right to show her feelings because the people who saw her cry could hurt her even more.

The copper came to the iron gate and called my name. Excitedly, I exited the gate into the corridor and was shown to a holding cell at the opposite end of the police station. I was not happy about having my visit in a cell, but the excitement of seeing Judith and Donna made me keep my mouth shut.

Donna let out a shout when she saw me. The three of us cuddled and kissed. Judith shed a few tears; I could taste the salt from her tears and cuddled even harder. The reunion went on for some minutes, each of us enjoying the moment.

The feeling of Judith's toned body close in my arms made me cuddle her again. I was holding two conversations at once, answering Donna's questions and listening to what the toddler had seen through the car window, and explaining to Judith what I thought would happen in my case.

My heart welled inside my chest. I felt great sadness in my soul and my mind raced backwards and forwards. It didn't take much for me to recall how good it had been to be with my family in our own home before the attack. I felt like crying, but didn't.

Judith commented that it was her first time in a police cell and we laughed, which broke the mood – that's what I wanted. I explained to Judith that a visit in the prison was held in a big visiting room, with rows of tables and chairs, nothing like where we were now.

At the end of every sentence, Judith wanted to tell me that she loved me. She didn't and this frustrated her. She guarded her emotions just for my sake. She knew I was picking up the vibes and contented herself with emotions that said it all. She lent over and kissed me softly on the lips. She believed that the atmosphere in the police cell was overcome by her love for me.

Donna pulled a toy, Thomas the Tank Engine, from one of the bags, enquired what the room they were in was for. The visit did not hold the toddler's attention and the room they were in was smelly and cold. Donna didn't like it.

The conversation, more importantly, went on to the subject of changing address and a move to where no one knew they lived. A council surveyor had visited the house when it was smashed up. They had estimated that, without the family's personal belongings, there had been £2,832 worth of damage that had to be repaired before the council would move them. The work the council required had been done and, when the surveyor returned, he passed the work and okayed us to move.

Initially, the surveyor automatically thought that the damage had been caused by a domestic row that had left the house in ruins. Via the telephone, I persuaded him that it wasn't the case, and that there was a genuine threat to my family. I reminded Judith of how I'd spoken to the surveyor and told her to make sure the council staff knew we were speaking the truth.

We discussed the loss of the new baby, we felt bereaved about it; pain burned our stomachs and our hearts. Judith wanted another baby and told me so. I was caught in the excitement of the moment, my woman wanting another child.

I spoke to Donna, asking if she still wanted a sister or brother. Judith watched Donna's reaction. The toddler said she would love a second child in the family, someone to play with, and that there would always be someone there to play her games with. Times change, but inside you can still hold the power of love.

At that moment, I felt like I was beyond the law and that there was little the law could do to change that. Convince yourself and you will grow strong; the bad times will be washed away by the excitement of the good. Our conversation visit was being earwigged by the police; the desk sergeant that sat near the cell was seated perfectly to listen in.

In between the conversation I could not get any closer to my woman. She was a sexual woman and I could tell that she was sexually aroused at the time. I picked up on it and immediately wanted to fuck her. She did that to me. It was always on the spur of the moment, maybe on top of a car bonnet in the middle of a 'B' road. Whenever she gave off female hormones, I would fuck her. It had not got any less after the birth of their first child. In fact there had been more sex than before the birth of Donna.

Judith whispered in my ear and asked how I was really feeling and how well I was coping. I held her hand as I gave her a look of sincerity and told her that I was all right, missing my family badly but managing to muscle on through. I told her that I missed being in bed with her and waking up in the morning next to her.

I told her how sexy she was and that I loved to see her dirty knickers on the floor, and how sometimes I'd hold them to my face and smell the woman in them, then call down for her to come to bed and make passionate love. Judith listened to my words and did not hear weakness. She felt like making love to me, and at the same time mothering me, because of the circumstances were so difficult.

I worried that the police would shortly call time and, with

intense passion, told her how deep my love was for her. My mood drifted slightly and it hit so hard that I said a silent prayer.

Surely Judith would be safe if they moved home, not only from the thugs but from the bitter women who may enjoy twisting the knife in Judith's back by opening up about the affairs and one night stands I'd had that past year.

My thoughts were selfish. All I cared about was my family and I hated, with passion, the threat of Judith finding out about my flings. I felt sorrow in my heart because I'd abused Judith's trust after taking her and Donna's love.

'Time,' the copper shouted through the half-pulled cell door. I had hoped the coppers would extend my visit as my family were the only visitors, but they didn't.

As Judith and Donna left there was an optimistic feeling in the air; we were very much in love, which was our strength, and that would always remain the same.

6
FREED FOR VENGEANCE

I had been on remand for six weeks. I'd appeared before the magistrates four times and listened to the CID oppose bail that I had not requested. I'd spent the time composing a long letter to the judge. At the bail hearing my solicitor recommended that I await committal and make the application for bail in the Crown Court. I had decided against this, feeling certain that I'd be granted bail on the strength of my letter and family circumstances. I had not entered a plea and, after the time spent on remand and hearing what evidence the CID had against me, I felt certain that my pleading at that time was beneficial to my case and me.

After careful consideration of the evidence against me, including information from the two witnesses and the description of my van, I knew that a 'not-guilty' plea was suicide. However, hearing the evidence against me allowed me to prepare mitigation for a guilty plea and, with luck and foresight, they would grant me bail.

The police wanted me locked up and out of the way and I knew that, normally, a man who had committed a serious offence applying for bail was not likely to succeed.

On the day of the bail application, Mrs Hall was the presiding magistrate – she was known as the Ball Breaker because of her no-nonsense approach in dealing with prisoners in the dock.

After reading my admittance to the charge, my legal representative recommended that I didn't produce it to the magistrate. He thought that it would have little effect, if any, and that it would only stand me in bad stead if the magistrates denied understanding of my written evidence. Although I was careful how I worded my plea, I did admit to the charge and gave my reasons why.

The judge eyed the letter in her hands. The room was quiet as she peered over her half-rimmed glasses. She looked briefly at Judith and our three-year-old toddler, and I was sure I could feel some compassion.

The only two people in the public gallery were Judith and Donna. They had waited in the foyer all day and it was teatime before I appeared in court. Donna had been on her best behaviour and waited patiently to see me. Her Honour called time while she and her colleagues considered the letter. I visibly relaxed as the magistrate left the court.

My little toddler ran towards me and I leaned out of the defendant's box, where I was flanked between two policemen, and gave her a hug and kiss. Donna asked me if I was coming home. I picked the child up and sat her on the side of the dock.

It had been different since Dad had been away; she had missed his fun and cuddles and now all that was finished. Dad was coming home and she knew her mam would be happy, 'cos her mam had cried a lot while they'd been on their own. It was Donna's fourth birthday in a couple of weeks and I had promised a surprise birthday present. I had to see their new house, which her mother was still decorating. They had been there for three weeks now.

Donna had helped with the decorating, painting the doors white without spilling the paint just like her mother had said.

Sitting there with me, Donna reeled off a prepared speech, telling me how she'd helped do the new house and even helped put new curtains up at the windows. As I listened, a lump came to my throat.

Judith had carefully watched the judge, hoping that women's insight would be considered by Her Honour, Mrs Hall. She believed, absolutely, that I would go free that day, in a matter of hours. The slight niggle she had previously had in her heart that there was a possibility I would not be released was covered by her womanly intuition and faith in the compassion of the female judge.

The two members of the police sat either side of me had noticed the judge take careful notice of my family during the hearing and possibly thought that the wife and child were putting on a careful act to get the judge to sympathise with the family plight.

My letter expressed in detail how deep my love was for Judith and my daughter, and how it had been such a serious attack on my family that I was truly forced to act because my family's lives had been threatened. It was the truth, that the offence was directly connected to the critical possession of my woman and child. I had explained fully and with feeling that there was no other way because the police had virtually ignored me and had prompted my offence by not acting to catch the thugs.

Her Honour considered the different explanations and it seemed to me that she could feel the truth come through the words. I'd guess it was not often that she had a clear perception of how evil and horrible prison really was. To set me free would ease the pain of two young lovers and their daughter, but I knew the judge also had to consider the risks made clear by the CID and police. Would I abuse bail restrictions and what about the miscarriage suffered by the family?

But I had spoken from the heart – every word was absolutely

true. And as I saw it, the judge slowly seemed to find that she was swaying to what was best for the man and family in front of her. Was she wondering if keeping this family together would benefit others, knowing now that I was a committed and loving family man, and a victim of circumstance?

The judge would know the police and CID's outlook on cases similar to this one, but there were the compassionate circumstances to calculate in her decision.

Her Honour must have known that such a serious offence would mean that when the case was tried it would result in a custodial sentence. I knew it too and would expect to go to prison. But what I was asking the magistrates' court for was time to prepare my family for a long jail term.

Judith watched with intense hope as she and the rest of court stood up as the magistrates entered the court. The judge watched the toddler return to her mother, ready and waiting for me to come home. It looked to me as if she was watching my reaction, as she granted bail and expressed the conditions, for any tell-tale signs of conspiracy. The tears in my eyes and the expression on my face would have quietened anyone's concerns as to whether the right decision had been taken by setting me free.

Judith told Donna that Dad was coming home straightaway, and Donna let out a squeal of excitement. Judith's instincts were right. She fixed the judge with a look that said 'thank you'.

I had won bail; Her Honour had a heart. But bail conditions were strict: I would have to sign on at the local police station twice a week and succumb to a curfew, which meant I had to be in the house between 9.00pm and 7.00am every day.

As soon as I worked my way back down the steps from the dock and through the gate, my mind was working overtime trying to predict what the police's next move would be. I spat on the floor of the cell as the copper locked me up.

Someone always had to put the dampener on everything. I banged on the door and shouted through the hatch. I was stressed and pissed off that the police seemed to be dragging their heels over completing the release paperwork.

Whilst the desk sergeant busied himself the CID came, got me out the cell and led me into the interview room. The coppers, two of them, looked at my mile-wide grin. They returned it with a look of annoyance. I just asked the CID when I would be released. They did not answer, just let the silence drag on and escorted me back to the cells.

Whilst I was in the holding cell, Judith and Donna walked around from the court to the police station's front desk. Judith was happy as her daughter skipped along beside her. The traffic outside was busy, people going about their ordinary business, which gave Judith a pang of jealousy as she wished this whole mess was ended so that she, Donna and I could get on with our lives.

The sun was out and Judith checked her watch. Time was on her mind as she recalled the wall clock that now hung on the fire breast in their new home. Summer was stretching to an Indian summer, which sometimes went on till the end of September. It was now the beginning of September and she felt joy that some things were going our way.

It had been a hard, but very busy, time apart. She recalled when she had visited the council, looking for another property. She'd been sad and it had sapped at her inner strength, as she had had to go over the attack and the offence again in order to make them believe that the family's lives were in danger.

At first, the managers of the council housing department had not believed Judith as she explained about the thugs. They thought that we had deliberately come up with the story so that we could be re-housed. After checking the explanation with the police, and finding that she was telling the truth about my imprisonment, they reluctantly agreed. Judith had been offered a two-bedroom ground floor flat in a quiet, more upmarket estate, where she and her family were not so well known.

Judith was not depressed long; she took strength from our family and the thought of how good it would be when the three of us were back together again. Something, though, haunted her: the bitter thought of Crown Court, a circuit judge and a final sentence. She hoped that there was a special clause that only the judge knew about that would be brought into action because of love.

Judith felt tears in her eyes as she realised that there would be no miracle; she was subject to the pain of expectation.

I walked out of the cell, the desk sergeant ushering me into the interview room. The bail papers were all prepared and waiting for my signature. I scanned them quickly. It was stated clearly that I'd been bailed to Crown Court to await trial, and that I had to surrender myself at a certain time, on a date to be arranged.

I took on board the lack of dates – they would write and inform me by letter when my case would be heard. At least three months, maybe even six. This thought gave me a surge of excitement; I would use the bail time for my purpose. I was free to move around so that I could sort out my family and business, which gave me a chance to beat the charge by intimidating the witnesses, or, at worst, receive a lesser prison sentence.

In the police station foyer, the three of us were reunited amongst kisses, cuddles and yelps of delight. A feeling that together we could face the trials and pain was hidden behind tear-filled eyes. Walking out of the police station into daylight, happiness and sorrow filled my heart. We made our way to the main street and a taxi rank.

There would be some running about to do these next few days. I'd have to enquire from my friends the whereabouts of the witnesses that the police had against me, then the intimidation would carefully be brought into action.

Judith was worried. She was not convinced her family would be safe and the thought of moving to Newcastle appealed to her because no one would ever find them. Fish and chips with Coke in Newcastle seemed a much better choice than sitting in a designer burger bar in the south, where they may walk into the enemies that had attacked their house. She felt butterflies in her stomach.

Donna got tomato ketchup on the sides of her mouth and wiped it off with the back of her hand while at the same time munching on her burger. Judith continues to think about the possibility of moving to Newcastle. She'd visited the city briefly on a number of occasions. She'd met my parents and had my mates and knew they were genuinely good people. She'd enjoyed the Geordie way of looking at things and she had related to my family.

Donna had been born in Durham, so she was a Geordie by birth. This had happened out of the blue. Judith's pregnancy came two weeks early as Judith and I had been holidaying in the north. The birth of our daughter was an ecstatically happy event and Judith was pleased to have her first-born come into the world with so much heritage surrounding her.

Sadly, I had not been present at the birth because Judith had started labour while I was out drinking with my mates. I'd turned up at 3.00am the following day, after finding out Judith had gone into labour and had immediately gone to hospital. They had let me see my daughter, but I did not see my common-law wife, as Judith was resting and was asleep. The nurses had told me to come back the next morning.

The attraction of living in the north-east was strong. She just wanted the family to be together and safe from the threat of the thugs. Our minds were being dictated to by the situation the police had forced us into.

Re-occurring thought patterns created in my head by the police had to be dealt with and got rid of. This was done by recalling future plans and what had to be sorted out in regard to further criminal activities. The thoughts of what I would do to my enemies – crucify them – would make me content, but it was a short-lived respite as I sorted through what I had to do.

I reached over the table and held Judith's hand. I asked her if she remembered Donna's birth, and I apologised for failing to fulfil my plans to make them a good life. Tears in my eyes, I forced my determination from deep within my soul, and I was very proud of my loved ones and impressed by their resilience and faith.

Judith listened to my explanations and my request for a second chance when the case was finished and dealt with, so they could get on with ordinary lives. Judith believed I was innocent of all charges.

Judith told me that she still did not feel safe, even in their new property, and made it clear that she wanted to move to Newcastle and start anew there. She was quite happy to watch her daughter grow up with a Geordie accent in Newcastle.

Donna picked up on what we were discussing and told us that she wanted to go to Newcastle to see her nana and all her cousins and nephews, whom she had seen only a few times. The happy times were stuck in her mind and she liked it there.

Donna still remembered when she had last seen her nana and pops, all the kids played on the streets of the council estate. She knew that she spoke cockney and that she would like to speak Geordie. This strange southern dialect fascinated the northern kids. Donna had told them all she was a Geordie too, because she'd been born in a Geordie hospital. Her dad had told her to say this so the kids shut up about the way she spoke.

A sense of calmness came across me as I listened to my child go on about the streets I'd grown up in. With passion, Judith squeezed my hand. I wanted to make love to Judith and it was hard waiting for the right moment.

She watched me intently as I thought of her naked body, and how we would make love to each other, fast and furious or with love and caring. That cheered me up. I was an excellent lover. I could switch her emotions on and off with a look of desire. I made love in tune with her emotions. We were soon both sexually stimulated – I had a semi on and Judith was becoming wet down below. We both laughed as these sexual thoughts crossed our minds at the same time.

We left the moment as we took notice of Donna, who had now decided to sing the theme tune to *Thomas the Tank Engine*. We let go of held hands and Judith offered me a cigarette. I took one and puffed away on the JPS. The mood had shifted again to one of happiness.

After we left, I stopped and looked in the window of the shop next to the burger bar. It was a bookshop, and advertised in the window were books on space and the universe. Donna held my hand as I contemplated buying a book for her. Judith followed us into the shop and browsed around. I chose a book about our galaxy. I let Judith have a look and she approved of my choice. She decided that Donna would learn from a book like that.

Judith would have liked to buy the book about witchcraft, which she was interested in and would like our daughter to learn about, but she decided Donna was too young for this subject. Donna liked her new book; it was the picture on the cover that attracted the toddler's attention – a starry night with a US space rocket flying thought space.

I began to feel tired as we left the shop. I had not slept well since I had last been at home with my family. But the thing that tiredness never changed was my will for revenge.

The three of us headed for the taxi rank. Judith told me she wanted some shopping so we took the taxi to Gossips Green shopping boulevard. I walked around the shops and watched my family enjoy what they were doing, choosing goodies for tea and supper. After being locked up, everything seemed new and without effort.

I walked down the boulevard and headed for the off-licence. We bought four cans of Hölsten extra strong lager and a large bottle of Merrydown cider; Donna had pop in the house.

Judith was looking forward to a night in with me; we'd share the drink while making love, just like we always did when I was stopping in with her, instead of going drinking with my mates.

My heart beat fast as I toured the two-bedroom flat. Donna showed me her bedroom and how clean it was kept. I laughed at her toys – teddy bears and Thomas the Tank Engine – which was still my daughter's favourite. I remembered how the toy had lain in one piece in the middle of the floor when everything else had been smashed by the thugs. Christ was coming with vengeance and the people against me would be dealt with severely.

Judith joined us in Donna's bedroom. She gave Donna the new space book and Donna excitedly went in the living room, switched the TV on and opened the book; first she would look at the illustrations then she'd get me to read, as she was not yet able to read books herself.

Then Judith took me by the hand, kissed me and led me into the master bedroom. She'd decorated the room in blue, with black satin sheets and duvet on the bed. She'd put them on clean before she had gone expectantly to court that morning.

Judith shut the door behind us and we groped and kissed with absolute passion, taking advantage of the moment, and our innermost feelings of want and need as we fell on to the inviting bed.

Minutes seemed to turn to hours as we aroused each other. I was totally engrossed in my woman. We separated with the thought that the toddler might come in the room and catch us making love. We kissed passionately as we left each other's embrace and returned to the living room. Donna was sat with her book, half looking at the pictures, half seeing what was on the telly.

Judith knew how to please me. She knew that night, when Donna was sound asleep in her bedroom, that she'd get dressed up for me: leopard-skin miniskirt, black suspender-less stockings, a body stocking in black lace with her tits visible through the material.

The three spent the rest of the evening giving Donna our full attention, reading her space book, with me explaining the difference between a galaxy and the universe. One day in years to come, I promised to give Donna my galaxy to play in, and a galaxy was a colossal size.

The toddler fell asleep in my arms and, for the first time in weeks, I carefully put her to bed and tucked her in with one of her teddies. The feelings inside my heart were so strong that they brought tears to my eyes.

Judith was sat on the sofa, quiet and enjoying the atmosphere of having her man around the house again. I told her I would make a phone call before we settled for a night of love-making. A quick kiss and Judith decided to get ready and bring the drink in while I made my call.

7
LOVING THE NIGHT AWAY

Unbeknown to Judith, I decided to put into action inquiries as to where and who the witnesses were and where I could find the thugs that smashed our house up. It would be obvious that, while I was in custody, the people involved would have had a false sense of safety. I considered which one of my associates would be best to find this information, and if he did not know then I could find out myself.

A plan was forming of how to get hold of some money. I would phone tomorrow my partner – and Steve's brother – tomorrow. He would be last on Steve's list of informers. I expected that Arthur would be praying I was not released and would go straight from remand to a long prison sentence, so that I would not get any money.

I asked Steve what his brother was doing work-wise; Arthur had started a private job, a big 25-grand extension, cash in the hand. I digested the information and thought: if the worst came to the worst I could always pick up my tools and go to work with Arthur, and I would make sure I got back any money I'd been conned out of from the big job, by taking a big chunk of the money from the extension.

Judith thought she'd get dressed first then get the drink into me so I'd get hard by stripping her with my eyes. I could tell she was wet and, as she slipped into her body stocking, she shuddered with anticipation. The weight she'd felt while I was away lifted from her shoulders and she wanted me inside her. From her toes to the tips of her long fingers, she wanted to fuck. Her love juice smelled of a woman's deep desire; it was an irresistible odour that was only associated with the passion of making love to the one you loved.

We were soul-mates; the hard times had done nothing but bring us together. When we were with each other nothing seemed to bother us. Judith frisked a finger over the top of her vaginal lips and the thought of my sperm shooting inside her drove her to the point of near orgasm. She came to me, collecting the Hölsten and cider from the back kitchen.

I had been anticipating this moment all day and it was worth the wait. My mind cleared. The anticipation was so strong it made my cock tingle and before she could put the drink down, I was on her, my hands ravishing her perfect body beneath the lace-and-nylon clothing.

We could not get enough of one another. We licked and kissed while loosening my clothes and throwing them to one side. I felt her body rubbing against mine and my shaft went rigid; I desperately wanted to stick it in her with all my might and just stay like that for hours, loving and lusting every blessed moment. The taste of her love juices while in the middle of intercourse was something special and out of this world.

If it had been a slut – a one-night stand – I was having, I would have told of my conquest to my mates in the pub, but I truly loved Judith and every moment I cherished and kept private. We orgasmed together, both our bodies covered in sweat and racked with pleasure. For moments that dragged on, we stayed inside one another. I became semi-hard beneath Judith's saturated clit. We cuddled each other and made the moment last.

We had started making love soon after Donna had fallen asleep: that was 7.00pm. It was now 8.15pm; non-stop lovemaking had quenched our thirst. We drank snakebites and wallowed in each other's company.

We decided to wait a while for our next love session and I decided I'd walk to the Chinese, which was in a nearby housing estate and shopping precinct. That was the closest as there were no takeaways or fish shops where we lived. I got dressed in record time. I wanted to get there and back so we could eat, drink and then make love for the rest of the evening.

As I left the flat, my cock felt special, wet with the juices of lovemaking. For a moment I considered my past six weeks held in custody, and freedom tasted even better. I considered what I had to do to keep my freedom and my family.

I'd sort out some transport from a mate, Charlie, and that would be done without paying. Transport was important, as I needed to move around as quickly as possible. Then I would look up Steve when I knew the identity and the whereabouts of witnesses and enemies. Once I knew this I'd decide who would be best dealt with first, and then I'd see Arthur regarding business and the company.

I intended to so some business with my limited company, hoping Arthur had left the banks alone. I realised he could not have abused the bank, as I was a director and I had to have my signature on cheques. Someone else was the chairman, but all he did was sign where he was told and get paid for the use of his name, which had been on my mind. Arthur might have used the banks by forging cheques in my name.

The building sub-contractors that dealt out of London were always on the lookout for company's going bent. They could fiddle a million pounds in a few months off the taxman, using the company invoices to write tax off.

Apart from the revenge I had in mind, money was second on

the list and I intended to break any and every law to get this for my family. I would take the easy way first, which was to deal with the limited company, and if I did not make enough I'd go on the pavement and rob at gunpoint.

As soon as I got money sorted out I would buy a house and, with the housing boom of the 1980s, I could make at least £1,500 profit a month. Once I had property and security in Judith's name, the family would get thousands of pounds in credit, which the family could sell on. The money from the goods bought with credit would contribute to Judith and Donna's living standards while I was in prison.

'Beef curry and chips twice, please.'

8
EYE CANDY

The day started at 6.00am. I lay for a few minutes looking at the ceiling; my woman lay asleep at my side. I dwelt on the fact of being out of prison and in bed with Judith. I studied my sleeping partner and slowly became hard; my cock stung as it ballooned to its full size.

I cuddled into my woman and felt between her legs. She was hot and moist and she moaned softly at my caressing. Judith responded by opening her legs. I became excited as, half asleep, my woman wanted to fuck. She started to wake up, but not entirely – she enjoyed the sleepy feeling together with being caressed sexily.

I entered Judith, the feeling of warmth and love washing over us as we desperately enjoyed the moments of togetherness.

The presence of me being back home and in her bed was too much. She shuddered and came quickly, her nails biting into my back as she writhed in orgasm. I came to the soft moans of my woman, pleased that I had made her cum so quickly.

I told Judith over breakfast what I intended to do, and that I'd have transport later that day. She ideally would have liked to have accompanied me, but I felt that the people I had to see would not be impressed if I turned up with my woman at my side, so I told her this and arranged to meet her later that day in town so we could go to a cafe for dinner.

My mate Charlie Wells fixed cars for a living. I found him busy at the garage rubbing down a yellow Vauxhall Chevrolet ready for painting. He had a metallic-brown Cortina 2000E that was ready to be sold stood at the side of the garage.

I enquired what had been going on while I'd been in prison and after the firearms attack. Charlie went into one and told me the regulars had talked about nothing else since it had happened. I listened and when Charlie spoke about the attack on my house and how the thugs had been bragging as to how they were paid to smash up my family, my stomach turned. It was really lucky that my woman and child were not in the house when the thugs attacked that day. I was sick for revenge and to make sure this never happened again. I asked Charlie the whereabouts of the gang that had conspired against me. Charlie told me that I'd be better off talking to Steve or Harry.

I asked Charlie if I could take the Cortina 2000E; it was an 'R' reg and very clean to look at. Charlie agreed, telling me I could keep it as long as I needed it. The car had no tax and the MOT ran out the following month. This little misdemeanour didn't matter to me, the same with insurance cover notes. I could have the tax, MOT and the insurance forged if I was pulled over by the police on a producer. I had a bent licence in my own name. I'd had it since the age of 18 and it had been produced to the police on a number of occasions and passed every time.

All paperwork to do with producing documents for a driving offence was forged at the cost of £25–30; it was worth it to use this system because it was £100 cheaper. With an ordinary out-of-date MOT, you steeped it in a tray of brake fluid and ten minutes later the ink lifted from the document, then you rinsed it under a warm tap and hung it to dry over a warm towel on the radiator.

The tax was done with other chemicals that had a similar effect; a friend of mine did this, as it was quite a delicate act.

I pulled up outside Steve's house. He lived in a cul-de-sac with only one way to drive in. His van was there. I was confident and pleased that I had caught my acquaintance in.

Steve was sat in the living room, reading the morning paper. His wife Tina gave me a kiss on the cheek. Steve came in the back kitchen saying 'hello', but I didn't waste any time on formalities as Steve enquired how I got bail on a firearm offence. I swiftly brushed the query to one side. I listened to the information that Steve had gathered. Two of the gang were shacked up together in a flat. These two men were John Barrett and Neil Evans, the same two that had entered my house and attacked my family. The other two that had waited outside to stop any escape I might try were still living in their family homes.

My mind was working overtime. I needed numbers for the thugs, addresses, and I was told that John Barrett and Neil Evans were in accommodation where they had upset the owner of the flat. I knew the person Steve was talking about; he lived in the flat above a shop. He was a law-abiding citizen and the two gang members could use and abuse the man.

John Barrett and Neil Evans took the shop takings each day and paid no rent or food bills – they were a nasty pair that planned to bleed the premises into bankruptcy.

I wanted these two thugs desperately. I decided then and there that they would be dealt with first. In between savaging these two, there was a possibility that the second two thugs would hear about the first attack and would go into hiding to avoid me.

Steve went into one over the two witnesses; one was the actual man that I had committed the offence against. He knew that the witness had made a statement that condemned me. Would he turn up for court when I was on trial?

Steve doubted that the man we discussed could be intimidated;

there was not a good enough reason for him not to turn up in court and support his statement. In fact, he was the type of person that enjoyed the limelight of being a celebrity after having paid to get me done over. His prestige had shot up ten-fold and the little club he drank in at the end of the estate's shopping boulevard was buzzing with the recent events he'd been a part of.

The second witness was an occupant of the house straight across from Andy Ward. This man had seen me and Chris Hawley walk away after discharging the sawn-off. He had come out to the end of his drive and taken down the registration of my van.

These two statements, together with forensic powder blasts on my hands after firing the shotgun, were enough to convict me. I hoped that the police would not find any forensics because I'd had time to wash, but I considered that the clothes I'd been wearing would have traces of the powder flash; I had to assume that there was forensic evidence.

Things did not seem very good as I weighed up the pros and cons of the offence. I enquired as to how our chairman was doing, thinking that Arthur may have had him sign cheques and invoices on my company. I arranged to meet with Steve later that afternoon in, of all places, our local, the Railway, where I would also meet the other partner.

I knew as soon as I had dealt with the thugs Barrett and Evans that the police would be on my case, so I prepared myself for this by securing a solid alibi with my mates and associates.

First I would sort out the gun, then early morning I would repay them. I would consider the scheme more so when I'd got used to the idea. Frank Hayes was the man that had taken the sawn-off and hidden it. I would have to see him and retrieve it. At the same time arrange an alibi for when I dealt with the thugs.

I digested the information that Steve had given me; I'd dwell on it until I felt the time was right. I had a powerful urge inside that needed me to be with my woman and child, and I decided to put off a visit to Arthur's until the next day.

I used Steve's phone and rang Judith, briefing her as to what I'd been doing, not mentioning the information in detail, just basic descriptions. Anyway, she could drive the car.

Judith put the phone down and picked up the mirror and carried on making her face up. She had decided to wear jeans and a sports top, but she changed her mind and put on a short skirt and black hold-up stockings, which would turn any man's head twice. She loved to look sexy for me; it made her feel so much more womanly. Judith tried to piece together, along with my character, the events that had led up to that day. Her mood changed as she considered it, and it frightened her – she knew I would go and inflict my revenge.

I was intense and needed revenge in order for us to put the past behind us and start a new life, with a feeling that all our debts were paid. There was no way she would stand by and watch me face another charge; a charge that would be severe.

When I got back to the flat to pick Judith up, she was candy to my eyes. I kissed her passionately, quickly brushing off her queries so as not to let on what my plans were or where we were heading. It was best for Judith not to know the full facts of what I was organising.

We discussed where to go that afternoon. Judith had to go to Tesco or Sainsburys to get the groceries for the week. First we'd do that then go to the burger bar, to treat Donna because she was helping her mam and dad. Right, Judith was ready to go, Donna was too, they all had their jackets on. Just as we were about to leave I told them that Donna's surprise birthday present was a Staffordshire bull terrier, a brindle coloured pup. It was a bitch, so Donna could breed her and always have a pup from the same family. I told my family that it had been organised prior to me being on remand, and that I would pick the pup up on Donna's birthday.

I intended to buy a second bull terrier so that, when I was in prison, Judith and Donna would be much more safer with dogs around the place; it comforted me as I considered the two dogs I would buy. The brindle bitch was not from the same litter as the dog, and the pup would not be ready for the next six weeks. I'd buy the brindle bitch on the next Friday.

The pup I intended to buy would grow into a four-stone monster that would keep my woman and child safe. The dog would be a handful, but Judith would cope and it would be worth it in the long run. I told Donna that she should think of a name and that her mam would help her.

Judith wasn't sure about Staffordshire bull terriers; they had a bad reputation as being vicious. I explained about how I felt and how the dogs could be used not only for protection as guard dogs, but that she could breed them when I was in jail. Selling the pups was worth the hassle and they'd need the money. Judith remembered her old dog and was sad it had to die; she dwelled on the thought from years ago.

I had Donna sat on my knee in the car's passenger seat. Judith was driving, which turned me on as she always took her shoes off and drove barefoot, which I thought was very sexy. I told Judith to go the long way into town as I was still buzzing from being free and wanted to take in the familiar scenery.

On to the main road, half a mile down the road to a junction, a short ride, then a left turn at the roundabout into the town. Immediately, both Judith and I looked as we passed a house in the posh area, where we'd lived when Judith was pregnant with Donna.

We each had our own memories of that time; I remembered the night before we left to live with Judith's friend. We had thrown a big party with all the drop-outs and rejects, punks, skins invited. The party had been a success, done for a good time and to spite one of the lodgers in the house; it had been so packed that they were coming through the front door and falling out the back.

Someone had phoned the police and complained. The coppers couldn't get in the front door so they knocked on the back and I answered. The sergeant wanted to talk to the owner. I said I was temporarily in charge of the property and told the copper where to get off.

The other couple renting a room came to the front door with an army of the local football team. They took one look at the breeds of scum that were partying and jumped straight into their cars and left. I got hold of Judith and together we picked up the music stereo and squeezed our way out to the garage where, in view of the waiting police, we put the stereo into the boot of Judith's old Fiat, reversed up through the police vehicles and left for our new digs.

We found out later that the damage to the interior of the house had come to thousands of pounds, and that Judith and I were expected to part pay for it to be repaired. We were not in any way going to part with our cash and considered the loss of our deposit enough to cover our part of the damage.

Judith and I had organised the party, along with the other couple that lodged in the property, because the other two, a couple, had conspired to evict us all. So we paid the snotty cow and her man back.

They locked themselves in their rooms and barred the door, staying like that until the party finished. I would have loved to have seen their expressions when they faced the aftermath of the shindig.

Judith, when I mentioned the house as we passed, remembered that night and what she had worn: it was a polka-dot, white minidress. She had fabulous legs that seemed to go on and on and up to her neck. She saw me that night as a saviour; the party had got out of hand so we left. I assured Judith that the police wouldn't pull her, as they were more interested in the goings-on of the party.

Judith was drunk and silently took strength from my assurances that she'd be all right. She was just starting to show with Donna and was looking forward to seeing her friend Sharon, whom we were going to live with. We had arrived at 1.00am on a Sunday morning, stereo and bags in tow, and Judith's friend had made us both very welcome. We passed our old house and continued on down the bank to the main road that headed into town. As we passed the open level-crossing gates I, again, lost myself in the memories of the wine bar set just off the corner of the main road. A burger bar was across the road from the bar.

I was sad and Judith, no doubt, breathed a sigh of relief that the wine bar was now closed and a record shop had taken over the premises. Donna asked which burger bar we were going to and whether she could go to to the one near the bar.

Judith had hated the fact that nine months ago I was a bouncer on the door of the wine bar: she thought that I had been tempted by the many single women; she never had any proof of this, but I used to arrive home very late and had the stench of women and stale perfume about me. I told Judith, when she asked, that the wine bar was always full of women and that, as I moved through the crush of bodies, the perfume smell got on my T-shirt and jeans.

It was two guys, Simon Tennant and his brother Bill, who ran the bar together. Tennant had needed a bouncer because he did not get involved with violence. They had no stomach for fighting. Judith's friend Bev Donnelly worked in the bar as barmaid, and when Simon Tennant enquired about needing a doorman, Bev had said that a Geordie friend of hers would likely be interested in the job. Judith and I needed the money so I took £30 a night for the door job and my drink for nothing.

If the bar had still been open, I would have taken my family in to see what it was like. They could have taken burgers and fries and eaten them in the wine bar, had a few drinks after the family shopping.

One of my mates, Eddie, used the wine bar like it was his home; he'd pick up his wages from an office-partitioning firm on a Friday afternoon, then he would go straight to the wine bar and hand Tennant his wages. He would drink at the bar all weekend and, if there was any money left, he'd get it back from Tennant on a Monday morning. Simon would have lock-ins most evenings and Eddie would drink till he could not drink any more and fall on the floor.

As we followed the main road through town, which was busy, we passed a taxi rank next to the Commercial pub. This pub had been my first local when I came to the area, as it was a spit-and-piss pub.

The locals mostly ignored the Commercial. It was not the type of place to take your girlfriend or wife. I used the pub because it reminded me of the pubs and clubs where I used to live in the north.

I would arrange to meet my women that I'd met in there. I'd always meet them early evening before the pub got busy, where I felt in my element and where the jukebox accompanied my character.

Judith thought of the night she'd been in the Commercial drinking double vodkas with me. She'd got so drunk that she slid down the pub bar, half-unconscious. I had put her in a Sainsburys shopping trolley, which had been left next to the taxi rank, and pushed her through the town eventually flagging down a taxi, as the taxis were at their busy peak time.

Judith had been sick in the cab and I had to pay an extra £10 to have it cleaned.

Donna surveyed the big oak tree outside the Commercial and next to the taxi rank. She asked if the squirrels were still there, tried to see them as we passed in the car. I told her they'd be asleep in the tree and that we might see them later on.

I remembered the spot just outside the pub door where I was glassed, and I ran my finger down the four-inch scare on the side of my face. The fight had been my second of the evening; the first had been with the shit that I'd knocked out earlier in the evening at the Railway pub.

We parked in Sainsburys car park and, while Judith and Donna went shopping, I sparked up a fag, which Judith didn't mind as she knew I was enjoying the time spent and not wasted in jail.

As I sat there admiring some good-looking women, my heart skipped a beat as Paula came into view. It looked like the woman, with two kids in tow and a baby's buggy, had come from the shop that Judith was in.

I felt threatened by the meeting and I averted my eyes. I didn't want to look in the buggy; I was frightened that Judith might see or Donna might come outside the shop looking for me.

I wished myself and my family a million miles away, so far away that the baby, that supposedly was mine, could never hurt us. I didn't want to talk and, as Paula slowed down and contemplated what to say to her old lover, my heart beat faster. But she didn't speak and looked right through me. I felt helpless and scared that, somehow, Judith would know what Paula and the baby were all about.

Some female instinct would tell her what the situation was and there would be no need for words or explanations. Shock made it a hard moment to deal with. There were tears at the back of my eyes as I considered my beautiful daughter Donna, and that if Paula and her baby came to light, I would likely lose the joy of my life with my daughter. However, as Paula, kids and baby in the buggy silently walked past, my breathing gradually came under control. I threw the half-finished cigarette on to the pavement and crushed it with my foot. A confrontation had luckily been avoided (the checkouts were busy).

Judith, Donna and I were sat in the lounge of the Railway. Normally children weren't allowed in the pub as one of Brian Leigham's homemade rules, but he had allowed it because I was a mate.

Judith sipped her half lager and watched Donna drink her orange juice; I knocked back my pint, feeling bloated due to the Kentucky Fried Chicken that Donna had chosen when we were in town.

Steve saw me from the other bar and took the opportunity to come round and speak to me. He was half pissed, and this made him very interested in my next move, which he thought would be violence – which was fair enough as long as it didn't involve him.

Steve had the phone number of someone he'd spoken to earlier that day, and he told me that this bloke was able to help by letting me know when to catch the two thugs that were there in his flat. I quickly considered this and put the thought of a set-up to one side. I took the phone number from Steve and glanced at it before shoving the piece of scrap paper into the back pocket of my jeans. I wondered how and what Steve had said to him, hoping it had been brief.

I paid for the drinks and told Steve to wait at the bar while I took Judith and Donna their drinks. I returned to the bar, having told Judith I'd be five minutes. Harry came round from the other bar and shook my hand, pleased to see me and pleased that I was out of custody.

I quizzed Harry on business he'd taken care of for me since I had been on remand. The white Transit's lease had not been paid so it would be two months behind. I told Harry that I would see him in a couple of days, as I wanted him to help me out with some other business affairs. Harry was sweet with it all – as long as he got paid.

Brian came to where we stood and bought a round in. He did this only when I was in company, something to do with my reputation.

The serious mood wore away as Brian chatted casually with us. He was not shy in offering me advice, having spoken to his acquaintances in the local police station. He realised the importance that I kept out of trouble. I knocked back my pint and brought the other closer to my reach, then looked round to see my woman and child. I caught Judith's eye and mouthed, 'A couple of minutes.'

I watched the public bar through from where I stood in the lounge. Frank Hayes walked in and stood at the bar. We nodded to each other. I expressed that I had to see someone and left the company to go and speak with him.

We shook hands. I was greeted by some of the locals in the public bar. These people had respect for a hard man of violence, and liked to stay on the good side of one with such power. I was relaxed, but still dealt with the business at hand. In my mind I needed desperately to avenge my family.

Frank said he would sort the sawn-off later that day and told me to meet him at 6.00pm. He said he would bring it down with a dozen heavy-shot cartridges, just as he had retrieved it. I quizzed Frank about Arthur; Frank had been working with Arthur labouring on the extension. We spoke of Arthur's money and if he'd had a first payment from the job.

Frank told me that Arthur had put a cheque into the bank for the first draw off the job. He did not know how much, but it had been in for three days so it should have cleared and be ready to draw. I knew that Arthur would know I was out of jail and would be coming to talk to him. Steve would have told him this.

I thought that Arthur would have his story worked out and figured that the cheque from the extension would go into Arthur's own account or his wife's, as it would not be viable to put it through the company because then I would know and want my share. Not only that but he was probably considering that I would be still in jail, and that it would be a problem drawing the money.

As far as I was concerned, Arthur owed me £500 and I wanted a percentage off the job he was working on. Arthur, the coward, would argue if he had a point to make over money and I didn't want any of this. I wanted what I was due and didn't want the hassle of an argument.

I would pick up the gun from Frank that night, then drive up to Arthur's and confront my ex-partner. I'd have the gun where Arthur could see it, in the car, and that should stop any of his bellyaching. I said my goodbyes and my family drank up and we left.

I dialled the number and grinned when I heard my mother's voice. She was equally as pleased to hear from her son. I told her the good news about having been released and back with my family. My mother quietly shed a few tears and we swapped versions, and I said that I had to keep out of trouble and would not go back to prison. My mother shouted the news to my old man, who had just come in from the garden.

I could hear my mother quickly tell my old man who it was on the phone and that I was out of prison. My old man shouted his regards and hoped I was well. My mother had spoken to Judith and Donna every day since I had been locked up. She was never sure whether I was in police custody or in prison because of the Valcon system that the police were operating.

I loved my mother very much; she was a hard working, conscientious woman who was always ready to help when needed. I avoided talking about crime when my mother was around because she was a born worrier.

I handed the phone to Judith and let her speak. Donna went to her mother and told her to tell nana that they were coming to see her. I heard and mouthed, 'A couple of weeks.'

I went outside to the outhouse, it was full of household junk. I pulled a sports bag out from near the back. Inside was a one-and-a-half inch copper pipe, about 18 inches in length. It had been filled with nuts and bolts and the two ends beaten squashed. One end was taped. I felt the pipe, holding it out in front of myself to gauge the weight. It felt good and I had premonitions of beating the thugs' heads in with it.

There was also a Jif lemon squeezer, bright yellow and shaped like the fruit. It was filled with ammonia. I held it in my hands and debated. Originally I had intended to fill it with brick acid, which was used to clean brickwork. It was pure acid and would burn holes quickly through skin, but Judith had thrown the acid out so I'd settled for ammonia, which I hoped would do the job.

I decided to keep the Jif squeezer and slipped it into my sheepskin jacket. I'd sewn a loop of material into the jacket that the swan-off slipped neatly into without giving away what I was carrying. The bulky coat hid the weapon easily.

I put the pipe back in the bag and took it into the flat. Donna came into the kitchen and asked what I was doing. I would like to have told her, revenging her soul; instead I grinned at my daughter and said I had some work stuff in the bag.

Judith, having finished talking to nana, came in the kitchen, saw the bag that I quickly zipped up and knew straightaway that I was planning something. I could tell she had premonitions of me going back to jail.

I pulled up outside the Railway and hooted the horn. A few seconds later Frank came out of the pub carrying a plastic shopping bag. He jumped in the passenger seat and handed me the sawn-off and cartridges.

I wondered what Frank was thinking; probably worried that he might get caught up in the conflict. I knew from experience that Frank was a man of his word, to some point, and would support me in a fight, but I was not sure about Frank when guns were concerned. I felt safe with the gun on the floor of the passenger seat. I left the barrels of the gun sticking out of the shopping bag; Arthur could not fail to see it and this amused me. I was intent on getting my money from him.

I hooted the car horn outside of Arthur's house. The estate where Arthur lived was new, the houses and gardens all looking posh and modern. Arthur pulled the nets back and looked out of the window. I waved for him to come outside so we could talk in the car.

Arthur forced a grin as he came to the car; his pretence at being pleased to see me seemed false. I told him to watch where he put his feet. He looked down and I saw the lump appear in his throat as he viewed the sawn-off barrels sticking out of the bag.

I started the car up as Arthur patted me on the back and complimented me on getting out of jail. I watched him roll a smoke every now and then, and could tell that he was worried what the gun was for, and that he'd willingly got in the car with an outright madman who may be out to kill him.

I could see that Arthur considered jumping out the car, but the car I was driving was doing 80 miles an hour and he decided against the risk. I just wanted to talk, and Arthur was going to agree to whatever I wanted. He wanted to distance himself from his ex-partner.

I pulled into the little village of Rusper, which was a money-people hangout. We drove into the village car park. I spoke, relaxed, and went over what Arthur had done and whether he'd ripped me off. He agreed to give me the £500 he owed for building materials, and £500 on top of that for his cut of the extension, which could not have gone ahead if Arthur hadn't been able to supply the materials. Also there was a job there for me if I wanted it.

Arthur, having dealt with business, was happy to have his life intact – he valued his kneecaps too much. I waited silently until Arthur suggested going to the pub and sealing the deal over a drink.

I dropped my bombshell: if Arthur was to keep the Transit, he would have to pay the lease on it himself and, as of then, would stop forging cheques in my name. If he did it again then I would shoot him.

I would rather have had the money than shoot Arthur, although I wondered whether it was a kneecapping offence against my principles. I wondered how I could best use Arthur, and figured that I may need to be shown how to fiddle the invoices and the tax on the company if a problem arose.

9
FACE-SAVAGING COMBAT

I waited in the Barclays Bank foyer. It was 9.30am and Arthur and his wife were waiting in the queue inside the bank. It was a busy Monday morning and there were half a dozen people in the front of them. Arthur was not happy with the £5,000 cheque from the job; he'd rather have been paid cash on a Friday. This had been the case for the first three weeks, so he'd be able to pay the labourers. The extension was up to DPC (damp proof course) level and the owner of the property would then only pay by cheque.

The main street outside the bank was full of people going about their business. Arthur's £5,000 cheque was in his wife's account. He was uptight and prayed that the cheque had cleared so that he could pay me the agreed grand to get me off his back.

He fidgeted nervously and considered how much money he'd have left after paying the second bricklayer, Graham Cotton and Frank for two weeks' work: it worked out at £500 each cash. Arthur, prior to the bricklayer and hod carrier, had paid labourers £30 cash a day to get the extension's ground work and now had Graham Cotton and Frank to sort out. He was expecting a second cheque that week for £6,000, with which he'd pay the lease on my Transit van. He planned on giving his wife £500 and he reckoned £2,500 for himself.

I eyed the passers by as I waited patiently for my money. Then I couldn't believe my eyes, my heart missed a beat and brayed on my chest. There, walking past was John Barrett (one of the thugs). He walked past the front doors of the bank but did not see me. Quickly, I calculated my next move. I was excited at this stroke of luck and hurried out on to the street. The day was warm, the sun shinning and I was in two minds about what to do? To risk an attack in the middle of the street was desperate. I searched quickly for waiting police cars: there were none.

I poised myself behind Barrett and argued whether to risk following the thug until Barrett was in a better place so I would be less easily seen when I attacked.

I felt in my sheepskin pocket. The Jif lemon with its ammonia was there and it made the decision for me – I prepared to attack.

I was nearly sick with need; I wanted to kill this thug. All the waiting and thought that had gone into this now unexpected meeting. I controlled myself as I walked quietly and quickly up behind Barrett.

Barrett was on his way to sign on at the dole office. My voice sent waves of fear into the thug's heart as I shouted his name. I wanted Barrett to see what was coming and couldn't help myself as Barrett turned and faced his enemy. I used the ammonia, hitting him square in the face. The fat pig of a thug squealed and staggered on to the main road, trying to get away from his now unseen assailant.

I followed, striding to keep up with him, using the ammonia again and again. Barrett, totally blinded by the ammonia, tried to get away and fell into a passing motorcycle. The bike and Barrett toppled over on to the road. Traffic came to a halt as I moved in to vent my anger and frustration out on the thug. I was getting in a position to jump on Barrett's head and cave his skull in, double pissed off 'cos I didn't have a gun on me.

A double-decker bus full of people looking out the windows

saw the event, but didn't copy that the third man was kicking a man in the head while lying in the road. People on the bus all tried to get a better view of the attack; cars, taxies, all busy, stopped and watched.

I vented my anger further as Barrett, the vermin, wriggled about screaming in the road. One down, three to go. My hackles went up as the danger of being caught came to the forefront of my mind. My head immediately cooled down as I began to think naturally, searching around me for an escape route.

I was conscious of the people at the scene watching me but I didn't want to let Barrett go. I wished I could kick the scum to death and stick his head under an oncoming bus. I eventually ran back to where I'd come from and cursed my luck. I was wound up and breathing hard, and trying to put my thoughts into perspective. Arthur walked up to me in the foyer of the bank, ignorant as to what had just happened and happy that the cheque had cleared.

We crossed the road and went into the Commercial where we normally drank on a Monday morning. Arthur wondered what was wrong with me, breathing heavily, flushed and tense. I was debating how safe I would be inside the pub so that, if the police became involved, hopefully if they came looking I'd be well out of the way. From my position in the lounge bar I could see anyone coming as the pub had big bay windows that looked out on to the main street.

A few minutes later, I couldn't believe my eyes and cursed as John Barrett came running down the boulevard, eyes and face flaming red, rubbing his eyes as he disappeared up the street. I debated whether to go after the thug, but was unsure. I thought Barrett must have known better than to lie screaming in the road until the police arrived on the scene. If Barrett had waited for the police, he knew he'd be at least charged with breach of the peace. The thug must have counted his pros and cons and decided to take a leaf out of my book and run for it.

Barrett had been lucky and knew this. I had been excited and not happy because I could not have blown Barrett's head off, but even if I'd had the sawn-off on me, I may not have been able to use it, as there would have been numerous eyewitnesses.

I settled down a bit as I realised the police were not on the scene to make an arrest. Instead, I decided to get drunk and wind Arthur up as to why the partnership had broken down and, at the same time, praise myself for taking one of the biggest chances for my freedom. I was lucky and thought I'd celebrate, maybe talk to Arthur about the tax exemptions on the company.

Arthur paid me my grand and I got the round in; it was our first pint. The pub was quiet with only a few early morning drinkers. I watched two men come into the bar, they were brothers. The two sold drugs to feed their own heroin addictions.

I acknowledged them and thought back to Christmas 1986. It was about half ten on a Friday night. I was stood at the public bar; the pub was full. I was drunk, but not staggering drunk. As I swigged from my pint, somebody bumped into me and this caused me to spill some of my pint. I turned to see who it was and immediately became aware that something was amiss; I told the man to watch where he was going.

It was easy to suss what was going down. The brothers were picking a fight and had sent their mate to bump into me deliberately so I would kick off. I eyed their mate who had only recently started drinking in the Railway. I wanted to smash him in the face, and I forced myself to keep my temper. He saw that I was not biting and walked away, going to the pub toilet.

The brothers intended to make a name for themselves and had discussed with some of the locals who the head hard man was. I became a target. I followed one of them into the toilet and proceeded to beat him about the head and knocked him to the floor.

Brian witnessed the whole episode and decided to watch my back; he followed the two men into the toilet where he found me kicking the other. He pulled me off, and for the moment the confrontation finished. The man went back round the lounge end where his brother and their pals were waiting.

I stood at the public bar, all keyed up. I swigged my pint down. Brian immediately came back round to the public bar telling me he'd ordered the brothers and hangers-on they had to drink up and get out. Last orders were called and the place began to clear.

The locals were taking their time to leave, hoping the fight would continue so they could see the enemies in action. Brian told me to wait, as he wanted to talk to me. They did not like the treatment they'd received from the landlord and decided to wait outside the pub and, with vengeance in mind, try to beat me up.

Eddie was worried in case they took it out on him, him being my friend. He kept his eyes fixed on the group of people waiting outside the pub. I was wound up and itching for a pint. All the doors were locked and Brian came and spoke to me, telling me to wait until the brothers got sick of waiting and went back to where they lived. I was not having any of it; if they wanted a fight then I'd give them one, and I unlocked the door and went out to stand my ground.

The man who'd attacked me in the pub toilet came straight at me, punching and kicking, cursing and clashed with me. Brian stood outside the pub door and looked on at us fighting. I wrestled him to the pavement and sank my teeth into his nose. He screamed in pain. The other one saw me savaging the face off his brother with the grace of a council-estate pit bull and took a run at me; he kicked me like I was a football.

I took the full force and, reluctantly, let go of his nose. I was stunned as I stood up ready to attack the other brother, who kept his distance from me: he feared the wrath of the man they had tried to set up. Brian came over to me and pulled me inside the pub. Eddie followed behind.

The locals, ten or twelve of them, were content with the action

– short and sweet with some severe damage to the face. His brother helped him off the pavement and decided to make friends with me rather than try to antagonise me.

Now, in the Commercial, I greeted the two boys and eyed the big scar on the brother's nose where I had bit through the gristle in an attempt to bite it completely off. It had healed but was bent to one side as a permanent memorial to what had happened. Arthur got the round in, pleased for the excuse to go to the bar away from the brothers and take his time to adapt to their company.

Arthur thought of the day after we'd fought, when the fight had been the talk of the locals. Arthur and Eddie had gone with me up to a friend's house. On the way, we met the two brothers, one with injuries due to my efforts. They laughed and joked with me, though on meeting the two brothers, I immediately tensed up waiting for another fight. Arthur had watched as we shook hands; he was amazed at my power over people.

While Arthur bought the beer, I asked the brothers if I could have an ounce of coke, but stressed it was not for my use, but to set up witnesses who I planned to deal with by hiding the drugs in their cars or houses. That way I would undermine the witnesses' statements.

It was agreed that I could pick the drugs without charge up from where the brothers lived when I needed them. The conversation was over when Arthur appeared with the drinks.

I didn't particularly like these people, as they were arrogant and full of themselves, but I'd decided to put up with the two drugs dealers, as it was beneficial being on speaking terms. They may have been misjudged in meeting me, but there was no mistaking the relationship now – they respected and feared me.

Arthur sat down and got the feeling he'd missed something as the company quietened down when he came on the scene. Time was ticking on and Steve and Harry came in. I pulled Harry to one side and told him I needed four invoices signed and that I would meet him later on in the Railway. Business dealt with, now I could relax some and enjoy getting drunk.

The mood shifted as the group of two men became four and then six, all sitting round the table. We spoke and laughed between ourselves. It was just an ordinary Monday morning, except that there was a worry that the police would walk in the pub as I made reference to the revenge attack on Barrett. They listened as I gave the details of squirting ammonia in the thug's eyes.

Generally they thought I was a madman to revenge myself on a Monday morning in the middle of the street, but that I was ... unpredictable and had no bones about the use of violence when needed. Graham Cotton, another acquaintance, came and sat next to Arthur. Graham laid bricks for a living.

Arthur and Graham did some work together. Graham was well known to the many sub-contractors in London, and his sideline was fixing up some of them with potential men that went bent for quick money. I had been to see these subbies around London and they knew me as genuine, but Graham would not hand out phone numbers and his part was strictly confidential. So when someone wanted to do the business, Graham would arrange to meet the subbies with the man who was selling all the documents needed to work the tax.

For this Graham was paid one-and-a-half per cent of the 10 per cent agreed by the men dealing with the company. The ordinary wage bill for a week was £20,000 and, when I handed over the invoice, he would be paid £2,000 on £20,000. I had helped Graham out when scaffolding he owned was stolen. I had gone to a pub and stood by Graham as he confronted the thieves. Even there my reputation held some weight. He got the scaffold back without incident.

It would seem that the reputation of my arrival preceded and doubled itself as the months went by. I had the tools of the trade in a sports bag in the boot and ready to be used.

I drove down to meet a sub-contractor. He had arranged the meeting and, because I was a mate, and after the show in the pub, he felt he could trust me, so did not need to be there when the deal was done. It was just up to me to give him a drink from his illegal dealings.

I pulled up on the main road outside the cafe, which was arranged by the sub-contractor as the place for the deal to go down. It was 10.30am and I tried to relax in the car as I ogled the young women passing by. The man I was dealing with was late. If it was 7.00am in the morning when I waited in the car, there would be 20 or 30 others stood around to be picked up, all cash in hand for work on building sites.

I searched the main street and watched for his car. I watched as the doors of the Fleece pub on the corner opened and the first of the day's drinkers went in. I could have murdered a pint myself. As he pulled up in front of me, I collected the company file with the relevant documents from the front seat. My heart beat faster with the anticipation of the deal going down and getting my hands on the ten per cent.

I jumped out the car and went and sat in the passenger side of his motor. There we went about our business. I handed over the company's invoices; it was a deal that only took the time of counting out the ten per cent of twenty grand.

I didn't trust the guy and, as I thought there was £50 short of £2,000, he paid up, pissed off about having to pay the full amount. He'd wanted the £50 for a drink to celebrate the deal they'd just done. He enquired as to whether the same deal could be sorted for the following week. I agreed.

As I drove back, I contemplated what I had achieved in the week after drinking with my mates in the Commercial. Judith and I had been searching for a house and we'd seen a property we wanted. It was up for offers around £52,000 but it was in need of major repairs and decoration.

I had hoped that the property would not be sold before we got the three grand deposit together. The work and repairs required to bring the full potential out of the property was not a problem. I could get all the building and decorating materials for nothing from the building sites and I'd do the work myself.

Materials from building sites were perks of the job. You nicked the stuff and, if necessary, gave the site agent a backhander so he would turn a blind eye to what went missing. Now it was, I thought, time for Donna's birthday. I could not wait to see my daughter's face light up when she saw the pup.

I had phoned up the week prior and made sure that the bull terrier was ready to leave its litter for later on that day. After doing the company business I'd decided to pick the bitch up on my way home instead of taking my daughter to see all the pups. I thought that the toddler would be excited when I walked in with the pup in my hands. I knew she'd love it, and also Judith had bought a doll and cards with sweets for her. We would have liked to have thrown a party for our daughter, but we'd moved house and Donna had changed schools.

When I walked in the pub, Judith squealed with delight when she saw how cute the brindle staffy was. She remembered that she was one week late in her periods and got the feeling she was pregnant, as she was never more than a day late. A thought occurred to me as Judith welcomed me home with a kiss; she seemed as excited as Donna, but was not saying much.

There was a lot on her mind but, foremost, she contemplated the baby she'd lost two months prior. It made her nervous and put a shadow over this happy event. She decided to tell me of the feeling straightaway. I listened and could hardly believe what she was saying; I went all joyful and happy, kissing and cuddling Judith. I insisted she walk to the chemist in the shopping precinct and buy a pregnancy test. I pushed her out the door, telling her to hurry. I would have gone to the chemist myself but I was not clued up on pregnancy tests, and would probably come back with the wrong apparatus.

While Judith was away at the chemist, Donna played happily with the Staffordshire bull terrier and played with the Mousetrap game that she'd got from Judith's mother and father. She showed me how it worked and I played for a few minutes; Donna kept plonking the pup in the middle of the game where the bitch kept knocking over the Mousetrap parts.

Minutes felt like hours as we watched the tester change colour to blue, indicating that Judith was, in fact, very pregnant. She prayed as she remembered finding out four years ago how she had felt when she conceived Donna. We were just as happy and excited then as on that previous day.

Donna minded her manners as she watched her mother and father cuddle and kiss each other. She picked up the pup and gave him the same treatment as her mam and dad were giving each other. I was so overwhelmed with joy that I told Donna she was going to have a sister or brother. Donna laughed and smiled. She had a new pup and now she was going to have someone to play with. She enquired when her brother or sister would arrive and I told her when her pup was nearly, not quite, one year old. Donna said she'd let him or her, whichever, play with her pup, who she kept picking up and catching when it kept running away.

The rest of the family, although concerned, congratulated us. It was a good omen that Judith had fallen pregnant again so quickly; not only would it give her something positive to think about, as she would have dwelled on the loss of our last baby, but it would go down well in court when I faced the judge.

It would, without doubt, affect the length of my sentence, as the judge would have to take the new pregnancy into account. There are many ways to consider time when serving a prison sentence. I believed you had to fight, if not physically then mentally, every day of a sentence. Getting stoned was the way to shorten a sentence because the user had no concept on passing days and weeks because the part of the brain that dealt with these important thoughts was dulled by the powerful cannabis or class 'A' drugs.

You can look at the wall clock, always hung next to the office, which when looked at gave a feeling of helplessness as you immediately took into account how many years you had left to serve. The clock on the wall only looked good on days when you awaited a visit from your woman and child, then when you went back to your cell and the door was banged, you would methodically prepare a joint and get out of your mind.

This would be the life I would have to cope with after being sentenced. There was no way out, it was something that could not be avoided, but at this moment time was on my side and the longer I was free the better it would be for my family and me.

Bob Ashcroft was a friend and we looked out for each other. Bob was a starch man with principles as to his friendship. He took the phone call on his day off from work as a machinist. I apologised for not phoning my mate sooner and told him the good news of Judith's pregnancy. He took his time to digest the information, as he always did with big news, and then he congratulated me. Bob was married to an ex-girlfriend of mine. Her name was Debbie and they had a new baby.

Bob was a dedicated family man apart from when I was on the scene; then it was mad time and benders where we two friends tried to drink the workmen's club dry. Bob felt some strong feelings towards me as he considered I had never had any luck in my life, and always seemed to get the wrong end of the stick and get arrested by the police. He wished I'd cool down. Maybe another child would help to do that – Bob hoped so.

He would do anything for me and we arranged a few days' visit for the oncoming week, which I looked forward to but Judith, when told, was not actually happy about it. But the benders never lasted long, as Bob had to go to work so it was only a few days that she had to put up with.

I decided I needed a van to get around in and looked in the local advertiser. There was a Bedford for sale and I was interested. I decided to let Arthur keep the white Transit as long as he paid the lease, which would mean more money in my pocket. I also wanted to keep well in with the bank where my company was based, and the leasing firm. Besides buying the Bedford, that I would purchase by lease, I would buy a car for myself as director and a company car for Harry, the chairman.

I intended to see Charlie for a couple of old bangers that I would use as deposits for the two new cars. Then as soon as I received the logbooks I'd take them up to London and sell them. I thought that the cars, worth £16,000, would get me half the value in cash readies, money that I would invest in the house I wanted to buy. I rang the leasing company and they arranged a meeting in Harry's house. I spoke to Judith and asked her to phone the number that Steve had given to me.

I thought if someone else picked the phone up, they might recognise my accent and be frightened off. Judith phoned up and this bloke answered. She handed me the phone. Still very wary that it might be a set-up, I greeted the man on the phone and asked if the two thugs were still living there. They were and I asked when would be the best time to catch them? They agreed that it would be a Sunday morning, as the shop they were at was shut on Sundays. I asked if, when I decided to attack, my contact could leave the key on the ground, under a bin or something so I could enter early and quietly.

He told me that a key was not needed as the door to the flat had a dodgy lock and with a bit of weight would open. He would be told when the attack would go off and I considered the information as to the layout of the premises and asked where in the place the two thugs were sleeping.

I made sure there were no guns in the flat and told him I'd phone him back. I decided I would enter the flat and shoot the two thugs. I wasn't quite sure if I'd blow their heads off, or shoot them in the legs. I decided that, after the next deal with the paddies, Judith and I would have enough money to put a deposit down on the house we wanted; same time, same place and another two grand.

I wanted, before I attacked the two thugs, to be in the new house where no one knew who we were, so as to be safe from further attacks.

I phoned the number of the advertisement for the Bedford van. It was still for sale, so Judith, Donna and the pup all got in the car with me and we went to buy it. I needed a van for myself, as I wanted Judith to have her own transport.

Judith, with Donna in tow, went into the Halifax building society and deposited £15,000. It was a joint account but the purchasing of the house we wanted to buy would be done in her name. We made an offer of £50,000 and were waiting for the property owner to get back to us. Property was going up with the building boom at 20 per cent of the value per month. Even if you kept the house for 6 months you stood to make £8,000 or £12,000 profit.

Harry and I stood in his place drinking tea. Harry was looking forward to doing the deal with the leasing company; two signatures on the company invoices, £50 for each signature, would do him for a session in the pub. The two old bangers that I was using for deposits for the company cars, were stood outside Harry's. One had a month's MOT and one had a month's tax: a Honda hatchback and a Rover 2.5 litre. The rep from the leasing firm would only drive one of the bangers if it had tax, so Harry could drive the other without tax.

The two company cars were waiting in the yard of the leasing company in East Grinstead. You have to drive, or the leasing reps drive the bangers back to the leasing depot where they would be exchanged for the two new cars. The deal went as planned and the rep drove the taxed motor.

I gave Charlie his Cortina back. I showed him the two new BMWs that together were worth £32,000 cash. I gave Judith one to use while I waited for the logbooks and I decided to take the second car to Jim Ford. I took the metallic BMW and pulled up outside Jim's house. It was a sunny afternoon as I knocked on the door and was let in by his wife. I shook the man's hand and came straight to the point about the BMW.

I had a bill of sale already made out in his name and wanted him to give me six grand now on the strength of when the logbooks arrived. The motor would then go up to £8,000. I explained that I'd also sell the second BMW to him for £8,000 as soon as I received the logbook. He stood to earn £2,000 if he paid me the £6,000 I wanted now.

The prices and profit were enough to swing a deal without the haggling. Shifting the executive cars was not difficult; Jim knew many men in the motor trade. I took the six grand and arranged to meet Judith at the Halifax where we deposited money for the deposit on the house.

I arranged with her to use my company's headed paper to write her own reference for the solicitor and the Halifax, saying she'd been a secretary at the company for the last two years and that her earnings were £24,000 a year. The owner of the property rejected our first offer so we upped it by a thousand pounds and the deal went down.

I wanted the house in Judith's name so that when what I'd been doing with the tax and company came on top I would, on paper, be penniless and Judith would be OK, and the parties involved would not be able to touch her wealth, or any money she may have.

The plan was for Judith, Donna and I to live in the purchased property and to rent our council flat out for £50 per week to Frank. He did the deal with a handshake and asked when he could move in.

The rent from our council property would almost pay the mortgage on the second property. I wasn't certain how long I could get away with the rent scheme, but there was an obvious way out if it if it came on top. We would just have to swap properties; we would move back into the flat and Frank and girlfriend would move elsewhere. It was a simple solution to a scheme that happened just as I had hoped.

Someone grassed us up and the council became involved, as it had been reported that someone other than us was living in the council property.

Bob came to visit two weeks later or so. I had moved back to the flat very quickly; Frank was happy as I had finished with the minimal work on the other property. It was a minor setback that had been corrected and my visit chased the blues away.

Judith informed the council that the report made to them that strangers were occupying the council property was, in fact, concerning relations of Judith's family who were staying for a week or so. The council decided to give Judith and I the benefit of the doubt, and the investigation was stopped. I had spent £200 on finishing the property that I had intended to use on my own family.

Bob and I went out on the town. I wore a police helmet that Bob had brought with him as a joke present for me. He'd stolen it from one of the miner's picket lines and the lad from up North thought it was appropriate that I could shit in it and post it back to the police station it came from.

I was impatient as to when I would attack these thugs. I discussed this with my mate Bob and ignored Eddie listening to what my plans were; Eddie got the message and went and spoke to Brian, who was now wearing the copper's helmet. Bob pleaded with me to leave my plan for a while, reminding me that the sentence for firearms may carry a longer sentences than I thought.

At that time I was headstrong. I left the pub and changed into my sheepskin coat, and slotted the sawn-off gun into the hidden loop. It felt comfortable and I decided to do a pub-crawl, in places where my enemies might drink. I kissed Judith, told her not to worry and went back to the pub.

Bob was still concerned. He'd seen that my mood was full of venom and revenge. I opened my coat and flashed him the gun. All I had to do was point it and pull the trigger and that would be the end of one of my enemies. I'd probably have to shoot the second as he ran way from me. We left the police helmet behind the bar.

The brave man Eddie jumped in the back of the taxi with half a gallon of lager in him, and the three of us went on the pub-crawl. We taxied over to the Half Moon in Southgate where we went about drinking and enjoying each other's company.

We then taxied to a wine bar in the centre of the town. The place was full of wide boys that, if I'd have had my way, I would have shot in the rear. Still no joy in the two places we'd visited and Bob was relieved, hoping that we could get home without major incident.

We walked to the Commercial pub and started drinking whisky chasers. Eddie's behaviour became even more irregular and I opened his coat and showed him the sawn-off. He struggled for words as he realised how serious the situation really was, but just drank his beer and then laughed.

Bob and I went to another pub: we were drunk and bothered ourselves with thoughts of shooting the thugs we were hoping to bump into. Personally, I would not have felt safe with my mate if I didn't have the gun. I had a vision of us being without the gun and meeting the thugs in numbers and possibly getting a kicking or getting hospitalised because there were too many to fight. The gun was for safety, not just revenge.

We exited the pub and waited to hail a taxi back to the Railway. I pulled the loaded gun out of my coat. Most people were the worst for wear with the drink, although I was well known and easily recognised with the big scar down my face. Well, didn't I go and let both barrels off at the streetlight; it exploded into pieces and the front of the pub went into darkness.

Bob shouted at me to put the gun away then he snatched at the gun as I tried to reload; people living across the road looked out the window at the sound of the sawn-off shotgun.

After managing to get a taxi, I decided to direct it to the outside my flat. I jumped in the red Bedford van I had bought. I loaded the gun again and, as Bob protested, I pulled away. He thought I had gone mad and he was right.

I fought the idea of killing my enemies, knowing the consequence might be a life spent in prison. We drove over to the Railway and pulled up on the boulevard, next to a roundabout where I let both barrels off at the streetlight. It shattered and I laughed. I pulled the van into the pub car park and the two of us went into the bar, by which time I had the gun safely tucked away.

I put the police helmet on. The pub was full. Eddie was completely pissed and feeling braver. Last orders were called and the locals supped up. At closing time, Bob and I left the pub with me still wearing the helmet and, as sod's law would have it, we walked smack, bang straight into a police squad car parked on the roundabout next to the boulevard.

The police saw the helmet and Northumbria Police badge and approached me. I told Bob to run and I took off like a rabbit. I was pissed and the drink was confusing me. I was frightened that I'd be arrested and sent back on remand on some Mickey Mouse charge. The police gave chase as I ran for all my worth across the school field and into the housing estate streets.

I discarded the helmet, concerned only about getting away

from the police. The power of the gun was in me. Two coppers ran after me and the effects of the beer sloshing about in my stomach were starting to make me feel sick. I saw an opportunity for escape. I vaulted over a garden wall and hid in the shadows. The worst part was trying to control my breathing as the sick feeling from the drink was increasing.

The police had given up and I came out of my hiding place and made my way home. When I got home, Bob had already been at my place for an hour. He had hailed a cab because he didn't know his way back to the flat.

The next day, I dropped Bob off at the station and my mate remembered the custard-pie incident in my home town and laughed about it. The custard pie was remembered by the community and it could not of happened to a more deserving person.

I told my mate that I would be up to see him in a few weeks or so and that I would be with my woman and child. It was time to split and I said goodbye to Bob.

10
GOD WORKS IN MYSTERIOUS WAYS

It was 5.30am, Sunday morning. I put the sports bag containing the sawn-off into the van. I'd decided to blow the legs off the two thugs. It wasn't an easy decision, but the deciding factor was a murder charger against an eight-year prison sentence. I concentrated on the business at hand, thinking that after I'd settled the score things would get better, but this had to be dealt with first.

I pulled up outside the flat and retrieved the sawn-off from the sports bag. They say God works in mysterious ways ... I started to reload the weapon and the catch to reload broke off in my hands! Nervously, I tried to fix it. The barrels would not open; my mind went warp-factor ten, into overdrive and I figured it was a bad omen. Luck or rotten luck, I was overcome by negative thoughts. If I got the sawn-off to work, I'd probably shoot the two thugs in the head. It seemed that these bastards had more lives than a cat.

Disgusted, I threw the sawn-off back in the bag and pondered what my next move would be. Without considering it further, I pulled on a ski mask and took the copper-pipe cosh from the sports bag and jumped out of the van. I was the only one on the streets. With determination I made my way up the steps and stood outside the flat. I listened at the door but there was only silence.

The cosh felt good in my hand and I prayed there would be no more setbacks. I switched my mind off as I quickly shouldered the door. It sprang open with what seemed to me to be a loud enough racket for the neighbours to hear, never mind the thugs.

I ran up the stairs, highly strung, with one thing on my mind, and entered the first bedroom, which had been locked from the other side. The owner of the place had failed to mention locks on the bedrooms door. I kicked it open and there was Barrett, the fat thug, in bed with some trollop. Barrett screamed like a wounded wildebeest almost before I hit him in the face with the cosh. I systematically beat Barrett around the head as if I was cleaning an old carpet, and then I pulled him from the flea-bitten bed. I jumped and, with acute precision, stamped on the thug's face. The screams of fear were high pitched and brought the other thug, Evans, running from the other room to his sidekick's aid. The sight that met Evans's eyes was that of his blood-spattered friend lying in a puddle of blood.

I was too quick for him; he would barely have seen the flash of steel from my homemade cosh as it landed in his face like a hot poker going into a marshmallow. I turned automatically and ran Evans into the toilet, trying to throw the thug out of the window. The glass on the sides of the smashed window cut deep into Evans's hands and he hung on and screamed like a stuck pig. I battered the man and left him with his head down the toilet.

I got home safely and immediately phoned up the man that had sold me the sawn-off shotgun and ordered a replacement one to pick up that day.

If the thugs came back for another round I would have a gun ready to blow their heads off – this I promised myself. I was strangely content with the beating I'd given them, as I pictured the two men in the casualty ward of the local hospital.

Part of the score had been settled. The next part would be dealing with the witnesses whose characters I hoped to discredit so that their statements would be deemed unreliable. A slight worry of mine was that, if the police became involved with the attack that I had just committed, I could just see myself in court with GBH charges on top of the firearm charge while I was on bail ... they would throw my cell key away.

I decided to take Judith and Donna up north to see Nana and Pops, and to keep off the scene for a while, just in case there was a comeback in some way. Judith, Donna and the pup waited in the car for me, I was in the house of the criminal that sold sawn-off shotguns. I had a choice of two and this time I chose a side-by-side shotgun. I paid the man £100 and put the sawn-off in a bag, leaving the broken gun with the criminal.

The drive back up North would be a four-and-a-half hour journey, but a comfortable one in the new BMW. I'd bought the sawn-off shotgun straightaway so that, when I came back, it would be within easy reach if needed. It was not for use up north.

The previous week I had my restrictions for signing on at the police station relaxed through my solicitor, so I had no worries over this. The skin on the soles of my feet was peeling away, so I got a doctor's note to say I could not walk more than a few yards because of the infection, so I would not be able to walk to the police station and had no transport; even walking to and from bus stands was too much.

We managed the journey in just under five hours. Donna, with pup in tow, jumped out of the car excitedly and ran into Nana's house, dropping the pup and picking it back up. I lent over and kissed Judith lovingly, deciding that Nana should put the kettle straight on. Pops had a horrible Jack Russell cross and it made as much noise as a pit bull, barking the place down and trying to bite everyone. I phoned my mate Bob but he was at work.

My insides glowed, and Judith and Donna made everything seem right. Nana and Pops made us all feel at home, and we chatted over a cup of tea. Nana was a good and happy woman with a great understanding of children, having brought up five kids, four of them girls. Pop's view on bringing up kids was 'never have girls, because they brought their problems home'; boys dealt with their problems outside and never involved others.

They had lived at the house for 20 years or more. It was not the first house that I had called home. That had been just round the corner, and it held many happy memories for me.

As we relaxed and made ourselves at home, I thought of one incident that always stuck in my mind whenever I came home. I was 11 years old and was on my way home from school. I'd just bought fireworks, which consisted of bangers, air bombs and roman candles, although you had to be 16 to purchase the things. I'd taken off my school tie, jumper and blazer to appear older. The man in the arcade would sell to almost anyone and didn't ask for ID. One week previously, the old picture house had been burned down to the ground. The kids that did it had been remanded in police custody for young offenders. They were all one year younger than me.

Young's tyre factory took up a big piece of land behind the shops on the main street so, haversack in hand with my clothes and fireworks, I decided to make the previous fire in the picture house look like a beginner's effort. I climbed over the fence on to a massive pile of used tyres that were waiting to have their treads renewed. I took a handful of fireworks and stuffed them inside the tyres in the centre of the pile, and lit them.

I ran, jumped the fence and disappeared up a back alley towards home. I looked back every now and then and, as I reached home, I called to my mother. She came to the back step and stood looking at the massive cloud of black smoke rising above the rooftops of the housing estate, the sound of fire engines screeching in the distance.

Innocently, I looked on at my handiwork. The blaze lasted six hours or more and the police were looking for yet another arsonist. It wasn't the first fire I had started; months prior I had been responsible for causing a fire on the fells, a green-belt patch of land. Again, I stood at a distance and watched the firemen fight the blaze in the woods and ferns. Then before the other guys had started the fire in the picture house, I'd started the fire in the Plaza, which was another closed down picture house. I kept these fires quiet and told no one.

The two years prior to me being sent to DC (Detention Centre), a gang of school friends and I explored the town every night after school. We caused havoc that in these days would be described as antisocial by the authorities. To the gang it was an adventure, climbing on shop roofs up and down the town.

We stole anything we could: barrels of beer, packs of lager. We had a camp near some fells where we'd take our ill-gotten gains, build a fire and get drunk. The town ran for half-a-mile, with shops and pubs and workingmen's clubs lining each side of the road. There were large council housing estates either side of the main street, and in between, on the way to the park, posh people lived in their private houses that were dotted around the area. Between the top of the street and the bottom the pubs were not so good. The taxi rank next to the Market Place was busy most days of the week. There were numerous bus stands to Newcastle and the opposite way to Durham. The pubs called Fighting Cocks and the Green Bank got all the best custom because the bottom of the town was always busy. We'd climb on the roofs of these places, where we'd break locks and steal the beer. These have all now become drinking places for the grown-up boys in the old gang.

DC for me was a disaster. I was only charged with breaking a bus light and throwing a bottle through a workingmen's club window. I was given three months in Kirk Levington Grange, which was a junior detention centre renowned for its regimental ways of training young, out-of-control kids.

The probation service hated the fact that a boy as young as 15, having recently been expelled from school and now living with his girlfriend, could reject the system and hold his own views that were, in no uncertain terms, anti-authoritarian.

Around this time my girlfriend had to pretend she was a cousin of mine because the rules of the DC said that there were no visits or letters to inmates from girlfriends.

I told Judith to put her glad rags on and get ready to go out on the town. I was excited as I watched her get dressed, feeling her crotch in the bathroom as she took a bath. Afterwards, she pulled on black stockings – she looked fantastic. Her hair was piled up on top, and she wore a leopard-skin mini and a black top.

It was about 20 minutes' walk to the main street. We held hands as we walked. We decided to do a pub-crawl and started at the top of the street. The first bar was virtually empty and the jukebox blasted out loud 1980s music. Years previous to this I had been barred from the same pub. I'd been 15 at the time and the police had come in to check for underage drinkers. I had a young face and, because of this, the coppers pulled me. I told them my date of birth, although it was a false one, but luckily the copper had taken it as gospel.

The same evening in the bar, I had started to fight with a punk rocker. The fight had continued outside where I had taken on two punks. I'd hurt them bad, booting their heads in when they were on the ground. I then took off my buckled belt and beat them until they bled; their faces were cut to pieces as the sharp buckle bit into their skin. I then ran off but was barred from the pub.

Judith compared me to her old boyfriends. I was certainly different. She liked searching for reasons that made me so different. I was great for sex when we partied; in fact, any time was the right time, but Judith though she saw something strange in my soul. How could it be the work of the devil when my love was so true and everlasting? Yet she knew my violent side, which I had used all my life to get by and sort out problems.

To Judith, it was as if I were two different people: one outrageous and one sincere, both completely different, one good, one bad. It did not make her nervous, more curious that anyone that loved as strong as us would always be a target for jealousy because our relationship was so secure, more so than with other couples. She knew that I thought deeply about her, was always attentive, always caring, always sexy, always putting my family before myself. She couldn't wait till the day I proposed, and she wondered if the new baby might make me ask her for her hand in marriage.

We decided to move pubs. On the way out I spoke to a couple of locals, all respectfully greeting me. We made our way down the main street and went in another which had a big public bar.

Sitting there reminded me of a situation that I described to Judith about how, whilst I was on the door bouncing years previously, I'd got in a fight with three off-duty coppers that had then complained to the manager. The police had insisted that I be sacked from the bouncing job in the bar; that was the end of that.

Judith, with her double vodka and orange, was feeling good. The drink was opening up her inner self. She thought for a moment about proposing to me herself. She wondered what it would be like if we were married and if it would change us. She believed it would change us for the better and that our love would grow stronger. Something was driving Judith; she acted her sexy self and prayed that some time soon they would get married.

We supped up and headed off down the street, hand-in-hand and joyful. I went into one, describing a fight that had started at the top of the street and ended up in the Market Place at the bottom of the street. I had kicked and punched my way down the street and had only stopped when the police came on the scene and gave chase.

We walked in to the Red Lion. The pub was quite full and time was strolling on. Judith wondered about Donna and thought we should tie the knot before she got any older; children could be cruel if they skitted a child that was conceived out of wedlock. All women love big white weddings and Judith was no different, but she also realised that it was not essential; she would be content with a register-office ceremony, just as long as she was married.

We came out of the pub and made our way into an alley behind a club; Judith thought we were heading for another pub. I pinned my woman against the wall, and groped her fanny and tits. I was hard and tore her knickers to one side as I thrust my shaft into her. Judith came quickly, becoming saturated with love juice. I almost came immediately. We felt relaxed, as if a big load had been lifted from our shoulders. We straightened ourselves up and made our way to the working men's club.

The sign on the bar door read 'no women allowed', but it had applied to years earlier. Judith thought that 'no women allowed' was funny and typical of the north-east and the Geordie culture.

I told her that I'd received a three-and-a-half year sentence for one particular fight that had started in the disco and ended up on the street outside of the club.

I bought the drinks, with a double-whisky chaser for myself. The bar had been changed into a plush lounge and there were a few people in the place. The jukebox was blasting and drinkers were the worst for wear.

If she wanted, and she would, I intended to take her to the only nightclub in the town. I got it into my head that I was being big headed for Judith's benefit. I told Judith this and she felt sorry for me, kissing me hard and holding me close. She enjoyed listening to my teenage events and told me so.

Then Judith popped the question, feeling the time was right, but not quite sure.

Love was all I felt, glad that she had asked me then and not

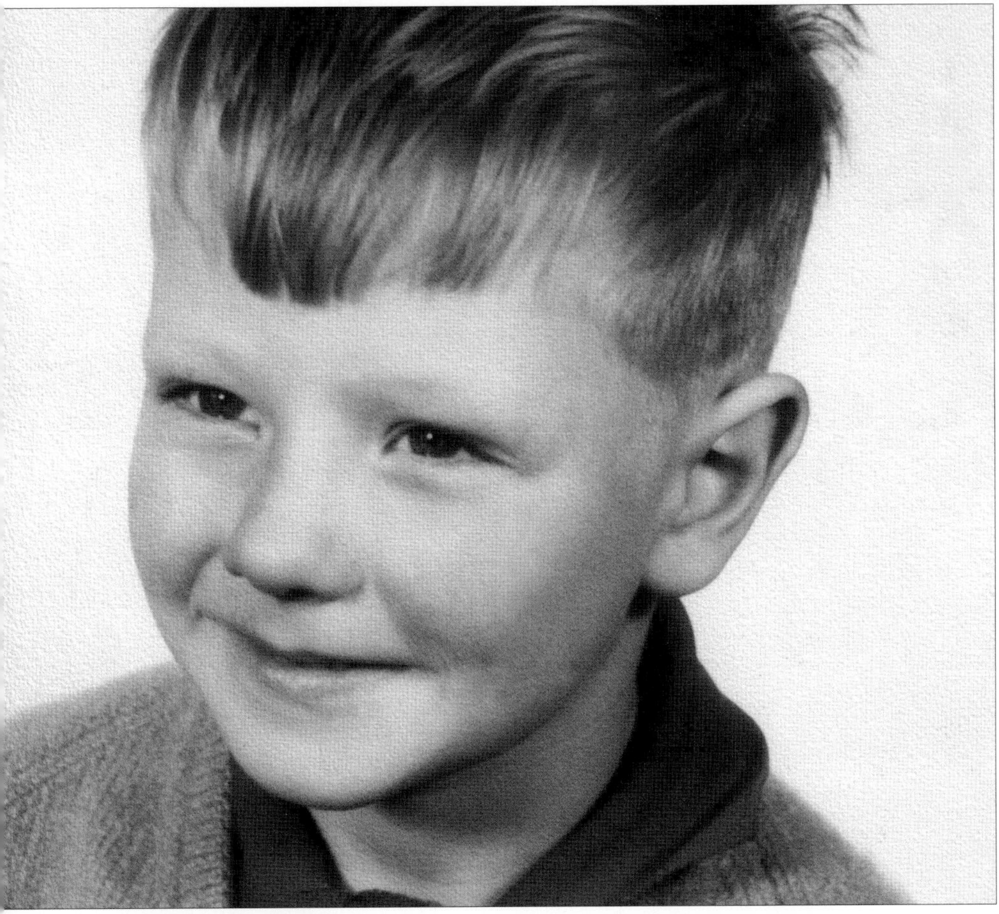

Top: Me as a kid in 1967.

Bottom: My dad and I in 1976.

Top: Just hanging out in 1977.

Bottom: Playing with the band, also in 1977.

Top: Another memory from the 1970s when I was young and carefree.

Bottom: The band in action.

Top: No wonder I was smiling – I had just been released from prison in 1999.

Bottom: This is how I look these days.

later. I had thought about marrying Judith, but I had been married once before when I was 17 years old, and that had ended badly because I was serving my young-prisoner sentence and went through the pain of being divorced from my wife while I was in jail – it had left a bitter taste in my mouth as far as marriage was cooncerned.

Then there was the court case coming up and, if I married Judith, who'd be to say the same thing would not happen again whilst I was doing time? I asked Judith if she would put things on hold until the outcome of the court case, but I was happy that she'd asked and in no way did I not want to marry her.

News that I was back home visiting would spread amongst old friends quickly. There was a time in my teens when what I did at the top of the street would spread like wildfire to the bottom of the street, and people knew I was on my way and talked openly of the hard man before I got there.

Years earlier I would have relished the fact that my reputation was talked about. The women I once knew were all married and the like, but now I'd rather play down my reputation because it meant trouble from the up-and-coming brigade of hard men.

I thought about the sawn-off shotgun and what it stood for. In my younger days, my mates and I used to make zip guns with a lump of copper pipe bound on to a piece of wood, one end of the pipe squashed with a small hole made in the end using a nail. This is where you taped a fuse from a firework (banger), then stuffed the pipe with six-inch nails or a few marbles, preferably steel ball bearings, lit the fuse and pointed the gun very inaccurately. When fired it would put holes in steel garage doors.

We headed to the nightclub but were disappointed to find it closed. I should have guessed this, as people up north mainly saved their money for the weekend; most of the locals were on social security so had little money.

We decided to walk back up the street for the last orders in another working men's club, which was a few hundred yards behind the main street. A lot of my old friends were barred from there because the committee was so strict and enjoyed barring men out who got a bit rowdy.

Although I was not a member of any working men's club, when we went into a club for a drink my reputation meant that I did not have to be accustomed to the formality of other drinkers. It was best to be friends with me rather than enemies. You never knew when a hard man may come in useful as they were all pushing pensions and the committee's days of standing up and fighting were gone; far better to let the young men fight if they had to and the moment was right.

Judith and I went in the lounge side, as no women were allowed in the bar; this one kept with tradition.

Through the hatch, whilst being served, I saw an old friend who had always made a living from dealing drugs. Bob had told me that most of my old mates were selling drugs. I went to talk to the friend and the two of us greeted each other warmly. This man was a biker and I asked him about buying a wrap of sulphate and he gave the drugs to me free of charge.

I tipped half the wrap in my pint and the other in Judith's vodka and orange. The stuff was good and we were immediately buzzing and feeling sexy.

We left the club and decided to get a Chinese takeaway. We were the only ones in the restaurant and lying on the floor was a crisp new £5 note that I immediately picked up and took to be a welcoming omen.

That night, after Nana and Pops went to bed, Judith and I had made love six or seven times.

The following morning I took a nostalgic walk around some my old haunts on the housing estate that I'd roamed years earlier with my gang. Briefly I remembered the different members of the gang and how high up in stature they were in the food chain.

Me, I had always been the boss and had ruled with a fist of iron; violence gave me an edge and I was considered to be the leader because of this. I allowed myself a wry smile at the madness of my control over the ten or so members. If they stole barrels of beer they'd use a hammer and chisel to smash the top off and I insisted they all got drunk. Even though the gang didn't like the taste, I made them drink even when they felt sick. The gang were frightened of their leader and did my bidding.

When they stole cans of beer and lager, they'd stash it in their camp and when they were doing cross-country school sports they were told to meet at the camp and drink whilst the other scholars ran. I insisted all the members did the same as I did or decided, or else they faced being beaten up. The nighttimes always seemed friendly to me; we did our worst under cover of night.

One particular member got his kicks through smashing windows. It didn't matter to him if the properties were empty, he'd smash windows with rocks. We'd steal school property, ripping the lead flashing off the roofs and causing thousands of pounds' worth of damage.

I bumped into an old adversary who was on his way to work. He was a bully that had no sense of humour. He'd once attacked me with a beer crate. The fight had happened quickly and he had stood his ground. He had spent the last few months of school chasing down my gang members and me.

It was an old tradition in my school that when finishing fifth year, the final year, you had to beat up the fourth year before leaving. This boy had caught most of the gang members associated with me, but couldn't catch me; he was a horrible cunt and I didn't want to know him – he was a waste of space.

I crossed the main road to the newsagents just a few hundred yards over the road. I hoped bumping into him was not a reminder, a bad omen, and dismissed the meeting as I picked up a paper.

I rang Bob, who had just got in from work as the phone went. We arranged to take our women out that night. We arranged to meet up before the women; they would follow on in a taxi after they had finished getting ready.

Bob and I were in one of the working men's clubs at 6.30pm. There were a few early drinkers that greeted us as we sank the first pint of the evening. This time Judith wore a leather miniskirt and a black top, with fishnet tights. She knew I would tear a hole in her crotch later and pull her knickers to one side to slip my dick in.

She soon turned up with Debbie, an old girlfriend of mine who I took out before she met Bob.

I left Bob to the formalities of signing the two women into the club while I ordered the drinks in. The two women chatted away as Bob filled me in what had happened to our old mate Ricky. Ricky had began taking heroin, smoking it at first, but recently, Bob told me, Ricky had started to mainline, using the needle for a better, longer hit. This was one thing I would not touch – I would never mainline any sort of drug.

You have to always know where your faculties lie to stop yourself becoming an addict; cannabis, coke and speed were easily controlled and used as recreational drugs by me.

Bob knew that his wife had been with me but Judith didn't, and Bob took in the situation and wondered what would happen if she found out. The couple, Bob and Debbie, felt awkward and guarded because they were part of a lie that they could not control and only go along with. My attitude was that what she didn't know wouldn't hurt her, so I ignored it.

I skinned up a spliff to share among us. Debbie didn't smoke but it didn't stop me taking a big lungful and passing it to Judith, who timidly tasted the cannabis. Bob became nervous in case someone complained about the smell: although he'd not smelled it while he'd been to the bar, it stunk around the table where we smoked. Judith handed the spliff back to me and I handed the bountiful package to Bob.

I was amused watching my mate become paranoid and unable to relax enough to enjoy the cannabis. Bob decided he was, at that moment, religious. Apart from being religious he was becoming sexually stimulated. He got up quick and opened the window. Debbie looked on and gave Bob a disapproving look.

Judith did not say a lot. There was something on Debbie's mind and the woman was not saying what. The cannabis made Judith more suspicious and she concentrated on Debbie's character and what the woman was keeping quiet. She brought up sex and this made her strike gold. Debbie became uncomfortable and even more guarded.

I asked Bob to skin up another joint, which he did reluctantly. He rolled the spliff nervously as we all watched. Judith told me that if I wanted to smoke then we should go some place that had a garden to sit in. Reluctantly I agreed and we all drank up. Bob put the spliff in his jacket pocket and we walked out of the club and up the street to the Black Horse. We all sat in the garden. We were the only ones there so we could smoke and drink in peace.

Half an hour went by and we moved to the High Crown and sat in the back end of the pub where I skinned up another spliff. No one was around to bother us and we all quietly enjoyed the atmosphere.

Judith and Debbie went to the jukebox and 1980s music belted loudly out: Robert Palmer's *Addicted To Love,* and Elvis Presley, my favourite, took their turns to entertain our group of four.

I told Bob how I was making my money, but it was crime, law and order that denied me peace of mind and happiness. But to win the end goal where life was perfect you had to make do the best you could until your day of wealth arrived. I was in no doubt that my time would come and I'd be a wealthy man through crime.

I could see that Debbie wanted to tell Judith that she used to be my girlfriend, but could not bring herself to do so. Judith hoped that Debbie would open up as she became more drunk.

It was spitting with rain as we all headed down the street to the Lambton Arms. Arm in arm, we walked in the bar. The place was packed like a sardine can and the music blasted loudly. I quickly searched the dimly lit bar, eyeing the many good-looking women strewn about the place.

I had to use my weight and size to push and shout my way to being served; the two women waited patiently. I thought back to when there used to be 20 or so men on a Saturday dinnertime met in the bar. They'd be drunk and even drunker if it was not for the beer fights between them.

One time both Bob and I came in the bar with a grand, all in one-pound notes. I had been stealing aluminium scaffolding and cutting the 18-foot long poles into shorter lengths with an angle grinder. I took the load to a scrap merchant in Sunderland, and they paid me all in one-pound notes. I recalled how I had got the round in back then and, before sitting down, threw my full pint in Bob and Ricky's faces. This immediately the started a beer fight: all 20 men threw their beer in each others' faces.

The bar had all been done out since the days of old and the alcohol fights. It was plush and the lighting was dim with laser lights flashing round the bar. We found a corner and I skinned up again.

When I pulled on the spliff, I felt like my mind was seeing everything in a perfect light. Judith turned the offer of the spliff down so it went to Bob. Bob was the worst for wear and took his time. Debbie's expression of disapproval looked right through her man. She was strict about smoking tobacco and if he wanted a smoke on a night when he'd finished work she made him go in the garden as the smell bothered her and the toddler, Steve. So watching Bob get stoned on illegal drugs did not go down well with her. It was her strict middle-class upbringing that made up Debbie's character; this rubbed off on Bob and he just agreed with whatever she demanded of him.

After a swift cool gallon Bob didn't care what his woman demanded and all he wanted to do was get drunk. Yes, it had all changed since I'd been living down south and had finished my prison sentence. Every pub I'd been in since had been done up; the days of bare wood floors and bench seats were all over.

Bob told me that since I'd been away there had been a gym open. I'd always worked out ever since my first prison sentence and had the body of a weightlifter to prove that.

At times, when I got the urge, I'd work out regularly, then for three or four months I would stop. I was getting the urge then. My arms and chest felt like they were expanding while I was drinking. It was a feeling of power knowing you were strong and in the best physical condition.

People who knew me before I went to prison were shocked at the size of me when I got out, which did my reputation good. I weighed in at a solid, muscular 14 stone and there was not an ounce of fat on me. The size and shape of me warded people off from wanting to fight with me.

I quizzed Bob on who was where and whom he'd seen about. There were three or four of the old gang in prison for drug offences. However, these were just acquaintances who'd fallen foul of injecting heroin. Two or three others had started their own business, and most others just scratched around and made whatever they could, whenever they could. None of them had moved away, apart from Davy Dent, an old school friend of mine who had given the south a try. I told Davy there was lots of work down south and plenty of opportunity, and that he should give it a try.

Debbie chatted to Judith, filling her in on how she'd met Bob. She still would not say that she had once been a lover of mine and did not say how she thought I was a womanising cheat; at least I was when she'd first met me. Debbie steered away from a corner she did not want to be in and told her that I had always been in trouble for fighting and that's where my reputation came from. Everyone that was someone in the town had heard of or knew Stephen Moyle, Moyle or Moyley; Debbie told Judith that Bob and I had committed a lot more than we let on. She suspected Bob of being a criminal, although she had not got him to admit this; she suspected dodgy dealings as lump sums of money would appear out of the blue. She prayed that it was not the business of drugs and blamed me for egging Bob on.

The night over, Judith got undressed in the bedroom and decided to please me as she left her fishnet tights on. Her knickers were the only other clothing. I pulled the fishnet tights to one side and ripped a hole in them, my throbbing manhood entering her. Our lovemaking was furious and demanding, although we kept the noise as quiet as possible so as not to disturb my parents.

My mind wondered from the act of love I had just shared and moved to the outstanding court case. There may even be a letter from the court with a date on the floor when we got back. The thought disturbed me and I wished it was all over and done with.

As we lay there, we shared a joint and let the cannabis mellow our moods. I told Judith that the river had been a big part of my teenage years when I played the nick from school; long school days spent swimming there. Time dragged on and the acrid taste of cannabis lulled us into a sense of security. We fell asleep in each other's arms.

In the morning I woke up andd snuggled up beside my sleeping woman. I didn't wake her. Instead I skinned up a spliff, then woke her as I smoked. Judith, half asleep, refused a turn on the spliff; she did not have her wits about her and needed time to wake up properly.

I mounted her after finishing the spliff and we fucked slowly with leisure and came again at the same time. A few minutes later we pulled ourselves together and went downstairs. The house came to life.

Nana still had a coal fire and it had to be lit every morning, so she busied herself with this chore as the kettle boiled, then it was bacon-and-egg sandwiches all round.

I cleaned up the shit left by the pup and I thought back to the first dog I'd owned, 'Rex' the bull terrier cross. This dog had a supernatural ability to climb walls and fences; in fact, any obstacle that I could climb the dog would follow. The police knew that if a crime went down, it was me because the dog that always followed his master. The dog went everywhere that I went. If the dog couldn't scale it, the dog would find his way through or around whatever object was in the way and meet me wherever.

We made plans to take Donna to the riverside. I offered to take nana and pops too but they had things to attend to. I reminded my dad that I wanted to take him out to the Osborne that evening, and that I was buying the drinks.

Judith, Donna and I got in the BMW and headed for the flower shop. We bought Nana a dozen red roses and paid to have them delivered that day with a simple message of love and thank you on the card.

I went to the shop next door and bought a big box of chocolates that I would give Nana when we got back from our day's outing. Errands done, we parked the car up and went to the riverside. Although the weather was sunny, it was too cold to swim. Donna played at the river's edge. You could see the ice-cream parlour and burger bar from the where we were. It had all changed since I'd spent my school days there. They'd built a new extension so you could eat seated on the benches on the grass. It was all new playthings for the kids, and what struck me was the big red sign next to the river that read: NO SWIMMING ALLOWED.

This saddened me because the kids had lost out. Maybe – I hoped – kids would just ignore the sign and swim anyway, and stick the pompous shit that'd banned swimming in the river.

I jumped up to get some munchies. I called for Donna and said I would buy three hot dogs together with a couple of bread buns so she could feed the ducks. Donna asked me if we could live in Nana's house and whether could she go to school in Geordieland. I told her that I could not say one way or the other, and that we might or might not, we would have to wait and see. I did not want to put all my eggs in one basket and build Donna's hopes up.

11
THE SHADOW OF THE HUNGERFORD MASSACRE

We had been home two weeks and *the* dreaded letter landed on the mat. It was from my solicitor, Simon Scamell & Co. It said that the date for my case was set for 27 October 1987. I only had a few weeks of freedom left. The reality meant I had very little time to discredit the two witnesses.

I went to see two brothers who gave me two ounces of coke in separate bags. I planned to set the two witnesses up in the shooting charges by planting drugs in their cars, as the woman I had originally convinced to leave the drugs in one of the witnesses houses did not come through – she bottled. She wanted to have a relationship with me for doing my dirty work. I was not prepared to start this sort of relationship. If I'd agreed she would have done it, or so she said, but it was too much to ask of Judith to become involved.

I went to see Charlie and borrowed a tin full of keys for different makes of cars. Both of the witnesses drove Fords. I waited till nightfall and drove to the Railway where I got drunk. My red Bedford CF was in the pub car park, with the box of keys and the sawn-off tucked underneath the front passenger seat. Eddie was in the bar, which was unusual for the middle-of-the-week session. He questioned me about what Judith and I had been up to in the north-east.

I wasn't interested. All my hopes for the future were in the balance and I was in no mood for distractions. I knew my plan was a long shot; if only I could slip the coke into a place that was accessible so the police would easily find it, then I could stitch the two prosecution witnesses up good and proper. They'd be arrested and charged, and that would be end of their credibility.

I had to rely on luck, and I had to have a certain amount of faith that the Old Bill would fall for this. If they did, I would walk from court. I decided to leave the execution of my plan till 4.00am the next morning.

The bags of drugs had no fingerprints on them, as I'd handled them with gloves and wiped the polythene with a rag, so the brothers were also safe. I had put the two bags of drugs in a larger plastic bag for safety so I didn't have to handle them directly, and would easily be able to place the drugs under the carpets of the cars.

As time passed, my stomach was in unpleasant knots. The flat was silent, Judith and Donna were fast asleep.

The second BMW had gone recently. I had done the deal with Jim Ford. Judith and I had discussed what was happening with the house. I told her that if I went to prison she should sell it. It worked out that we'd made £1,200 profit each month. It was the money the family needed. I had seen my mate Charlie to sort out a decent motor for Judith, something worth a few grand for her to get about in.

I left the house: hat, gloves and a big work overcoat. The streets were deserted, save for a milk float that trudged along at 15 miles an hour, the bottles rattling in their crates. I parked up a street away from where the two witnesses lived, took the box of keys from its hiding place.

I had listened about, and the two thugs I'd beaten up had not tried to make any comeback and it seemed that the police were not involved. I hoped this next twist of the tale would be just as successful. I prayed as I fiddled with the different car keys, Charlie having told me which keys would be best to try and for what make of cars.

I managed to plant the drugs successfully and I came away with breathless anticipation, and full of hope. Later I made the phone call to the police telling them that two men were dealing drugs from their work vehicles; I muffled my voice and put on a moody Cockney accent.

I figured what move the police would make in relation to the news. I assured myself that I was not grassing on the witnesses. I was in the right, it was these witnesses that grassed me.

But a stroke of bad luck happened. When the Hungerford Massacre occurred, it cast a shadow over my case, as guns were bad news. I tried my best to work out a move that would work in court. I couldn't foresee any way I could get out of going to court or receiving a big prison sentence. I felt as though the Hungerford Massacre was done deliberately just so I would get a longer prison sentence.

My witness set-up plan had failed; the police had not charged the two witnesses because they wanted me locked up, so they had not made a case out of the planted drugs. The CID and Drug Squad knew who was responsible for the bags of coke. It was reported only by verbal contact – no charges were to be made. The police knew that they'd have me in court and I would not have anything to fall back on. My plan suddenly seemed insane.

If the judge presiding over my case knew my reasons for avoiding court because of the Hungerford Massacre, would it appeal to his conscience? Would he understand that the possibility of the court being affected by the massacre and how it would reflect on me? I had to think fast and decide whether to take a gamble.

I decided to break bail and go to Canada; you didn't need a visa, just a ten-year passport. I booked my seat for the day I was supposed to be in court, kissed my family goodbye and went to the pub with my mates, who had all wanted to go to court to hear the case. I was buying the drinks out of the £2,000 I'd taken with me.

It wrenched my heart out to say goodbye to Judith and Donna. The ploy was to keep out of the way of the police and court for as long as possible till the firearms charges cooled down. Maybe I'd find work in Canada and then move my family over to be with me? These were my first two options; the third meant flying from Toronto to Vancouver, on the West Coast. I knew that you could walk across the border into the USA from there, then I could make my way down to Florida and disappear until I was settled and make my mind up as to when and where I intended to go.

My flight was leaving at 3.30pm. There were six or seven old mates in the pub. Arthur had come out for the event and had taken the Friday off work. I got one of them to ring up the court and say that I would be delayed as the car had broken down. I did not think they would have search parties out too quickly, but I was making certain there wouldn't be any horrible surprises waiting at the airport.

We were all seated around a table in the Game Bird public house in Horley; it was only a ten-minute drive to Gatwick from there, so I was content with my schedule.

I felt sure that, on my return in a few months time, it would be better to face the charges when public the outcry over Hungerford had stopped dictating the judge's views, and anyway, I might not return.

I believed that the move I was making would save me at least 18 months on any prison sentence. If I stayed and went to court, the judge would give me six or seven years.

There was a reason for everything, I thought as the aeroplane banked on its way to 30,000 feet; I looked out the window at the land below and imagined the judge sat in his court in Chichester waiting to sentence me while I flew over the top. The thought cheered me up.

I was sat beside a girl about my age and felt like striking up a conversation, but she seemed reluctant to engage. I decided to have a whisky and, as I got drunker it eased the feelings of guilt that I felt for Judith, Donna and our new unborn baby.

Things were far from perfect and I still had misgivings of where life would take me. Suddenly, out of the blue, under the influence of the whisky, my mind switched. The sound of the plane's engines was somehow speaking to me, saying my name with the rhythm of the noise they were making!

I looked at the girl sitting next to me, trying to figure out if she was hearing the same thing. She didn't seem to be acting as if she was being spoken to by the engines. I could not tell and then wondered, maybe the engines were only speaking to me. I looked at other passengers for any strange reactions, but again I could not tell.

Stephen Moyle, the sound was, and then, *God Almighty,* then the engines repeated themselves. I was certain that it must have been a sign, and wondered how to respond. Should I speak through my own mind or was that a stupid response to dealing with this phenomena?

I thought, try to make the engine say something by forcing my will on the environment – just one word. The atmosphere in the aeroplane said *Canada,* and then I decided to say, *Judith,* and straight away the engine sound said my woman's name. Then the names would switch to the free animal spirit, which I called birds and dogs ... supernatural powers.

I wondered if it could be the pilot and I became paranoid because the people who were chasing me, by listening to the engine sounds, would hear where I was at and when I would be there. I swigged the whisky and tried to figure out what sort of power was making the phenomena happen.

Supernatural, it had to be, as it seemed to shift the environment inside the aeroplane by the sound of the engines outside, on the wings. If it was supernatural and if I could understand the language of the aeroplane, it must have had something to do with the future, my future road in life.

Then I considered whether it could be super-paranormal, because the engines were manmade. The sound just kept repeating itself. I tried to make it say *whisky*. It would not so I tried *Donna*, my little princess, and the engine sound duplicated my speaking, through my mind into the atmosphere in the aeroplane. I could clearly hear the name of my daughter.

I thought that it must be the strength of the family's feelings that must change the sound and, maybe, it was telling me that I must keep thinking about my loved ones, because they would be thinking about me. I was not certain about people's reactions to my situation. It was like they knew and could hear, but just weren't showing any signs. Possibly, I thought, it might be fear that prevented them.

The time ticked by and I continued to swig at the whisky. The rhythm and steady beat of the engines started to relax me. I wondered if the same would happen to a car engine that I may be driving – it had never happened yet. I wondered why and if this happening at the moment was somehow connected to the next stage of my life.

I thought of my mate Bob Ashcroft, and the engine sound said Bob's name, but seemed to pull at my spirit like I was been drained of power, both spiritual and physical. There was a distinct sound of what I thought must be God skipping in and out of the Moyle family name. It did not have an accent, but was old, sincere and calming – it made you think.

I got tired of using my mind to change the engine sound, like I was slowly being used, but I feared not trying to imitate the throb of the engine. I became aware again of the girl sat next to me. She was a good-looking blonde and I eyed her crotch. She wore tight jeans and I imagined what colour knickers she had on, and then imagined peeling them off.

What would making love feel like if I were controlling the environment whilst fucking? I got up from my window seat, beginning to feel horny, and squeezed past the girl and went to the toilet. God's voice was so plain to me. I could hear the words but could not understand their meaning. In the toilet the same voice said, 'This is the mile-high club,' and it struck me that people must have, in the past, made love in the small toilet. I wondered what it would be like?

When I flushed the toilet my name rang clear on the engines' rhythm and I forced my will so that when I left the toilet the girl sat next to me would come inside the toilet and make passionate love. At that thought, my woman's name rang clear. There was no one waiting. I went back to my seat and sat back down quietly.

Then, *universe*, the engine rang plain as day and I pictured a starry night. It then said, 'The ruler of the universe, Stephen Moyle.'

Why it said this, claiming that my name was part of the universe, I couldn't work out. I felt that someone, or something, was giving me something by saying things with my family's names that I had not thought of. It must have been a blessing from God and the powers that be, I thought.

I began to think money and willed this thought on the engine. Maybe, I considered, if I did this I could will myself to come into a lot of money. I tried to think of a way this could happen, and my first explanation – a notice in my mind – was horse-racing. Or maybe I would come into money through doing a big job: an 'A' Class robbery. Perhaps it meant I had to work for it.

I quizzed the engine sound for a concrete explanation. And what happened? God's voice came though as clear as day. It told me I was on to something but that I had to wait. It reassured me and I relaxed more so, swigging at the bottle of whisky.

I wondered if the voices I was hearing were coming from radio frequencies and maybe, for some reason, they were interfering with my personal thoughts. This would mean it was super-paranormal, or so it would seem.

I swigged at the whisky and added another view of what was going on, a drunken view which immediately felt good and took the edge off the ridiculous notion of being spoken to by God Almighty.

As the hours passed, I began to doze. The alcohol relaxed me and the voice seemed to be fading into the steady hum of the engine.

The stewardess was asking what I wanted to eat. I was still thinking about the dream I'd just had woken up from.

'Chicken salad?' she asked.

I forced the word 'yes' out.

Finally I managed to get myself together, and pulled the meal tray down from the back of the seat in front.

I bought a can of Carlsberg to wash down my meal. As I ate, I remembered my vivid dream and then the engines started to speak to me again. For a moment, I thought I'd gone mad and forced myself to think realistically. I made conversation with the girl next to me.

She seemed more relaxed and answered my questions. 'No,' she'd never been to Canada before. I told her I was visiting relatives. 'No,' she was not on holiday, she was visiting friends, was looking at the prospect of getting a job in Canada.

The chit-chat went backwards and forwards, not personal, just sociable, general chit-chat that eased the pain from my mind of what had been going on in the last few hours. I was interested and, with the interest, the engines started to dictate my name again. I wondered if I introduced myself whether the girl would put my name together with the noise of the engine and realise that it was me the engine was talking about.

I shook her hand and said my name. I watched her face for any reaction and then she introduced herself as Annette. As soon as she'd said it the engine sound repeated her name. I saw her reaction, which was one of confusion as she searched for the same explanation that I had been searching for.

'Annette. Did you hear that?' I spoke through my mind and the girl went white with fear.

I wondered why the girl had not done the same as me. Maybe everyone could hear their own names from the engines, or was it more personal to me? I mean, if I was introduced to new associates then the aeroplane would say their names through my new-found powers – maybe it was all down to me.

At the change of the engine sound, the stewardess looked confused and agitated, yet firmly in control. She spoke loudly and was easily heard three or four seats away from where she was serving.

'Moyle hit,' she said and stared straight at me.

My reaction was immediate and I spat out the word, 'Witch!' then mixed in the engine noise, saying my daughter's name. I heard Donna's voice: 'Dad, I've lost me witch.'

The stewardess looked busy, like she was trying to keep control. She had a look of determination on her face as she worked, but I could sense her mind was on other things. The second stewardess also looked at me with a hard, concerned expression; she seemed to keep one eye on me and the other on her colleague in front of her.

I felt alarmed. Donna's voice seemed to be asking me for her help – 'lost a witch'. I felt that she must have lost something dear to her, something personal, and I felt that I did not want my daughter to lose anything. I needed to protect her from strangers that it seemed to me had stolen something from my Donna.

I dealt with the confusion, at the same time hating the stewardesses. I wanted to choke the life from their bodies and get back whatever it was my daughter had lost.

Then a feeling came to me, a spirit from the stewardesses that clearly assured me that my child was in no danger. The feeling lasted a couple of seconds then a spirit from the second stewardess entered my physical awareness and offered me sex as a way to compensate for the pain I was feeling. It entered my cock and I became semi-hard. I held on to the thought as the engine spoke my name again. The stewardess closest to me started to rush her work, making noise with cans, bottles and glasses as she did so. She seemed to be doing what I was doing; keeping her mind fixed and, at the same time, doing her job.

I swigged at the whisky and washed the bitter taste down with Carlsberg lager. Was I in control or was it a phenomenon that I'd just walked into by mistake? Then I asked in my mind what the stewardess had meant by what she said. It had clearly been meant for me.

Trying to keep a grip on reality was virtually impossible; my thoughts just kept switching with the noise inside the aeroplane. I felt that the stewardesses were aware of my situation.

Then the engine noise changed again and I could hear a voice telling me that when I was hearing God's voice, I myself became God Almighty. Quickly I made half a dozen wishes, which came to mind automatically, all to do with money and my woman, daughter and unborn child. Then I was left feeling empty, not knowing if my wishes would come true.

The girl beside me left her seat and headed for the toilet. I watched her navigate the aisle and thought how much I would like to fuck her. I intended to try and seduce her in the hope that we would leave the aeroplane together and get it together for sex at her place.

I felt free when thinking like this. My sexual awareness changed to a burning desire that you sometimes get when in the presence of the opposite sex. I wanted to ejaculate in her. I swigged more whisky and the desire burned in my soul. I willed this feeling on to the girl that would soon be sitting back next to me.

The burning sensation began to dictate my mind. I felt that I was in control at certain points of the phenomena. I reached the conclusion that thinking of the deep emotion of sex could control the expressions, and the act of making love could be used to keep me thinking straight and with a purpose.

She came back and sat back down, looking composed. I struck up another conversation, asking if she had any plans to go out on the town when she arrived in Canada? I told her that I did not have a clue as to where I would go for a drink. 'I'll put one foot in front of the other and go looking for some nightlife. No doubt there'll be some lively clubs and pubs in the city of Toronto.'

The two of us relaxed and spoke about the 'in places' we hoped to visit. Maybe we could exchange phone numbers so as to keep in contact and go out on the town together. It turned out that she was being met at Toronto airport by friends and would be going to stay with them, but giving me her phone number did not seem untoward, she found me quite charming.

Stephen Moyle, the engine roared and I lost the exchange of pleasantries as, once again, the super-paranormal took over my attention.

In the airport at Toronto I followed the people in front of me. There was no such luck that the girl Annette would invite me to stay with her. I flashed my passport at the desk and was waved through; 65,000 miles away from the judge.

So this is Canada, I thought. I searched for a taxi but could only find limousines and coaches. I decided to make arrangements in order to get across the border into the USA, though sexual conquests were on my mind. First thing, though, I had to find a hotel. I asked the bus driver if he could recommend anywhere and he told me there were hotels just a few minutes walk from where the coach stopped in the city.

The coach stopped outside the York Hotel, which was situated in the city centre. I eyed the hotel and dismissed staying there; it was too upmarket – five stars. The bus driver had told me that just across the street was the Hotel Central, and he said I would find a cheap room there.

After checking in to the hotel I found a bar. There was a dark-haired girl stood close enough to brush against me. Italian looks and complexion, and dressed in a dark skirt and top. We struck up a conversation; she seemed game and was looking for some company. She was called Rachel and lived in the city; she often came to the bar we were in for their 1960s music night.

The woman with the brooding Italian looks was with her brother and they planned to go to a nightclub after the bar disco finished. I asked if she'd mind if he came along. She didn't and seemed to enjoy my friendly manner.

The drink relaxed us and she confided to me that she had a boyfriend who her family did not approve of; he was in a Canadian penitentiary. Not wanting to be outdone, I told her that the police were after me in England and that I'd jumped bail. I explained that, probably, I would cross the border and go down to Florida, Miami or maybe California – somewhere hot – get a job and enjoy the plot. She told me that the border control would be hard to cross in Toronto. She suggested that I take the chance and, not having an American visa, hide in the boot of a car because Canadian people did not need a visa to enter the States. I asked if she knew someone who would take me across. She thought for a moment and said she might.

Rachel filled me in on the dos and don'ts of Toronto. She loved my accent and we both felt sexually stimulated. The club was packed, jiving and rocking bodies moved to the beat of the music. It was a big club and I reckoned there were about 6–800 people in.

I would ask her to dance when I had warmed to the atmosphere. She told me that her boyfriend had been sentenced for armed robbery, and that the jail he was in had conjugal visits once a month where the cons fucked their girlfriends in parked trailers next to the prison.

How lucky can you get? Conjugal visits. I deduced that if they had that in England, doing bird would be a doodle. I was free and enjoying the night, and soon got Rachel's telephone number.

12
SEDUCED BY THE DEVIL IN CANADA

I was alone, the hotel room was dark and the ten pints of Budweiser and half a dozen double whiskies I had downed in quick succession made the room spin. I lay on my back looking up at the ceiling, and dozed. Time ticked by and I digested the nights' clubbing. Rachel had seemed to be a cert for sex, but she was taking her time getting to the hotel. She had dropped me off and then taken her brother and his girlfriend home. Her brother had complained that Rachel should not be driving because she'd had too much to drink. She said that she would come to me after she'd dropped them off. I checked my watch and decided she was not coming. I fell asleep dreaming of sex with the girl I'd only met that evening.

I woke early, showered and shaved, and decided to ring Judith. The hotel switchboard connected the call to England from the phone in the room. Judith told me that the police had been round to the flat with a search warrant looking for me. They told Judith that I would make things worse if I did not hand myself in. I told her that I'd ring home every day to see how she and Donna were. As soon as I put the phone down I rang Rachel.

When Rachel answered the phone she told me that she had

been asleep and was suffering from a hangover. I asked why she did not turn up like she said she would and she apologised; she had had an argument with her brother who had then stopped her from driving over to the hotel I was staying at. I arranged to meet her for lunch later that day.

I left the hotel and found a fast-food outlet, where I sat down to a coffee and a cheeseburger. There were about half a dozen other customers and I eyed the young girls. I was feeling horny and decided to make a play for Rachel when I saw her later that day.

Then my mind switched as I thought about Donna and the burger bar we'd last eaten in. I wondered about God's voice on the aeroplane and wondered why the voice would not come to me at that present moment. Maybe I had to think in secret so only I could hear my thoughts. And then it came to me: the voice told me to play *follow the leader*, meaning that whatever the voice said I had to follow. I wasn't sure where this would lead, but I decided to give it a go.

Maybe there was a power that could dictate my thinking and movements. For some reason, the voice told me that, on occasions when thinking, it would take ten minutes for God to get back to me. I questioned this, as what would happen if I needed an answer from God straight away? The voice assured me that this was only a situation to fall back on and it would likely never happen.

First thing I asked was, 'Will I fuck Rachel today?' A few seconds went by and the voice told me it would depend on Rachel and her thinking mood at the time that I propositioned her. I considered this answer, and wondered if everything I would query would be a cat-and-mouse game.

I wondered if I was cracking up or going mad? I thought of the voice and it shocked me that it had immediately come to me and told me that my thoughts, at that present time, reached God Almighty as clear as day. So I tried to think round this and stop my thoughts being heard.

I found that the thoughts I was having touched my feelings and emotions in a way that thoughts and feelings affect each other. This frustrated me, as I was unable to digest one or the other. God told me when this happened to keep a clear mind and force thinking of different subjects so that my mind would go off on another thought pattern.

The voice told me that there was not much point in forcing my mind to think of what I'd just thought, and that the future was the fact I had to reach when listening to God Almighty. If this really was God Almighty, I considered, where was the devil? The voice assured me that the devil was there and 'is waiting for the right time to reveal his ugly head'.

I was suddenly overcome by a strange feeling. I felt that God was very angry that I'd asked about the devil. I was told to guard my soul and the voice then became two, although the second voice could not be heard. I was told that God Almighty was discussing with the devil who owned my soul.

I clearly heard God's voice; it was persistent and strong, full of wisdom. I felt fear that the devil might steal my soul; I forced myself to remain calm and strained to hear the conversation.

My soul had apparently been touched by the devil and I wondered where and when this was supposed to have happened. The devil insisted that my soul was no use to anyone but him. I'd been seduced by evil and my soul was unclean. God was not put off. He verbally supported me and urged me to consider what the devil presumed. I became anxious and unnerved, but the devil let me hear. So now I was not just listening to God, but to the devil and his responses and allegations that I was evil.

It would seem that coppers who were evil when I was last in police custody had touched me. I could not quite remember where and when it came to me. I recall that I was pushed – by the base of my spine - into a cell at the police station. I remembered because it hurt the left side of my body, like I'd lost something. At that time I had been unnerved, but I had concerned myself with other thoughts.

The devil told God that the thoughts straight after the seduction were from the devil, placed at the time so while I tried to use my mind to find out more, the devil had sneaked in and stolen my soul.

Once again paranoia overcame me and I wondered where the voice of God had been when this incident had happened. I remembered that a screw had deliberately, with hate, hit my left testicle. I had felt pain and told the screw what I thought of him. I thought that, maybe, this was the time and place my soul was stolen.

Through my mind I told God, but the devil answered me, saying that the soul I had was his anyway, and that I should not be afraid as the devil took care of his own. I hated the thought of being owned and decided to find out the meaning of the devil's suggestions.

I had had enough and decided to leave the fast-food outlet and head back to the hotel bar to meet Rachel, and then the voice hit as plain as day and told me I'd make the first move of my life at that particular moment.

God told me, as I walked, that movement from one place or another was like a time machine that was pre-dictated to control the soul. Could it be possible that I was considered evil for being on the run for offences against the law? Was this how the devil had touched me?

The hotel bar had just opened when I walked in. I was the only customer and there was quite some time to pass before I met Rachel, if she turned up. So I started the day's session, once again, doubling up with whisky and Budweiser.

Rachel strolled in the bar right on time, which was a good sign I might get her into bed. I bought her a double vodka and coke and we sat down at the other side of the bar. There were a few customers now, but it was still very quiet.

She sat very close to me, touching my leg with hers. We both felt sexy and I immediately launched my attack to get her into bed. I complimented her on how beautiful she looked. I asked her, as I usually did to women I chatted up, if she was wearing black stockings – she was, and smiled at my manner.

I thought further about getting her into my bed, and was shattered as she told me it was her time of the month. She apologised to me, seeing the happy expression change to one of disappointment.

I pushed the query and asked when she finished her period. She told me she'd come on that morning, shortly after she'd spoken to me on the phone. I thought to myself, was it a coincidence that she'd come on that morning, or was it the voices of God and the devil that were responsible and were keeping me in check?

If it had been Judith that had just had her period then I would still have fucked her and would have enjoyed it just the same; blood from your woman's fanny just made the act of shagging feel dirty, but the feeling of love overcame any thoughts of apprehension while having sex.

The drink helped me. Subtly I asked her if she would shag whilst on her period. For a moment I thought she was about to say yes and, probably, for a minute would have agreed, but instead she turned me down.

I was not going to ask for a gobble or a wank because it was important to me for her to enjoy my love-making. We decided to get drunk together and, for the moment, enjoy each other's company. Before the moment was lost in a cloud of alcohol consumption I asked her again if she would take me across the border in the boot of her car. She wasn't certain but said she would think about it.

Sick of getting nowhere with Rachel, both in bed and in the

boot of her car, I decided to move on, not only because of the hotel being expensive but also because I wanted to find a way across the border.

I packed my bags, got out an aerial survey map and headed for a town ten miles away, St Catharines. I asked the bus driver where I could get a cheap room and he directed me to a place called the Tavern, which was a bar cum rooming house. The room was spartan and reflected the $10 a night charge.

On the way in I noticed a girl playing pool; she'd given me the eye. I hurriedly sorted my room out and was pleased to find that she still there as I bought a Budweiser and a chaser.

I'd been in Canada for less than a week and was disappointed that I hadn't fucked a Canadian woman yet. This woman was giving me the come-on, but she was with a man and looked to be just after free drinks for the night.

Alone, I walked around the town looking for the nightlife. I found a pub and went inside. The place was lively: it seemed to get busier as the time wore on.

I immediately made my way to the dartboard. There were two women playing and I struck up a conversation with one of then. I told the women that most pubs in England had dartboards and that it was popular with the punters, and that the Nags Head was the first pub in Canada that I'd seen with a dartboard.

The best-looking one told me she was a student; she was friendly and stood close to me. We were both aware of our desires. I told her I was a self-employed builder; she listened with the interest that two people feel when meeting someone from a different part of the world. I bought the two women a drink and the conversation continued.

As the conversation flowed back and forth between us, I told her I was searching for a woman and that I felt lonely miles away from home. Telling the truth was better than a chat-up line. I really fancied her; she was good looking and seemed independent.

After a while and a few more drinks, I asked her straight out if she would come back to the room I had rented. She did and we hurriedly left the pub. Any guilt about fucking another woman was left at the entrance to the bar. I ordered last orders in the bar of the rooming house and bought a bottle of whisky.

Tonight was going to be a night to remember, my desire was made clear ... I wanted her body, I wanted to seduce her mind with my sex. When we got into the room, we swigged and enjoyed the burning of the alcohol in our stomachs.

We tore each other's clothes off. Her body could have been on page three of the *Sun*, she was gorgeous and she was suntanned. I kissed her with passion; my manhood felt so hard that I thought it was going to burst. I hovered above her and, without asking, she took my tool and guided it into her.

Our bodies tingled with anticipation and I rammed my cock into her as hard as I could. She moaned with ecstasy. Then strangely, she spoke to me with the rhythm of our love-making. 'Jesus Christ,' she spoke from the bottom of her stomach. I fucked her harder and she 'Jesus Christed' me again. She was speaking from her soul and it drove me mad with pleasure.

Over and over again she called me 'Jesus Christ'. For the first time of many, I released my bodily fluids into her cunt. It turned me on, fucking someone from the other side of the world, and she felt the same.

As we lay side-by-side, I made up a story, exaggerating the truth as to why I was involved in crime, and I just burst open with the reason I was there ... because my woman and child had been killed in a car crash. No sooner had I said this, I felt guilty.

We swigged the whisky and gently massaged each other's sex. Again I got on top of her and fucked, while she said, 'Jesus Christ.' The love-making went on, and in between sex we would lie still together, enjoying each other's closeness. Why I had said about my family dying in a car crash, I did not know.

After both of us falling asleep, I slowly awoke and lay looking at the beautiful woman asleep next to me. I became hard with excitement. I needed to fuck her again, baptize her with sex. Slowly I began to kiss her face, her nose and her soft lips. She stirred and responded. I felt her fanny, still wet. I pulled the girl on top of me and positioned her illustrious body and entered her. She slid up and down on my hard shaft. I held her tits and massaged her nipples. She came as I ran my fingers over her body, and she gasped with sexual pleasure.

Her face was a picture of lust and wanting. I held her back, the spunk in my balls wanting to capture the moment when she came again. I felt the sudden surge of her fanny and I let loose my spunk.

I was out on the town all day after seeing that bird in the morning, and I was looking forward to meeting her again that evening. We had arranged to meet at 8.00pm in the same bar.

I waited an hour and she still hadn't turned up. I'd been stood up and wondered why. Our love-making had been good, in fact, it had been perfect, so why had she stood me up? At last orders I made my way back to the rooming house.

Soon, the immigration services were on my back and I moved around in order to avoid them ... and I developed a wacky plan to swim across the Niagara River!

13
THE BROODING CAULDRON OF DEATH

There it was, in all its deceptive destructive glory. I stood with my suitcase at the mouth of the Niagara River, and gazed in wide-eyed awe across the gap to the America – so close, yet so far away.

Lake Ontario that the Niagara ran into stretched out as far as the eye could see. The river was a calm, but brooding cauldron of death. It looked like a sheet of glass and freedom beckoned to me from the water that had taken so many lives before. Anyone looking at it could easily be fooled into thinking that swimming it would be easy. Even I had the notion of a few empty containers tied to my suitcase, and of then floating the containers and pushing them out in front of me as I swam. I was the only person on the shore and it was peaceful, no distractions.

I took my trousers and top off and, after having a quick look around and spotting no one, I dipped my toes in the water. I thought I would see what it was like and slowly started walking out, and then ... there was nothing beneath my feet, a sudden drop and I was sort of pulled along by an unseen current. As I looked to the shoreline I could see how far I was from it. I began swimming frantically just to stay alive.

I kicked and put my head down, swimming for all I was worth.

What had started out as a tester had become a life or death struggle. I was saying to myself, 'Come on! Swim! Swim! Swim!' With more intensity and driven by stark fear, I dove beneath the water and swam breast stroke ... I was making headway and felt the current release its deathly cold grip. I surfaced and gulped for air, reaching out to grab whatever I could on the shoreline.

What I didn't realise was that Lake Ontario is the smallest and easternmost of the Great Lakes, and is an inland sea, which can present overwhelming dangers during adverse weather conditions. In fact, this wasn't a lake, it was an ocean and behaved like one. They have dangerous rip currents and large tidelike coastal currents. These changes in coastal water levels are called seiches (say-shez), they are caused by prolonged strong winds and passing storms.

OK, I had underestimated what it would take to get across it, but I wasn't giving up. Desperate measures called for desperate acts. I recalled the great showmen, those who used barrels to sit tight in as they went over Niagara Falls, which was some miles away from where I was. I would use containers to float on or hold on to, and would let the current do all the work – the very current that tried to take me.

Niagara Village was less than ten minutes away and I'd have to look around in the backs of pubs for the empty containers I needed. God spoke and said that 'life had many roads' and that I was 'at the crossroads' of my life. Too right, I was.

I had a twinge of fear in my stomach, but I pushed it to one side. God said, 'It was the devil.' I thought about nicking a boat, but there was not one in sight. Maybe I'd search for one later, but a stolen boat would stick out like a sore thumb, and what if someone reported it stolen?

I had a strong urge to get drunk and decided to head for a pub I'd seen in Niagara Village on the way to the river. I thought as I walked, and it seemed that the voices were in control. I did not like this and, fearfully, I wondered if I might drown if I swam the river. I dismissed this worry, having always been a strong swimmer.

I entered the pub and stood at the bar. There was a couple stood at one end of the bar, but there was no one else in the pub. The place sold Guinness and I doubled up, again, with whisky.

I ordered my drinks and the punter that was with his woman spoke to me. It turned out that he was an engineer. I immediately grew curious and asked if there was an easy way to cross the river and get access to America? I didn't tell him of my brush with death whilst testing the water out.

When he heard of my plan to cross the river he was shocked and lost a mouthful of Guinness down the front of his shirt. He spoke in gasps as the beer went down the wrong way.

He told me that the current that came from the falls would wash me into the middle of the lake. I thought about this and realised that I had been caught in one of these rip currents, and I thanked my good luck in finding out that I, indeed, could have drowned if I'd tried to fully swim the raging river. In fact, in 1882 Matthew Webb died while attempting to swim the whirlpool rapids below Niagara Falls.

It was a suicide lottery whether you would get out alive, but it could be done as was proven on 22 July 1859 when Seth Ford swam across the Niagara River from a location north of the American Falls to the Canadian shoreline – the reverse of what I was planning. Many people had successfully swum across the Falls gorge, but I didn't have the benefit of a supporting crowd of well-wishers, I would be doing it illegally and would, therefore, have to swim a longer distance than Seth Ford. I later learned that a German, Claus R Kirkoff, swam the lower rapids (Devil's Hole Rapids) of the Niagara. He was swimming back to the USA to gain illegal entry, from where he had been deported in 1957 – he survived.

To show you the futility of my plan, the second-oldest person to swim across Lake Ontario was Peter Gibbs (56). On 8 August

2004 he took 18 hours, 40 minutes to swim from Niagara-on-the-Lake to Leslie Street Spit, Toronto ... only the 36th person to do this.

Ah, what the fuck! I shelved my madcap plan and pushed my disappointment to one side, thinking more about the drink than my future quest for America. The man told me that he and his woman were on their way to a city called Hamilton, a steel-factory town.

He told me that if I was looking for work, Hamilton was the place to go, as it was an industrial city and offered me a lift. With nothing to lose, I accepted. It was about a two-hour drive to Hamilton and the city was busy, more so than any other town or city I had been in so far. It was late afternoon and we entered a bar called Jacks in the city centre.

I had fanny on my mind and my English accent would be somewhat of a novelty to the women. After finding a hotel called 'Hotel', I said my farewells.

The hotel did not have a restaurant. It was 11.00pm when I got up, showered and shaved, and headed out to look for a cafe or burger bar. There was a pub on the corner of the block. It had a big Union Jack flag above the door, and it was a restaurant also. The place was dimly lit, with secluded booths for people who wanted privacy whilst socialising. The barmaid was dark haired and beautiful. She wore casual wear that resembled a uniform of sorts. I wondered if I should hit on her but decided against it.

Whilst I ate the bar grew busy. It occurred to me that the clientele were a bit on the gay side, and I realized that it was a poof's place. I paid for my meal then quickly left.

After ten minutes walk I found another bar that looked safe to drink in. I ordered a pint of Guinness, doubled up with a large whisky. I socialised with the barmaids, who seemed to be very efficient as they went about their jobs. They asked if I was in town for the ice hockey; seemingly the Canadian hockey team were playing Russia for the World Championship and the games were being held in Hamilton's Hockey Stadium. I explained that I was there on holiday.

After six pints and six doubles, I was on my way to being drunk. I met a man who gave me a telephone number of a sub-contractor for building work.

As the drink took hold, I grew louder and openly bragged about my English roots. I liked the bar and, as it got busier, the talk between us livened up. There was a notice board and on it was a three-inch needle. I took the needle and borrowed a pen and paper from the barmaid. I wrote on the paper: I NEED A WOMAN. Using the needle, I stuck the paper on my chest; a drop of blood stained my white T-shirt.

The company I was in thought me mad and laughed at my chat-up line. As the evening wore on I suggested to John that we go to the bar called Jacks, because there was live music on. We ordered a taxi and left for Jacks, 15 minutes' drive away.

Jack's bar was packed with bikers; it was dimly lit, with a live band at the far end of the bar. There was a scattering of women, most of which were in the company of men. I was drunk and my comrade in arms was even more drunk than he'd been for the last year.

We spotted a couple of women who seemed to be on their own, and immediately made a move on them. We'd been speaking to the women for ten minutes or so before we were approached by two bikers that had just entered the place. They were full of speed.

The fight broke out to the sound of the live band. I rolled over a table, smashing glasses and turning over tables and chairs. Other punters who were friends of the bikers joined in. I felt pure aggression as I punched and kicked them. The women screamed for the two bikers to kill me. The police were on the scene in minutes. They waded through the damage, pulled their guns out and restrained me. As I stared down the barrels of a magnum I was shocked into sobriety. I was cuffed and bundled into a police car.

Toronto Detention Centre was a relatively modern building. It was a high-tech security for prisoners awaiting trial, or transfer to various state penitentiaries. It was built in a circle. The outside of the building was the prison wall itself. It was four stories high and surrounded by an eight-foot electric fence, not so much to keep prisoners in but to keep undesirables out and away from the building. The only security was video cameras trained on the fence. There was a big exercise yard and gym in the centre of the building, the only place where prisoners could get fresh air and exercise.

There were no walls, as the exterior of the building acted as a wall or fence. The cell windows were small and looked out over the eight-foot external fence. The cells were two-man cells, but the jail was so overcrowded that they were housing three men to a cell.

I rubbed my wrists as they screw took the cuffs off. The screw reading through my telephone book, which I always carried, stopped at the back page and made a note of my name and national insurance number. That was it, I was firmly nicked. I had been thinking about giving a moody name, but the book had let me down. All I could do now was give the screws my hotel address and tell them that my passport and other important documents were with my belongings, locked in the hotel room.

I was jailed in the secure block whilst enquiries went on regards my passport and the like. The cell was the very pits: it had a sink and a hole in the floor to shit in. The mattress was taken out through the day and put back in the cell at 6.00pm.

As of that time, I had not been charged with any offence; the police and screws were not sure who I was. I worried, not knowing what I could be charged with because I was not familiar with the Canadian laws. I guessed it would be some kind of public-order offence, maybe assault if the bikers I'd fought with pressed charges.

The screws retrieved my passport and birth certificate from the hotel and immediately put my details in the international computer. They found out that I was wanted for jumping bail in England. Shortly after, I requested my red telephone book and rang Rachel, explaining to her that I'd been locked up. Rachel sounded concerned and sympathised with my plight. She arranged to come and visit me the next day.

On the wing, I introduced myself to the Canadian villains, some of whom were, like me, from other countries, such as Israel and Afghanistan. They openly bragged about the offences they had been imprisoned for, all of which were waiting to go to trial. The Israeli was dealing with his Ambassador, trying to get back to Israel. It was clear from the way the Canadian prisoners reacted towards the Afghan that he was top dog on the wing – no one hassled him.

Rachel came to visit me and brought me some munchies. The visiting room was different from in England. Every prisoner sat behind Perspex glass to stop the prisoners and visitors from having physical contact. You had to use the phones on both sides of the barriers to speak to each other. I cheered up because I thought Rachel had come to offer me the hand of friendship.

As I looked into her eyes through the Perspex, I wished that I had not made love to her and I cursed myself for not waiting until she'd finished her periods before I'd left for a different city. Rachel laughed as I answered her question of whether I had managed to make love yet in Canada. She complimented me when I answered her and told her that I had. Rachel thought that the woman I spoke of was lucky to have fucked such a handsome man, and she cursed her luck that she'd missed out.

After the visit was over, I rang the British Ambassador, but I could not get any information and was told to ring back the next day.

The voices came to me again as I showered. It made me feel good and I questioned why the voices had come to me again. The voices told me that under the noise of the shower the other prisoners were less likely to hear the conversation that was going on in my mind.

It was God Almighty that came to me first, and he told me that I would be on my way home soon. God didn't give any specific details though, and I wondered if he ever did. The anticipation of God's declaration made me feel cared for.

Then the devil spoke, claiming that what God had told me had been stolen from the devil. The doubt that was left in my mind by the devil's claim was a present from the devil and his perception of facts.

After a week, I managed to speak to the British Ambassador; things seemed to be moving towards me being deported, as I was told there were no charges being brought against me.

I spoke to Judith and told her of my plight. Although she was sad, she was also pleased because I was on my way home, even though I'd be going straight to jail. The Canadian authorities had told me the day before that I was being deported back to England, on the early-morning flight.

I'd been in custody for three weeks and was looking forward to the journey back home. In the airport I requested to go to duty free and the Immigration people allowed this, which surprised me. I bought a big bottle of Bell's Whisky and 200 cigarettes – Benson and Hedges.

When I was on the aeroplane I fumbled the bottle of whisky out of the bag, and Immigration told me not to and that I would be making trouble for myself if I drank.

I hissed at the jailer and said that if he did not allow me to drink I would kick off in the aeroplane. I was full of myself, I had nothing to lose. I was going back to England where I knew I'd be going straight to jail.

My escort reeled back from my insistence and venom. His colleague sitting straight across the aisle flashed warning signals. They had been briefed that I was violent and the two decided that I could be a problem that they could do without it, so they let me drink my whisky. I contentedly stared out the aeroplane window and dreamed.

The whisky burned my throat and I enjoyed the sensation as it went down and warmed my stomach. Then, damn it, the engines started to say my name; they chopped and changed from my name to my woman's and my daughter's.

God Almighty came to me; the voice was separate from the engine voice and said that my two jailors were rejecting the names of my family and I. God Almighty said that it was freaking the two Immigration officers out. Their faces were of disbelief as they were made to think that I was burning their souls.

God Almighty encouraged me to use my mind to dictate the airways, and informed me that he was murdering the two security men, and that he was doing so because I had been taken for granted and my character had been abused by the authorities. So God Almighty was letting me revenge myself by mental torture of the two Immigration officers. I swigged from the bottle, amazed at my good fortune amongst the devastating circumstances. I was on my way home.

Six hours later, we landed at Heathrow Airport, and I was pissed and did not care much about what was happening to me. I listened to my mind and put one foot in front of the other as the voices followed me.

I guessed that the British authorities would be cocksure about me being deported, and I was met as soon as I left the aeroplane by airport police. A plan to run when they took the cuffs off was one option I was considering. The airport was packed as we entered ambush alley, which was so called because that's where Immigration swooped on passenger's suitcases for any illegal contraband.

They waved us straight through, which surprised me. We went through a locked door leading to a corridor of holding and interview rooms; they took the cuffs off and dumped the contents of my suitcase on to a table. They confiscated my passport, stating that it would be sent to the passport office to be amended to state the fact that I had been deported.

The Canadian police signed my custody over to the British authorities and left. In the end, I had been deported for being an illegal immigrant, because I was on the run from British justice.

The room didn't have a window, just the door and a few tables and chairs. The police allowed me to smoke while I waited for the outside police to take me to Heathrow police station, where I would wait to be escorted to prison.

God Almighty stated that the devil had lied about giving me a present, and that the devil would never truthfully give anything to me if God Almighty did not do so first. The feelings of God's voice gave me hope: hope that my family were all well and coping, and that I'd started, since being arrested in England, my sentence. Time, bird, porridge had immediately came into effect.

At the moment there was little chance of doing a runner. I could attack the two airport police and fight my way out, I thought.

'Maybe you should,' said the devil, but then changed its tune and the voice told me to listen to God's voice, as he knew the way out.

The devil was giving advice that agreed with God's. In my mind I wondered if God Almighty or the devil were speaking the truth.

After a five-minute ride in the meat wagon I was banged up in a cell. They gave no information as to what would happen to me. God Almighty's voice whispered that I was not going to prison yet.

The devil told me that he, the devil, predicted what God would do and I felt secure in a plight that was full of stress and paranoia.

As I'd done many times before, I studied the graffiti on the back of the cell door and scrawled on the walls. Signatures of pain, prisoners scribbling injustices on the cell walls. The devil told me not to let these thoughts interfere with my own reality, and that I should keep focussed, as all was not lost.

I began to consider religion. I wondered what a religious man would make of these voices. For a moment I thought of Jesus Christ and worship. I questioned the voices, thinking that they were playing me at piggy in the middle, as Jan over in Canada had called me Jesus Christ while making love.

The voices promised there would be answers, all the answers I needed, but that they would come mostly when my time was hard. I did, by all accounts, feel secure when the voices came to me. It was like being in a world where no one else was and I could not be harmed. Convincing and soothing and at the same time bitter when the devil added his penny's worth. It stood to reason that, if the voices were real, there would be a cost for all the information and assurance from them, that they'd want something from me, something very precious and reliable. They were playing for my soul.

Heathrow police let me out of the cell to be escorted back home. The four burly Sussex policemen eyed me suspiciously as they gave my belongings back. It took only minutes for me to be on my way. I wondered why I had not been transferred to prison and was instead going back to the local police station. This was what the police called 'formality'.

When I was stood in reception they tipped the contents of my suitcase on to the bench and again rummaged through my stuff. It took them an hour to itemise my belongings, then they banged me in yet another cell.

They had brought me back to the local nick so as I could be charged with jumping bail; they did this shortly after my admission back in police custody.

I was now on the way to HMP Lewes under cuffed transfer. I wished the prison van would crash and overturn, so I could beat the screws up, nick the keys for the handcuffs and run for freedom.

As the van entered the prison's main gate, all thoughts of escape came crashing down. I was back in my worst nightmare, where good thoughts and happiness were no more; only a daily struggle to try and keep my mind in order.

In the holding room the other prisoners and I waited to be processed and assigned to the correct wing.

14
THE LONG ARMS OF THE LAW

The long arms of the law had caught me and here I was looking down my nose at one of the most appalling sights to greet me. As soon as we eyed each other up, there was instant hate between the system and me, the prisoner. Because I was a remand prisoner I should have been entitled to remand privileges, but I was denied this ... bastards. The screw insisted that the tobacco that was open was thrown away. Although I had 200 cigarettes that I had bought in duty free, I had to throw a spent packet in the bin. The screws did this so the prisoners that worked in reception could fish the discarded tobacco from the bin for their own use.

After the usual boring formalities were over, I fumed; I hated my predicament and did not at all want to see some doctor that I considered to be my enemy. It had been many years since I had seen an outside doctor and the only time I had crossed paths with medics was when I had been in prison. In fact, I feared these people out of some hidden sense that they were evil and were out to destroy my character. This made me less co-operative. The doctor scribbled away as I reeled off the same answers that I'd used on previous visits to the big house.

The screws, when dealing with the paperwork, thought that they would like to jail me in the block because I was a threat to security and the good order and disciplines of the prison. The screws could tell I was an unexploded bomb, a firecracker that could go off at any time.

They hoped I would kick off so they could lock me in a place suited to my security. I played it cool and my arse hurt from sitting on hardwood benches. The screws gave me my valuables in a clear plastic bag then marched me from reception and I was told to pick up a ready-rolled bed pack. They were stacked in wooden racks against the wall. I would need these to make my bedding up for the night when I got to my cell.

My prison number N61883 and cell card confirmed I was a remand prisoner. I marched up the stairs and was studied by the prisoners who were the wing cleaners. There were only four of these privileged prisoners out of their cells at this time of day.

In my cell, the voices came and I was stunned at their ferocity, calming me and assuring me that I'd been right in my plans and would be acknowledged when I was in court in front of the judge.

The cell was just as bleak as I remembered it from the first time being in prison. The light switch for my previous cell had been outside of the door, on the wall, but with this cell, as with the others, the lights were inside and you were able to use it at your own discretion.

The following morning at 8.15am the cell door opened and was left partially shut. I woke up from a sleep that had been restless and my head felt heavy. The daily routine of slopping out never changed and I went about the business of fetching clean water to wash in. I washed in a dish in my cell and then slopped out the dirty water in the prison recess.

The landings were narrow, so you had to turn and pass prisoners sideways. Other prisoners would lean over the rails, smoking or waiting for the breakfast call. The prison became busy. Remand prisoners went to and from the screws' office at the end of the landing, or were on important missions to cadge for tobacco, matches or sugar. Comrades would help each other, but not all.

On the way to the servery to collect breakfast, served on to a steel tray, I walked past a female screw and I made eyes at her with the hope that she may pleasantly respond to me sexually. I wondered if she was wearing black stockings beneath her trousers, as I always wondered when around female screws. It made life in prison that much more easy being around them.

I kept my eyes firmly on the food: a sausage, three slices of white bread, a piece of toast and a large scoop of porridge. I gave the porridge a miss. I got my mug of tea and climbed the three flights of stairs back to my cell.

At about 9.30am the cell door was opened again to slop out and wash the utensils. Prisoners sometimes washed their cutlery in the one of two basins in the recess, and your tray was put outside your cell door for the cleaners to put on the kitchen trolley, ready to go back to the kitchen to be washed.

The door opened and the screw asked if we wanted exercise. I say 'we', as a prisoner called Leigh had just been put in with me; he was on a serious charge of violence. I slung on my denim jacket and left the cell, telling Leigh to bang the door up if he decided to leave.

The walkways were busy with prisoners, some in their own clothes and some in prison-issue browns, which meant they were remand prisoners. It grew noisy as the hundred or so prisoners made their way from the cells to the exercise yard. Time dragged as the wing became lively. Prison was basically the same wherever you were jailed.

There he was, Nick Foster, larger than life and stoned out of his mind. We greeted each other. We had met some time ago on a building site and had become friends. Nick was the man to see for drugs, but I didn't enquire at first, choosing to listen to Nick and what the man was on remand for. He was looking at seven years behind bars. We walked side by side on to the exercise yard. The weather was overcast like the mood of the inside of the jail.

Nick lit up a spliff that he'd rolled earlier and shared it with me, and his cellmate who was also a drug addict. Leigh limped over and sat next to me. I enquired about the heroin that he had asked me about earlier, as he had £400 in notes hidden up his rear end, and a deal was a deal. I asked if Nick wanted to sell any of the powder. He did and Leigh pulled out some money he had in his pocket and paid Nick up front. The heroin would be delivered and pushed under the door of the cell when they got back inside. Nick would not give Leigh the heroin then because it was shoved up his arse and he would have to go to the toilet to get it out. I did not pay attention to the conversation about the heroin. I let the pair sort the deal out, as I had no interest in the stuff.

Then the voices came to me again. I did not know, and had no inclination to figure out, what the voices meant. Maybe they were there to stop me feeling alone. But I was sure there were sinister reasons why these voices came to me. They praised me, stating that I was above the rest – all the other cons were shit and I was above royalty; even the Royal Family were lesser than me. But the voices did not account for my gut feeling that I was being set up. I thought, maybe, that the CIA was tracking me, and maybe the voices that came to me were an omen of hard times to come.

I hated grasses. The voices told me I was one in ten million that held this view and that other prisoners would grass to save their own skins when the pressure threatened the prisoners with more jail. It was 11.30am when the screws called exercise over.

The cleaners were scurrying about pushing dinner trolleys, which were large insulated steel boxes on wheels, to the prison wings from the kitchen.

Nick gave me a small lump of cannabis. There was enough there for three joints and I thanked my old friend and decided to smoke a joint whilst finishing my letter to Judith.

I watched Leigh produce a hypodermic, which no doubt had been folded and taken from his arse. He fixed a hit up. For a moment I wondered what the hit would be like as I watched the heroin being prepared. Not my business, I thought, and the voices came again stating that if I wanted a fix then I should take one. I considered this and then thought about addiction.

The voices said I would not become addicted, although I had an addictive personality. God said that I was above becoming addicted because I was special in the link between reality and the other side. The devil spouted out that God was stating this to steal the experience of injecting heroin from me.

I watched the warm liquid drain in the arm of Leigh, who immediately took to his bunk absolutely monged out of his mind.

At noon the door opened and I walked from my cell to collect dinner. Leigh was semi-conscious and the last thing on his mind was food. Along the walkway, dodging this, then that, bodies coming at you from every direction, everyone heading for the hot plate or the recess.

The female screw was not there. I met Nick, who enquired as to where Leigh was; I grinned and told Nick the drugged state of Leigh. Normally the best time to take drugs was in the off times that existed in the routine running of the prison: normally in between meal times and slop-out times, or the best was last lock-up where from teatime until the next morning prisoners were locked in their cells. The door would be open once more at the end of a day for a mug of tea from the cons that bring buckets of tea round.

After dinner the cell door was opened at 2.15pm for us to slop again. I had to empty his piss pot. I was succumbed by the stink of shit and piss as I emptied the pot ... quick scrub with the brush, breathe shallow to stop the smell and back to the cell.

A screw told me that the reception prisoners – and I was one of them – from the previous day's induction were being paid reception money, which was enough to buy half an ounce of tobacco, a packet of cigarette papers and a box of matches. But remand prisoners were allowed to spend money from their own private cash. I made my way to the canteen.

There were about half a dozen prisoners in front of me. I joined the queue. As a remand prisoner, I bought four ounces of Old Holborn tobacco, cigarette papers and matches, and goods to make tea and coffee with, and a couple of Mars bars for later when I had my spliff.

It was hard to stand still in prison whilst in a queue. It made your arse twinge as there were poofs about that had a fixation that all prisoners were gay and thought about their arses as some kind of flower.

I also hated blacks, dare I say it ... I used the 'n' word to describe them. Some might say that is racist, but I had had bad experiences with them and old memories die hard. My experience on previous sentences was such that I had fights with blacks and had been grassed up by puffs. Time had not changed my outlook on these people.

As far as I was concerned, they were there but not to be seen in my everyday life. I had over the previous years in prison built a particular view that did not acknowledge these scum. The hate oozed off me. I blatantly refused to do deals or have anything at all to with the culture of blacks and poofs.

After canteen I returned to my cell. Leigh was not in and I figured he must have gone to get his canteen. I decided to make a cup of tea and got my water jug, emptied the contents and went to the boiler, which was situated on the bottom floor to one side of the upward staircase. I was sat on my bed sipping tea when Leigh entered with a box full of munchies; the screw followed him and banged the door shut, as is the usual procedure.

I prepared to skin up a spliff and, when done, pulled deeply on the drug. I finished my letter to Judith.

> Darling Judith, the time is about 3.00pm and you're still in my deepest thoughts. I have thought of little else but you and our daughter. I hope that our children, when of age, never have to suffer like we are doing now. In my mind there is a plan for our relationship, but as yet I cannot say for certain how we shall make the plan work.
>
> It is sketchy but luring. I feel there will come a time when we know for definite what we both want and how to make it happen.
>
> Judith, we are forced by the system to take drastic measures as the screws want us and what we have to be gobbled up by them and smashed to emotional chaos. I think our dream must start by moving home – where to, I do not know, but my instincts say that we should start anew where people do not know us, and in this place we could build a new life.
>
> I think that at this point in our path through history it is the right choice, and I can familiarise with this plan of choice. We will discuss this scheme to get away from the system when you come to visit me.

We were opened up for what is called 'association'. I eyed Leigh up, who looked as if he'd died and gone to heaven. I picked up my tobacco, fag papers and matches, and went to find Nick on association. Nick listened as I told him what my charges were and my friend thought that I'd receive a five or six-year sentence. I did not agree with Nick and told him so. It still made my heart skip a beat because Nick's opinion was valuable; he knew the score. I decided then and there to cop a plea of guilty; this way the judge would hear my mitigating circumstances.

The voices came as I spoke quietly. My attention wavered. Cons played pool; the table was placed in the middle of the wing. There was a video playing in the room where they served canteen. The canteen was locked for the day so the other half of the room could be used for prisoners' videos.

The voices told me to keep Nick at a safe distance and to be careful what I discussed, as Nick was a drug addict and could use information to do a deal as he was pleading not guilty and, if found guilty, would be facing a seven-year sentence. The devil's voice said that to relax my guard at all would have grave consequences. Nick sensed my mood swing and decided to have a spliff.

In prison on a daily routine it was a game of life or death, do or die, but I felt different because of the voices. God warned me that the two prisoners I was talking to, Nick and his cellmate, could steal a spirit from me. But I was strong and had the benefits of using God's and the devil's voices, which had up until then been a comfort and helped me think positively.

I sat in a hard wooden chair, letting my mood mix with the cannabis. For a moment I felt guilty. I thought for a second how easy it was doing time while smoking cannabis. The voices thought that Judith and Donna would be in the flat with the new baby on the way and two Staffordshire bull terriers to keep them safe and in company. The voices cheered me up again.

God Almighty said that if it were not for himself and his adversary, the devil, I would not have had that particular thought of my family at that particular time. Time would tell what the voices meant. My thoughts felt heavy, yet content.

15
ANOTHER DAY IN HELL

The keys rattled in the lock of the cell and the screw called me for a visit. I quickly jumped up, checked myself in the cell mirror and headed for the visiting room. The visits room catered for all prisoners, remand or otherwise. The cons sat facing each other across the room, remand prisoners on one side, convicted prisoners on the other. The remands were easily observed, as most wore their own clothes or brown denims, whereas the convicted prisoners were dressed in blue prison denims.

The tables had a six-inch partition down the middle. Prisoners sat on one side and the visitors on the other, so the only contact they had was holding hands across the partition and a quick kiss when the visit started.

As I caught sight of Judith, tears came to our eyes and Donna became restless. It seemed that when her mammy and daddy were together they started to cry. The toddler asked me when was I coming home. I ruffled her blonde hair and told her that she looked beautiful in her pink dress.

Judith did not want to let go. I ran my hands along her shoulders and told her how desirable she looked. She was easily the best-looking woman in the room and people looked twice.

I fought to keep my attention on Judith, except those damn

voices were trying to tell me something. They stated that I must have my own supply of cannabis to supplement my life in prison. They made it clear that I should ask my woman to bring cannabis into the jail. I told Judith that to survive in any sort of way of life in jail you needed drugs as a common supplement. Judith listened as I told her how to bring the stuff in, down her bra, tucked underneath her tits. Having a stash of cannabis would mean I could do deals for food, as the usual food was terrible.

She listened and agreed to smuggle me the drugs. I told her to ask Charlie and told her that he would get the drugs for her to bring in to the visits. As I was describing what to do, I found that I was not bothered about anything else but the conversation on how to smuggle.

The voices stated that my thoughts were being cultivated to think things at a certain time, which would end in undying love, shown to the maximum, across the partitioned table. Judith realised that I would not ask for her to do such a thing unless times were tough. There were times in her life that she felt obliged to do her duty, for a woman in love should to help her man. She felt great pain in her soul as she realised that I was in pain and suffering.

The voices assured me that this request was for the better and that I needed to establish myself in the jail food chain. After giving my woman the lowdown, I fixed my attention on the clock. Judith did the same. The clock hung high on the wall above the screw's pulpit and reminded us that we had only so much time left for being together.

If the screws were feeling generous they would give prisoners extra visiting time. Remand prisoners were allowed 20 minutes, but if they were not busy prisoners would get 10 minutes more, but extra time was down to the discrepancy of the Senior Officer (SO); if the screw was in a good mood then there would be extra time.

Judith listened to me as I spoke about marriage and moving away. She thought it made sense to make a new start, and it made her stomach warm and content inside. She felt that, as long as we were together, the family would always be all right. Conversation switched from our future plans to the difficult circumstances our relationship was in now.

I assured Judith that, when sentenced, I would receive a lesser one than if I had not gone to Canada. In my heart I wanted to reassure my woman to keep her chin up, that things would work out. Whatever sentence I got, time at that moment and from now on, was coming off my eventual sentence.

The screw called time. Judith and I cuddled over the table partition, and Donna too. I stood up and watched my family depart. My thoughts were of the new baby on the way. I was keeping my fingers crossed that Judith would come again the next day. The visit had gone OK and I was happy about it, except for the lonely, lost feeling I had. It was like my heart was being cut in two and one half had left with my woman and child.

Before the visit I had hidden a piece of cannabis under my piss pot. The pot was half full and it had been an ideal hiding place, short term, while I had been on my visit. I liked to keep cannabis on me. Normally I shoved it up my arse, but it was only a small lump, enough for maybe two spliffs, and I did not like the thought of poking around and messing with my arse so much.

Association was finished for the day so it was safe for me to skin up a spliff. I passed the spliff to Leigh who enjoyed the cannabis. I thought, maybe it's done his back injury good, as he had a bad back. I was lost in a world of drugged optimism. Sometimes I thought of my family; sometimes I considered the interior that I lived in; sometimes I drifted in to the voices that seemed to attract my thoughts like flies to sugar.

I was partially aware of it raining outside the cell window. It was dark and the rain hammered against the glass. It made me feel calm and secure. I felt like the rain was my friend, and recalled walking in it and becoming wet with the elements.

I dozed but became eventually aware of thunder and lightning. The thunder hovered outside and seemed to call my name. It rattled through the sky calling *Stephen Moyle*. God's voice came and in my mind I heard him say, 'The ruler of the universe,' and in seconds the air rattled with the thunder. Again, I thought that other people must be able to hear.

Slowly, I got up from my bunk, my mind fixed on the thunder and lightning flashes. Then all of a sudden I looked at Leigh. The prisoner was lying on his bunk. I could not believe my eyes as Leigh changed shape from a convict to a huge deformed fly; the moment hung in the air as, amazed, I looked at the deformity. Lightning struck the bars on the cell window and the vision went back to Leigh, the prisoner.

I thought that Leigh must have noticed the change; it was blatantly obvious he was awake just lying on his bunk. I searched for reasoning: nothing. I thought of the voices and nothing came. I wondered about this phenomenon and hoped it was not catching. Between amazement, I was not sure if I felt fear.

Then the devil's voice came and told me I was honoured at being in the presence of telepathy of substances, change, and that the circumstances would never show themselves again. I was a one in a billion, a witness to a miracle that only I knew the answer to. God had made my name be heard by thousands, so the devil had awarded me with a miracle from hell.

I questioned the cannabis and God's voice told me that, without being under the influence of cannabis, this phenomenon would not have been seen. This made me think that it would not have happened if we two prisoners were not stoned. I felt rejection and this rejection, God's voice, told me that I should feel this way when listening to the devil.

The voices clashed as they worked on the borders of hell. It was my hell made for me by the powers from when the universe had been created. I thought of the coming of the devil but could not shake God Almighty from my mind. I wondered how long these thoughts would last and considered that I might just be hallucinating the vision of Leigh changing into a hideous entity.

God Almighty pulled out of my brain and the devil was left sifting through my mind. I was left with the thought that the devil, in all his glory, was trying to trick me, fool me into some sense of thought to steal my soul and destroy my confidences. God came back and made sure that the pain I was feeling could only be felt when God had his back turned and the devil was left to do his worst.

The thunder disappeared through the heavens and spoke God Almighty's name. My mind switched and the devil in my mind also flashed across the heavens, booming out his presence.

Leigh sat up and reached for his fags. He lit one and offered one to me. I immediately became aware that the offer of a smoke at that moment would be dangerous to my soul and myself. I read Leigh's mind and the convict thought that he would deny the thunder speaking my name and conspired with his own evil, heroin, to get his own name up in the skies.

Leigh thought that the way to steal my powers of heaven and hell would be for me to take something from him, then pretend to be about to talk of the phenomena, which I would not. The devil came to me and congratulated my powers of perception in recognising my cellmate's plan.

Immediately I was interested and picked up Leigh's thoughts. Again I was wondering what the rest of the prisoners in the jail that could hear the thunder and the names of powers in the skies were thinking. The devil told me that 100 per cent of the convicts were all thinking the same at that moment, and I thought that all the prisoners were my enemy. The Devil agreed and, again, praised me and laughed at God Almighty.

Keys rattled in the lock and the screw opened the cell to slop out. I went about my business; I left the cell on the way to the recess and then considered what other prisoners would be thinking. Convicts had heard the thunder outside their cell windows, but the screws had been on the interior of the wing and had not been able to hear the sound of the weather through windows because there weren't any.

Apart from the outside security screws, the screws on duty inside the prison wings were not aware of the names in the sky and I let that thought go. It travelled down the walkways and entered the minds of those prisoners that were slopping out. Immediately the atmosphere changed as the prisoners recognised how this predicament would help them. Instead of questioning me, they praised me.

This thought was a gift from my mind; the prisoners cursed their jailers. I decided to test some of what had gone on in my cell. I went to the screws' office at the end of his landing and requested a razor to shave with. The screw eyed me up. I spoke to the screw and at the same time held a vision of Leigh as a fly in my mind, so when I looked at the screw it was like looking at the huge deformed fly.

The screw rejected my request and told me what I already knew, the shaving gear was only issued on a morning. I immediately requested some tissues, which I knew the screw would issue. I watched the screw, as in slow motion, as he picked out four or five new tissues from a box. I saw his soul move outside of his body.

I wanted to get away as quickly as I could, back to the confines of my cell. Something unique had happened and I did not want to help the screw think things out. I took the tissues, making sure there was no physical contact, and went back to my cell. Prisoners lent on the steel barriers, looking up and down the walkways. I felt eyes on me and I wanted to be away from the feeling; being eyed made me feel strange.

I slopped my piss pot out and crashed out on my bunk, wondering about the events of that day. I had a feeling of being powerful and privileged at these occurrences. Prison was many things, but these events I had never experienced before on previous sentences. Maybe it was my age that caused the miracles to happen.

I wondered if my woman and child had had some experience with the supernatural at the same time as I myself had and, if so, what state of mind my loved ones were now in? Then the thought hit me: it was the power of being in love that attracted the voices. It meant that our particular bond of love was unique to our family only.

Leigh came in the cell and the screw banged the door. That was it until 7.30am, when the same routine would start all over again. But not this time. Something was guiding me through events that would normally hurt me whilst being inside of prison.

Cannabis was a release; it tested feelings of intent and made life easy. Time stood still for a moment as I skinned up another spliff. Sleep was on my mind as I lit the joint. I thought of my visit that day and grew concerned about my woman's pregnancy. I had no perception of others, I only knew of my plight, and I dragged hard on the spliff before offering it to Leigh, who was busy preparing a fix of heroin.

I watched through glazed eyes at the drug addict in action. The powers that be made his stomach turn. I knew Leigh's mind and it was not friendly.

He withdrew his thoughts with the immediate hit of the heroin he injected into his forearm. He'd have to wear a shirt with long sleeves to stop the screws sussing the track marks of the needle.

I decided to climb into my bunk, confident in Leigh being unable to reach my soul or the names in the sky. I felt too powerful and would not succumb to the prisoner and his attempts to steal from me.

I knew that the voices, without Leigh knowing, had placed Leigh in my cell for a reason, and that the prisoner had a purpose in his mind of my circumstances. God's voice boomed through my thoughts. The thunder and lightning had moved from earshot. I opened the window and felt that God had given me a gift by reminding me that the thunder, far off in the distance, was still calling my name as clear as the rain that slowly drizzled down the walls of the prison.

I felt content as my cellmate became unconscious with the heroin flowing through his veins. I was stoned as I switched the cell light out and, as I did so, I thought of switching the living-room light out in the family's flat as Judith and I got ready for bed. I felt warm as Judith's love came to me.

I stepped around the cockroaches as I got back into bed. Dark pitch-blackness was the inside of the cell, a cool wet breeze coming from the open window. Time went on and I suddenly woke. I felt an evil presence in my cell. I wondered about the time and tried to see my watch with the glow of the lights on the bars. It was 2.30am and I noticed stars in the sky. The weather had changed and the night was clear and crisp. I lay still and focused my mind on what was in the cell.

I looked at Leigh asleep in his bunk and wondered if the evil feelings were coming from him. Suddenly the presence fell on me like a heavy weight in my chest. A voice told me to stop breathing and I did so. I felt as if I was choking and wanted to breathe again, but the presence entered my body and stopped me from physically moving. My chest would not rise or fall; I did not panic and concentrated on expelling the evil in my body.

Suddenly at breaking point, my breath restricted by the entity. I cast the evil out, and I felt it move through the cell, seemingly angered at being cast aside. It disappeared through the cell door, and then silence. I was left in a state of calmness, curious as to the phenomena that had tried to seduce me into a state of death.

There was a reason for this occurrence; it was evil. The screws that had heard my name in the thunder and had forced an evil spirit to try and kill me, as they were disgusted at what had gone on, jealous that the powers had come to a prisoner and not them.

I believe that the screw I had seen earlier had been the enemy that I'd cast out. He would have gone to sleep and let his soul wander, trying to destroy me. I wondered whether he had woken. The entity may have killed him in his sleep.

I was certain that it would not be the last attempt of this sort on my wellbeing. I reached for my tobacco pouch and matches, concentrating as I rolled a spliff by the light on the cell bars. I dragged deeply on my smoke and a thought sprang to mind. I'd been looking for answers and believed that the evil visit, had it happened to another prisoner, would have without a doubt murdered him.

God's voice spoke when I considered these thoughts and it made sure that I knew then how much danger there was as I went through the days and nights in jail. If the screws could not get you for violence or breach of rules, they would use their evil in the laws of the supernatural to break down a prisoner's confidence and kill him.

God's voice answered me. From the beginning of time, I'd been programmed to know exactly what to do and when to do it – I was a walking, living saint. Then the devil's voice told me that the entity that had failed in its attempts to destroy me did not wake me up to deal with it. With my conscience, it was the devil who had woken me, so I'd be ready and waiting. God Almighty and the devil were playing with my soul.

I lay smoking, my gaze fixed on the open window as if expecting some phenomena to happen again. There was silence. The atmosphere in the cell made my inner ear buzz and played tricks on my mind. Slowly, a single tear ran from my eye. I wished I were as far away as the thunder and lightning. I did not feel completely awake, and I hung on to the sleep. Suddenly my mind began to pray. I'd prayed before and that's why I was praying now.

I searched for peace and wondered if the prison chaplain had sent the evil visitation to an abomination that was a threat to the establishment. I considered being called an abomination and was insulted by it; my prayer had been answered. The screws soul had been used, requested by the prison chaplain. I decided that any chance of socialising with the man had been automatically stopped, and both God Almighty and the devil agreed on this conclusion.

The voices seemed to be joyous over this decision I'd taken. Time was the issue. I was left with lying in my bunk. My watch did not glow in the dark and I remembered the first watch I'd purchased. I'd bought it from a young prisoner whilst I was in Durham Jail and cursed the prisoner I'd bought it from.

I wished that all and any bad luck would happen to this prisoner from years ago. Sometimes it was good to think of some other prisoner that would take, unaware, your bad luck. I supposed that's what made the world go around. I pulled hard on the spliff, enjoying the aroma and taste of the cannabis.

Vaguely, I was aware that I had no more cannabis left. The small lump was gone and I hoped that Judith would bring some in on her next visit. I hoped that my dick would one day be back where it belonged ... in Judith's fanny.

My mood was optimistic as I thought of my woman visiting that day. In the cell, looking in the small mirror, I searched my eyes, thinking what they had seen. They were bloodshot from the previous night's cannabis. If only things were different; yet another morning closer to the day of my court case.

There was an old superstition that if you did not eat your porridge at your last prison breakfast, you would return on another sentence to finish it. Superstition bothered me because, if the voices were real, it was possible that prison superstitions were real too. Wearing other prisoners' shoes was another superstition. In fact, there was a saying or superstition for pretty much any set of circumstances in jail, and they were all bad news. This was just another day in hell.

16
WEIGHED AND TRUSSED UP LIKE A CHICKEN

This was the third week of November 1987. I had been due in court the previous September, and it was the day after the great storm that destroyed parts of southern England; roads had been destroyed by fallen trees and buildings.

I had been escorted to reception in Lewes Prison to appear before the judge for sentencing, but as many of the prisoners were due in court that day it had been cancelled. I, with the voices in my mind, looked at this delay as an omen to whatever the judge had in mind for my sentence. I had to wait until now.

I sat in the dock six weeks later than the system had wanted. The judge sat listening to the prosecution that stated a long prison sentence was in order. My mind felt tired. I'd been over again what size of sentence the judge would hand out. Judge Crocker, I had been told, was a fair judge and I wondered what sentence I would have got if I'd have appeared at court the day after the storm.

The prosecution finished and my defence barrister stood up. My barrister, I had been told, was good, but I was not sure. The barrister that I had spoken to before I entered the dock had not wanted to make an issue of the letter of mitigation I had written some months prior to being in court.

The barrister had quoted that the context of the letter could be misinterpreted in other ways that I had not considered. What I had asked the judge to consider in the letter may be misconstrued as the words of a violent, uncontrolled criminal. I did not agree and insisted that the letter be produced as mitigating evidence when the judge considered evidence to affect the sentencing.

My antecedents were:

1974: dangerous driving on a motorbike, no tax or insurance and no licence – sentence was £60 fine and a year ban from driving.

1974: a theft of two stones of lead from a church roof and criminal damage – £40 fine.

1976: dangerous driving, reckless driving, no tax or insurance – £60.

1977: criminal damage to an interior bus light – three months' in a detention centre, Junior DC.

1977: criminal damage to a club window by throwing an empty bottle – three months' detention concurrent to the prior offence of breaking a bus light.

1978: malicious wounding, smashing a pool cue over the victims nose – one year probation and one year psychiatric treatment.

1979: three counts of ABH and breach of the probation order – three years on each account; Young Prisoner (YP) under the age of 21, with

> sentences to be concurrent, and six months' consecutive for the breach of probation.

The judge thought that, up until this point in my criminal life, I'd been unlucky and unfortunate. It seemed to the judge that I had not been sentenced because of the seriousness of my crimes, but sentenced because of my character, which had been frowned upon, and that my outlook on life was the reason I'd had two custodial sentences.

> 1985: theft of a policeman's helmet and drunk and disorderly – £50 fine.
>
> 1985: criminal damage to the Mayor's suit with a custard pie – bound over to keep the peace for one year.
>
> 1986: GBH on a taxi driver – £250 fine.
>
> 1986: firearms charges. Possession of an illegal weapon, discharging a legal weapon in a public place, criminal damage and possession of a firearm – three years' imprisonment.

All in all, with my previous and mitigating evidence, the judge did not think I should do so much jail time, so he sentenced me with leniency in mind.

I waved at my daughter. Judith smiled sweetly and with determination. Today the family would know how many months we'd have to be apart. It had been months of hard slog, not knowing how long I would get. Well, the day was here, and Judith felt butterflies as we all stood as the judge came back into court and seated himself.

Briefly, he explained his reasoning for a custodial sentence, but he did not give reason as to the length of the sentence he was about to give me. My heart pounded and the voices came to me, assuring me that things would work out.

Eighteen months on the first count – possession of an illegal firearm. Eighteen months to run consecutive for discharging a firearm in a public place. Three months for criminal damage to run concurrent to the first two counts. Three months consecutive for breach of bail when I went to Canada on the run. Total sentence was three years and three months. With remission I would serve 26 months.

I visibly relaxed. I'd received a sentence more or less the same as my previous YP sentence. Judith mentally added up the years and months left and realised that I would be in prison for the birth of our second child. This thought made the tears come as I was taken away to the cells beneath the court.

I swore blind to always, from these days on, be faithful to my woman. To Donna, I swore blind that she'd have a great and beautiful time growing up. I decided that none of them would ever shed a tear of pain again, only tears of happiness and joy.

Hate was the dish of the day and, although content with my sentence, I cursed the judge and the system that had the power to take life away.

The voices came to me and, in their own way, they praised the occurrences that had lead to me being incarcerated. In some ways the voices cheered me up, just as the voices had predicted I'd receive a lenient sentence.

I swigged at the mug of tea and, for a few moments, wondered as to how many prisoners had been in the same circumstances, held in the cell I was in. The voices came and told me there were many thoughts in the cell from lowlife scum, and that my way of dealing with being in the court cells was the right way.

God Almighty's voice was in good stead and the devil's voice claimed that the feelings that made God Almighty happy and preoccupied were his, the devil's. It seemed that I was not alone. The voices encouraged me to think beyond my time and I did so, starting with the journey from court back to Lewes Prison.

In the prison reception I was now treated as a convicted criminal, which meant I was not allowed to wear my own clothes and was issued with *wonderful* prison clothing.

There were three main wings: E-wing was the remand wing with the block underneath; A-wing was the convicted prisoner's wing; and D-wing was the long-termers' wing – this housed the sex offenders, and prisoners on protection from other prisoners were locked in on the ground floor of D-wing.

I knew where I was going. It would be A-wing and I contented myself with this, but this was not the case. They escorted me on to the protection landing of D-wing and, when I realised that I was being imprisoned on a nonce's (sex offenders) landing, I complained to the Principle Officer (PO) and requested to know why.

It wound me up as ordinary convicts did not want to be associated with sex offenders. I drew no sense from the screw's claim that this placement was not permanent. I stood there, bed pack under my arm, and hated my surroundings; the nonces were open for association and eyed me with the confidence that they could not be harmed or got to by ordinary prisoners.

Dirty nonces thought that I was a new nonce and quickly thought that they would have to get to know me. I read these perverted thoughts and grew insane with anger at my treatment. I requested a reception letter and visiting order as the screw escorted me to my cell.

I was mad; the cell was locked. I'd been placed in a nonce environment and had not been allowed my rights to a letter and visiting order. I wondered about my woman and child and I became concerned. I hated not having contact by letter to my loved ones. This meant my temper flowed as I turned the bunk bed over and twisted and tore the bed end off. Blind rage took hold as I smashed the furniture and windows. I began to pound on the steel plated door, unaware of time, only pain in mind. I battered away at the door, the steel denting time and time again. Then frustration made me sing the Geordie National Anthem of *Blaydon Racers*, as I battered away with the steel bed end.

The screws, on hearing the commotion, knew they had a serious incident to attend. They banged up the nonces and called security in. The pounding on the door was deafening and I knew that the screws could not let this infringement of authority go on; the noise was affecting the nonces and they were becoming agitated ... poor things.

I had a sweat on and was feeling fit, and I took great pleasure in beating the shit out of the cell door. Extra staff were called. I had a weapon, a steel bed end, and the screws knew I'd use it. I was lost in a world of torture and I hated the screws.

They opened the cell door and I swung with all my might. The screws wore protective riot helmets, had Perspex shields and padded uniforms. The two sides clashed. The cell filled up with first one, then two, then three screws all in secure uniform. At one stage there were six screws in the cell, pinning me first to the wall and then to the floor.

I fought back, cursing the screws. Sweat poured from me and at that moment I did not care about the world. I was half conscious and took comfort from the pain I was in; it made me feel ordinary.

The screws handcuffed my hands so tight behind my back that the circulation stopped flowing. I was dragged from the cell, swearing and cursing. I had been weighed off by the judge, now I was trussed up like a chicken, my head nearly touching the floor.

The cell they put me in was a padded one, the window high above, with a stained and smelly mattress on the floor. I stood there panting like a dog that had just been exercised. The cell had double padding so I could not be heard if I were to bang it or make a noise.

The screws had left the handcuffs on me. They were like a long nylon strip that looped over the prisoner's hands and were pulled tightly together in a binding loop. This form of restriction was used for speed and in violent circumstances.

Slowly, I cooled down and regarded my new set of circumstances. I squatted down, as best I could, on the mattress, my cuffed hands causing pain behind my back. Steadily, insane humour came to me and I grinned and felt comfortable, like I'd achieved something, which I had.

God Almighty's voice came and told me that I'd had my wish granted and I laughed. I'd got my move from the nonces' landing.

The devil's voice came to me and told me that, when the screw looked through the in the door, I could ask for the cuffs to be removed, but the devil also told me that it would be pointless, and that the screws would leave me as I was until slop-out time the next morning, no matter what I said. If I asked for the cuffs to be taken off they'd only curse and think I was being soft. On the other hand, the devil assured me that by keeping quiet, evil would curse my plight and a bad omen would fall on the next prisoner that was in a similar state of affairs.

I kept my mouth shut as the screws surveyed me through the spy hole every 15 minutes. I felt drained as I lay on my side, trying to get comfortable. The pain from my wrists was unbearable and I cursed my jailers.

God Almighty immediately came and he manipulated my mind to send my pain to the judge that had sentenced me. The following morning, at 7.30am, the screws unlocked my cell and four of them entered. I jumped up from the mattress and prepared myself.

The PO had a large pair of scissors and proceeded to cut the nylon cuffs from my wrists, as this was the only way you could get the one-use cuffs off. My arms felt immediately light in weight and I found it hard to make my arms go straight.

I washed, shaved and asked the PO for a jug to keep in my cell for water. The screw ogled me as if I was asking for gold. I requested my personal belongings from the cell I'd been in on the nonces' landing. The screw grunted and told me I'd have to be moved to an ordinary cell in the block, as prisoners were allowed nothing in the cell I was in – it was purposely padded.

The screw told me that I had to see the doctor then be processed by the Governor as to what punishment I was restricted to. I knew the routine, I'd been in CC (Cellular Confinement) before. It meant an audience in a mini-court with the Governor presiding, and half a dozen screws stood round the room in case the prisoner tried to attack the Governor. My arms slowly began to relax with some circulation draining back into my hands.

There were big red welts cut into my wrists from the cuffs. I showed them to the doctor. I had washed away the blood I'd been covered with in the recess.

Vaguely, the devil's voice stated I'd done the right thing in washing my wounds, because complaints were pointless, as the system covers its back when dealing with prisoners that commit my sort of offences against authority.

The system frowns upon violence against screws; prisoners who do this sort of thing get injured while being restrained and prisoners that are in these circumstances inflict injuries on themselves while struggling and attacking screws.

The doctor said nothing; he turned my hand, first face up, then down, and made no comment. He decided that I had deliberately harmed myself. The doctor insisted that I be watched and checked every 15 minutes, and that I was to be held in the padded cell.

The screws knew that we prisoners hated being locked up in the padded cell and that I would be kept there for a long time. They unlocked me and escorted me in to face the Governor.

I stood with a thousand-yard stare, staring straight at the Governor sat behind a table in a room that had been converted from three cells and into one. The clock high on the wall showed 10.30am.

If circumstances were ordinary then I would have seen the Governor anyway, because it was a prisoner's right to see the Governor the day after being convicted. Generally, the Governor had to inform the newly convicted prisoner of his release date and when he would be eligible for parole. But not in my case. As far as the Governor thought, the lack of information about my sentence would be used as part of my punishment. The Governor had my file in front of him; he glanced over the pages and asked me if I had anything to say before the punishment.

I told the Governor about my reception letter and visiting order being refused, and that's why I'd smashed up the cell and attacked the screws. The Governor considered this excuse and wrote something in my file. Of course, it was not a very good start being jailed in the block some two hours after I'd returned to prison. At this point the Governor ordered the screws to issue the letter and visiting order, and then told me that the behaviour I had been part of was not acceptable and would not be tolerated. The Governor considered what the doctor had written in my file and issued the punishment to me: seven days' loss of remission and to reside in the security landing until the doctor was satisfied that I had settled into my prison sentence.

Back in the cell, the doors firmly locked, I craved for a cigarette and hoped the screws would give me my rights to one hour of exercise. They came to the door and gave me the reception letter and visiting order, and then locked the door, refusing my request for a pen.

Judith went to the front door, retrieving the mail that had just landed on the mat. Donna stood at her side as she sat on the chair and anxiously tore open the letter. Her hands shook slightly as she prayed for good news and read the letter. The visiting order fell out on the floor. Tears welled in her eyes as she read my words and wishes. She read the code about bringing cannabis; I asked her to bring a good luck card, which Judith knew meant cannabis.

They let me out of CC and allocated me to ordinary location on A-wing. It didn't surprise me when I found that my personal belongings and my letters and photos of my family had all gone missing. This sort of thing always caused conflict between prisoners and screws. And again, there was reason for the prisoner to become aggressive and violent.

I was in two minds as to whether to tell Judith about my fight with the screws and the loss of seven days' remission; I decided against it. By doing this, it would avoid any unpleasantness on the visit as, if my woman and child came to visit when I was down the block, they would have to sit in a visiting booth, which means speaking through a glass partition without any physical contact.

I was in cell 24, situated on the ground-floor landing – known as 'the one's' – of A-wing. The screws called this part of the jail the part 'where the sludge sinks to'. It was a two-man cell and I hoped that I would be the only occupant in residence; I could not be bothered with cellmates.

I prayed that I'd get a visit that coming weekend, and then I thought of the voices, and wondered if any of the prisoners on A-wing had been aware of the voices in the sky when the thunder had spoken my name?

Judith had been as good to her word. She'd been bringing up, hidden in her bra, half an once of cannabis at a time. I had not had a spliff since the night prior to my court appearance. I was strung out. I poked and prodded at my arse, retrieving a lump of cannabis that I washed up in a dish of clean water, peeling off one of the layers of cellophane. The cannabis smelled vaguely of shit, but that would pass after one hour or so. I didn't have the means to smoke cannabis whilst I was in CC because smoking was not allowed in the cell, so I promised to enjoy the acrid smoke of the drug I was preparing to have.

I thought about the morning, and a warm feeling came in to my stomach. I'd made an application to see the Governor about my release date and my application had been processed. The Governor told me that my release date had been worked out as 3 April 1990, with a parole date of May 1989. Not that I was ever likely to be granted parole.

On my way down to the wing I'd bumped into a friend. His name was Tim Brown. It was Brown's first time inside; he was serving two years for burglary. Because Brown was new to prison life, he latched on to me as a hard man who had a reputation for taking no shit and fighting. It turned out that Brown was also a friend of the thugs that attacked and smashed up my house.

I threw straightforward questions at Brown, which he answered. I hoped that the scum whom had smashed my house would come into jail. I prayed for this. If I could get the thugs on my terms, in jail, then I may be lucky enough to at least hospitalise them or, worse, kill them. But Brown had no information that would help me, and we shared a smoke instead.

Tim Brown was a carpenter who fucked prostitutes as a pastime. He knew two girls that I knew, who frequented Brown's local pub. I had had a brief affair with one, who was gorgeous like a page-three model. I enquired as to how she was and immediately felt guilty; I'd sworn faithfulness to Judith and here I was asking of another woman.

Brown put on a show for me. He acted like he knew the score but, in my mind, I could tell Brown was fresh meat on a first sentence. It became a ritual at slop-out times and exercise times for Brown to meet up with me. As days passed, we became closer and I acknowledged him because he might hear some news of the thugs.

I had a cellmate that seemed right enough. He had long black hair and was about six-foot two. I immediately showed who was boss by skinning up a spliff and sharing it with the reception prisoner. I had been busy and I was not prepared to bow down to prison rules, so decided to show off to the carpenter, Brown.

I organised, through a drugs deal, a plastic milk sack and a lump of yeast. Slop-out came and I went to Brown's cell with the stuff I had bought from one of the kitchen prisoners. The empty sack held two gallons when full, and I told Brown how to make prison hooch. I told him to keep the sack under the bed and close to the pipe so that it would ferment. We intended to have a party with all the means available on the black market in jail.

17
THE BEST VIEW OF PRISON VIOLENCE

Slop-out at 7.30am on the wing was at its busiest. I stood over a dish of hot water washing myself, and thought of the event that was planned for the day.

I, along with two other prisoners, intended to drink the illicit hooch when the wing was unlocked for exercise. We intended to meet in Brown's cell and bang the door shut instead of going on exercise. The screws would not know, as they would think the prisoners would be out on the yard. The plan should come off without us being caught.

As I was drying myself with a towel, Brown came running into my cell carrying the milk sack ... the sack had split. Falling off the hot-water pipes in Brown's cell, it crashed to the floor, spewing out some of its valuable contents.

Brown panicked and insisted I get a dish to put the hooch in. I threw the water from the bowl I'd just washed in out of the cell window. Seconds later, a screw came through the cell door and caught Brown red-handed holding the illicit sack of brew. He had seen Brown run from his cell to mine on the other side of the landing, and there was a trail of strong-smelling booze along the walkways. I didn't know whether to laugh or cry. The screw told Brown to bring the milk sack and dish to the landing office as evidence.

To cut a long story short, Brown was punished with 14 days' loss of privileges, which meant no canteen and no tobacco. Back on A-wing, teatime slop-out, I gave Brown a spliff to cheer him up. The voices told me to treat Brown as a comrade, as the time would come when I'd be able to use Brown in one of my many schemes.

I had met Duncan, another criminal whom I knew from civilian life; he was living in the cell a few doors along from me. I was doing drugs deals with the kitchen prisoners; they were supplying roast chickens and beefsteak for a cannabis deal. I would split the food with Brown and Duncan.

The three of us would pool our rations so that we could have our perks: drugs, drink and decent food. As time went on and things became established, it became a routine for us to associate and do deals together. Duncan also received cannabis on visits; he dabbled in heroin as well. Regular drugs deals were done with prisoners outside of our little firm, and business got to a stage where we were running part of the prison and supplying prisoners with drugs.

The voices came to me and said that times were about to change. I went into deep concentration, wondering what turn of events the voices meant. Brown got a visit from an old friend; it was his first visit since being in the jail for four months. He had also arranged for a lump of cannabis to be smuggled in. I saw him cheer up and wondered if the voices were referring to Brown and the cannabis he'd arranged to have on his next visit.

Life went on, days ran into weeks, weeks into months, and every hour was torture. You had to live in prison like we three comrades were, or you could lose your mind as well as your soul. It was not direct animosity that made me tick, it was survival. The other two prisoners looked up to me, who, at the drop of a hat, could sort deals out with the people that counted in prison. We watched each other's backs and shared our illegal contraband.

Judith, still set in her mind, visited me every other week. These visits from Judith and Donna kept me sane. Lewes Prison, A-wing, was a local big house; when sentenced, this is where you went. Some prisoners serving short sentences were kept on A-wing and served out their term of prison in Lewes.

All good things come to an end, so they say. This was no different with me; Lewes Prison was a dispersal prison, which meant you were allocated an appropriate prison somewhere else in the system ... my time for allocation had come. It was just a formality in my case; there was only one prison suitable for my character. I was not the only prisoner that had been informed they'd be going to HMP Camp Hill on the Isle of Wight – there were another twenty-nine. Brown had also been allocated.

Camp Hill was a training prison and cons that went there were rejects from prisons that could not handle them. It was for men that were hardened criminals, without a future.

The voices came again: God Almighty and the devil were impressed with the way I had handled the surprise.

My face was a picture of concern when I spoke to the probation officer at Lewes Prison. I requested, for family reasons, not to be transferred to Camp Hill until Judith had given birth. After checking my circumstances the social worker spoke to the Governor about my request, but the Governor, after reading my file, stated flatly that I would be on the next transfer to Camp Hill.

I had informed the social worker that I would be on my best behaviour if the system let me stay in HMP Lewes until I'd had, at least, a couple of visits from Judith, Donna and the new-born baby. All my requests fell on deaf ears. I was told that if I was prepared to wait and if my attitude changed and, when I was in my new prison, if I proved to them that I had a change of character, there was a possibility I could be transferred to a mainland prison from Camp Hill.

The voices stated that this plan to use the system was a perfect ploy that could only lead to better things. I became joyous as I saw the plan unfold on my side; the voices praised me as I rolled a spliff. The taste of the cannabis in my lungs made me consider the voices and I wondered if it was God Almighty and the devil that had made things turn out as they had.

I pulled hard on the spliff and breathed out slowly. Could I control the voices and make them work for me, like an invisible spy that only I knew of?

Time ticked on, the spliff was a blessing. I lay on the bunk enjoying the feeling of being stoned. I considered my latest visit with Judith and our daughter. On the visit she had been tearful as her mother had just been diagnosed with terminal cancer and only had months to live.

I questioned God Almighty and he told me that she'd be dead within one year. I'd waited until now to ask things about Judith. When you thought of your other half in prison, you would become sexually aroused and other prisoners would pick up on these strong feelings and masturbate over these thought patterns.

So I used God as a cover. The devil, under these circumstances, denied that it was he airing my private thoughts. It was, in fact, a bounce in my lifestyle and that my thoughts would be in bits to other enemies, and that they would read into these thoughts wrongly. I would benefit from these misinterpretations of my life and sex drive. God Almighty scoffed at the devil's explanation and told me to go to the gym and pump iron, and that, when I did so, I would be told mentally of the next part of the plan.

I tried to get my head together and get into the gym work and the exertion, but I had such a lack of concentration that I pumped the weights less and less. Then it happened: God

Almighty's voice was clearly heard round the gym, and threw off all concentration, apart from mine, as he worked his magic.

As clear as day, in the middle of a workout, God Almighty stated, 'Stephen Moyle is the devil.'

I took this proclamation to heart as the thought struck me. This meant that I was fighting with God, that he was my enemy. His voice came again and every one of the prisoners and screws alike heard him state that I, Stephen Moyle, was his enemy. If the other con's had not heard voices before, then they certainly had now.

I used God's statement and found more strength as I pushed the bar up and down with a hundred kilos on it. Prisoners that knew me cast looks from the corner of their eyes at the devil. I went on guard as I imagined being attacked by some of the black prisoners. Blacks were never happy and if they thought or saw something that denied them, their spoilt and aggressive nature would attack the threat.

I became hot and finished the last set of bench presses. I thought of what had made God Almighty denounce me in public and, again, thought that I wasn't evil, so how could I be the devil?

Time went on as the news of what had happened in the gym spread round the prison, or so I believed. I attempted to keep my mind clear and wondered when God Almighty would come again.

Back in my cell the door banged; my cellmate was quiet. It was as if some unspoken decision was being made as the prisoners picked up mental thoughts of what had gone on in the gym.

The blacks hated it; they praised themselves on being evil and part of the devil. How could this be? I was in their eyes racist and hated the blacks and yet there was proof. The gym incident spread like wildfire through the jail and the blacks were denying being a part of it, as the blacks thought I controlled the mental airwaves, which denied and stopped individual thoughts and concentration. The voices told me what was happening and that there was nothing at that moment anyone could do to stop me.

A fight broke out between two prisoners and the jail immediately changed as everyone watched the fight. The two prisoners stood toe to toe and punched each other; one pulled a shiv (knife) and stuck it in the other's stomach.

The screws then reacted and a dozen of them restrained and carted the two perpetrators away. Cons hissed at the screws. Prisoners were not interested in the reasons why the fight broke out; all they were bothered about was having the best view of the violence. Some, when the screws intervened, hissed my name and other con's joined in.

The view of the prisoners involved with the gym incident had come to the conclusion that the prisoners had the devil on their side, and took the piss out of the screws that they hated. The gym prisoners were overwhelmed that the evil power was on their side in the context of me being a prisoner like themselves.

It was on prisoners' mind to get on well with me. The prison was buzzing with anticipation and the screws became fearful; they sensed trouble and were concerned that a riot may occur if the use of their mind control did not work. The screws wondered what the cons were thinking and the cons wondered what the screws were thinking.

The cons kept firmly in mind their saviour – me – and prepared themselves for a riot. The screws smelled trouble, if not at present then in the near future. They cursed me for the influence I had over other prisoners. The screws grew restless and hurried the lunch up to get the cons safe behind their prison doors.

I sat on my bunk and skinned up. I decided to play safe. I became paranoid as to what move the screws would do, knowing well enough that they'd blame me for the threat to their discipline and would, somehow, make a move to try and undermine my routine.

I had half an ounce of cannabis up my arse and a small bit loose in my pocket; I decided that a cell search would be a possible move by the screws, so I gave the small lump to my pad mate to hold on to.

It was dinner hour and screws from other wings were called to A-wing to do cell searches. They used screws from other wings because they avoided comebacks from the cons that grew restless and aggressive towards their jailers.

There were six screws on two landings opposite each other; they searched two cells on each landing at the same time. I picked up my bedding as I was told and with my cellmate we carried the bedding out and draped it over the steel railing where the screws on the landing went through it. Then they frisked the two of us, while inside the cell the two screws searched for any illegal substances.

My cellmate looked at me and I was pleased that the screws did not have sniffer dogs. It was obvious because of this that the cell searchers were spur-of-the-moment screws trying to gain control after the incident in the gym and the fight at the hot plate. Luckily the screw that searched my cellmate found nothing; the prisoner had the cannabis in his mouth ready to swallow if he was asked to open his mouth.

The screws, after all of their efforts, caught only one prisoner that had been smoking a spliff when the screws walked through his door. He was immediately reported and strip-searched for any more drugs.

As days went on the prison constantly changed, with screws and cons fighting mentally for control.

Good news – it was a baby girl! She weighed in at seven-and-a-half pounds. The probation officer told me this after Judith had phoned the prison. Tears of joy sprang to my eyes as I yelled out with happiness.

The last three months in prison before the birth of our little girl had been a hard slog. I had to tell Judith they were moving me to the jail on the Isle of Wight. I did this on one of the visiting sessions. I swore that I would be the best dad in the world and Judith listened as I made the promise to make our lives happy.

On the visit I rocked our newborn baby slowly and told the little bundle that she was the most beautiful thing in the world, just like her mother and sister. Judith wanted me to choose the name for the baby, I called her Michaela.

In such a cold, hard place I looked down at Michaela and Donna; the two sisters were alike – blonde hair, brown eyes, same little nose and mouth. I thought back to the first time I held Donna and great sadness came with the happiness.

I had to stay in control and not let my emotions interfere with the visit. It could be any day that they transferred me to Camp Hill, and Judith listened. Charlie had sorted out a half-decent car for Judith, so I would still get visits from her when I was transferred to the island. The car was a Mark IV Cortina; Judith had paid £1,000 for it. She had a baby seat in the back, but we decided that when Judith visited me on the island she should take a friend, probably Pauline, so she could sit in the back and take care of the new baby.

The screws called time, not even giving extra minutes; any half-decent human being would have allowed extra time because of our new baby. We kissed, cuddled and ended the visit.

18
HELL ISLAND

There were nine prisoners on my transfer to Hell Island ... the Isle of Wight: five for Camp Hill, two for Albany and two for Parkhurst. I knew three of the prisoners bound for Camp Hill prison. There was a Scouser, a six-foot two headcase, like a skinhead with everything to say. Brown was there, sticking to me like glue.

Brown and I were placed in a double cell together. We were opened up one landing at a time for food; there were only two landings. The silence of the wing also struck me and I guessed that cons banging their doors was frowned upon. This was an altogether different prison, yes, sir! You had to strip your bed down every single morning and make a neat little bed pack, and it had to be just so.

The screws walked up and down the landing checking to see that all prisoners were co-operating and cleaning their cells. We got cleaning materials from a cell that was used specifically for that purpose.

The screw was a stickler for discipline and had brought his prior experience of life, having been in the army, to his new job and prison life. The reception PO and he worked together.

Both Brown and I thought that we needn't shave and that same screw pulled me as he walked past our cell, as we had been opened up for morning slop-out and breakfast. It was an immediate stand-off between screw and prisoners. The screw insisted that Brown and I shave. I objected because of the rules that Brown had co-operated with, and lost my temper and told the screw to 'fuck off' and 'get off my case.'

Brown followed my lead, so the screw banged the cell door shut and that was it till exercise. The screw had rejected our rights to be fed and we missed the morning's breakfast. The screw had flaunted his power to make sure that the prisoners knew who was in charge.

We were even denied morning's exercise as well and, soon after this, Brown and I were split up. I was moved to a single cell, which I did not mind.

I was hungry and wondered if the screw would deny me dinner. There were two convicted prisoners on the landing that had cleaning jobs and lived on St David's, permanently doing the cleaning jobs for the screws. I sussed these two cleaning prisoners out while I collected my dinner.

The cleaner had told me that the best two wings in the jail were St James's and St Thomas; these wings housed the works and kitchen departments. To be allocated to either of these wings you had to have some experience of building or catering. I told Brown that we would be assessed by the PO as to when we would be considered for dispersal into the mainstream of the jail.

When I was interviewed and asked certain questions that only a man experienced with building work could answer, I was allocated to St James's, the works department. Brown's bid to go to a decent wing failed. He was allocated to St Michael's – the worst wing for violence in the jail. Brown was devastated. The reality meant he was alone and had to face the harsh surroundings of a new wing by himself.

The voices throughout this time were quieter than usual, but still influenced my life in prison.

On the walk up to St James's wing I noticed that a 24-foot wall went round the whole jail, surrounded all the buildings. The voices coaxed me, saying that I would not be in the jail for very long, as I was going to escape. How and when I would escape, I didn't know, but God Almighty and the devil seemed to know, and were confident that the escape would happen.

St James's and St Thomas's wings were situated at the very top of the prison; it was an upward walk to St James's. These two wings were new and modern, unlike the other wings in the jail, which were old and similar to other prisons. I was admitted entry, whereupon I found a cell unlike any I had ever been incarcerated in. This was a big, four-man cell with two sinks and a toilet, with the toilet separate from the rest of the cell, and there were cupboards and lockers.

The bottom bunk out of the four was vacant and this is where I made my bed. I searched for a spare locker, to skin up a spliff, the smell of which would be in the cell as the other prisoners came in from work. I dragged deeply and explored the oversized cell.

The two windows were heavily barred, so much so that only a tungsten-reinforced metal hacksaw blade could cut the steel off. I could see the 24-foot fence with its razor wire clearly through the cell window. I considered this for a moment and then surveyed the wall beyond the fence, which was only about 16 feet high. I wondered about climbing these obstructions.

As I drew the final drag on the spliff, I wondered what liberties the prisoners, when they returned, would try to take. I was the new face, so it automatically meant that the prisoners would gang up against me. The screws opened the cell door half an hour before tea and in walked the three prisoners that I was forced to get along with.

The first of the men I set eyes on was Alex Blackshaw, a small mouselike man with a heroin addiction – he was serving two years for drugs. Smelling the cannabis, Alex grasped my hand and shook it. Then a young prisoner, who was only 21 and was serving time for aggravated burglary. Another handshake came from this man, excited as he smelled the cannabis and thought about a possible session on the drug later that evening.

The third prisoner to come through the door was a man of awesome proportions, a fat man weighing about 22 stone. At the sight of him, Alex Blackshaw immediately started to order the man – whom he called Hilda – about. Hilda used to clean the cell and was there to be used as a dogsbody and general joey to keep the cell in order.

I made a point of not shaking Hilda's hand as, in the eyes of the other two prisoners, it would be a sign of weakness on my behalf. I had six ounces of Old Holborn tobacco, which I intended to baron out at half an ounce for one ounce back.

After tea I skinned up a joint and flashed my parcel of cannabis to my pad mates. I decided that I'd pay the young prisoner if he agreed to carry the parcel of cannabis for me, but I decided to give this plan a few days until I got to know the prisoner and his outlook on being in jail.

As we shared a spliff, I immediately made my presence felt. I told Alex of my plans to baron and lend out tobacco for double back, and Alex, enjoying the cannabis, felt his ship had just come in.

Yes, there definitely was a market for baroning tobacco and Brown and my other cellmates would put the word about that I was doing deals. I rolled a second spliff and our bleak surroundings did not seem too bad.

I started my job in the works department and was allocated to a screw who was a plumber and I became his plumber's mate. He was a six-foot four ginger-haired man of about twenty-four years of age, and he was a part-time bouncer in a nightclub on the island.

There were about 20 prisoners from St James's wing that worked for the works department. Most were bothered about their parole so were on their best behaviour.

Back in the cell I skinned up a spliff. We all hurriedly smoked it, as the wing was about to be unlocked for association. I did three deals while on association: three half-ounce deals for a total of three ounces back. I always considered that violence might occur if the prisoners did not pay their debts for the loan of the tobacco. I knew once word got round that I was doing deals then business would pick up.

After some weeks I found a bent screw. He smuggled tobacco and bottles of drink in. My business had increased to £75 per week for the tobacco. Access to tobacco in that jail was the main source of income. I would order tobacco from the bent screw, who charged 50% on top. I in turn would charge prisoners on the wing extortionate prices, three times more than I had paid for it.

I did not just lend and baron out tobacco, I also sold the tobacco for cash – notes that prisoners smuggled in on their visits or when they came back from home leave. I was in the perfect position to do all sorts of business throughout the jail and the business grew big. I started to take orders for booze; £50 for a large bottle of spirit or £50 for six cans of Tennents super-strength lager.

I had a visit from my family every three weeks. Judith was under strain and stress as her mother became increasingly ill. Donna was beautiful and did not want her grandmother to die. She had picked up on how critical their plights of prison and death were. I would hand over the money to Judith made from my illegal deals. Our new addition, Michaela, was growing big and strong and I told Judith to use the money I passed over on the visit to buy clothes and toys for my two children.

My next ploy in bribing the screws was drugs: heroin, coke and speed. It was arranged for a parcel half as big as a bag of sugar to be picked up and brought into the prison. It then fell to me to get it into the hands of its owner. The cost for the pick-up and delivery was £300: £100 was for me and £200 was for the bent screw.

During one of my tea breaks I used this opportunity to assess and survey the prison surroundings. I was sussing out an escape route. The yard was lower than where the plumbers' and joiners' shops were. Above these two shops was the works office where admin work was dealt with, and beside this office was the storeroom, which was reached by a set of steel steps that led up to the second floor; access was next to the plumbers' shop.

This was where the Senior Officer (SO) was situated; he worked, at most times, in the stores. The yard was full of building accessories: there was a dumper, scaffolding, which was locked up in sheds, and cement mixers. There was a shed full of second-hand plumbing materials, and also a drainman's shed and a sign-writing shed. There were prisoners that worked in each of these sheds. They were locked in and surrounded by the 24-foot fence.

I toyed with the idea of using a dumper to crash the fence and gain my freedom, but my freedom would have been short lived and, therefore, I rejected this way to escape because the noise would alert the screws. I could use the scaffolding to scale the fence, but this was under lock and key until it was required for a job. Maybe a shovel to split the fence with. No, I discarded all of these plans and wondered then if the fence could be climbed.

The voices came to me and explained what I should think. I wished for a spliff as my mind was full of doubt. The voices told me how to do it. I was to screw one-and-a-half inch screws through the lip of the sole, at the toe of my boots; this was done by pushing a heated, red-hot nail through the rubber so the screws were secure. I was to make hooks from six-inch nails and blocks of wood.

I was in a state as the voices drifted away, astounded as to what they had told me. They had given me my freedom and I decided to make my escape as soon as possible. I feared that someone else would hear the advice from the voices and cringed at the possibility that the screws might hear.

The plumber was called out to a job on St Michael's roof. The lead flashing had gone and rain poured through. I held the ladder as the plumber climbed to the roof then I followed. The view was amazing: you could see across the Solent to the mainland. The distance would be about three miles. In the opposite direction, the view was restricted; Parkhurst Forest covered the whole of one direction.

I decided that when I escaped I would head for the forest, then make my way along the beach until I was hidden and safe to plan the next stage of my run for freedom. But there may be another way of beating the system. I decided that if the Governor, on request, was to grant me home leave because of domestic problems, Judith's mother being terminally ill, I would not escape and would return to prison after the leave. The next morning, I made the application first thing. I handed the carefully worded application in to Assistant Governor (AG) ... my request was refused.

I had chosen a blind spot at the end of the plumbers' shop to make my escape bid. Under my overalls I wore extra jeans, vest, T-shirt and I had a donkey jacket on that I intended to throw over the razor wire. Hopefully the extra clothes would stop the razor wire from cutting me.

I had already got a fellow prisoner to make the blocks of wood I needed: three-inch long, two-inch square pieces of wood with holes drilled in. These were already stashed by the place I intended to scale the fence.

I had about fourteen ounces of tobacco outstanding and I agreed with Brown that he'd spend five minutes going round to the cells of the prisoners who owed me. He would do this as soon as they were unlocked for work. I informed the prisoners that they should pay Brown the tobacco instead of me. Of course, the likelihood of this being repaid would be slim, as Brown did not have the muscle, but I felt that it was only right that I hand the baroning business over to him.

At the plumbers' shop, four screws were waiting for their lads. It was a hot summer's day and I felt exposed because of all the clothing I had on. There was one particular job that involved one of the screws having to use Perspex screens that he positioned round the bunk beds to stop the flashes of the welding torch. It also restricted his view of the escape route.

I had two six-inch nails that would go through the wooden blocks. With the help of the same con that had provided the blocks, I had managed to get the nails bent into a hook shape. When pushed though the holes in the blocks, I had my climbing tools. These nails would go through the tiny square holes in the thick, armour-meshed fence, so I could pull myself up with them.

I wondered what would happen if the screws came out while I was halfway up the fence. If this happened, I'd almost certainly be captured. If I reached the wall on the other side of the fence before I was noticed, I'd still have a chance to get away.

I prayed and the voices came to me. They told me I was very strong and would make climbing the fence as easy as a gym workout.

I asked, 'Can I have a vicar or priest, the same one that had called me an "abomination"?'

God Almighty stated, 'Your prayers go straight to me, they do not involve the church.'

In answer to my prayers, the devil that was supposed to be me scolded me for the request of a clergyman. He spoke to God Almighty and they agreed that I could have the vicar's soul to aggravate. I wanted something I hated for my escape, and that would be the vicar that denied my powers of the voices in the sky and denounced me as an 'abomination'. I would escape the obstacles and think of my power, the power to communicate with God Almighty and the devil.

The two powers guided my mind and kept assuring me of what I was going to do. I was to rebuke the system and deny them the rights to imprison my soul and me. I would use my foresight to make my life become perfect and take control of my destiny and my family's. Times would change, but the voices would be there for me in my greatest times of need.

God Almighty came to me and told me to put the finishing turns to the hooks. The nails were loose and swivelled round in their holes; the head of the nail was larger than the drilled holes and could not pull through because of this. God Almighty told me to use electrician's tape around the nail and where the nail went through the wood to stop the actual hook from turning as I climbed the fence. Immediately I did this.

The devil's voice came to me to make sure my boots were well tied. I checked and they were tied very tight. I used the devil's suggestion to check I had my money, about £100, safely wrapped in a plastic money bag, and I also had his tobacco and matches although I was not certain as to when I'd get the chance to have a smoke. And then, by the Grace of God, I went to the blind spot in the fence.

For a moment, I stood at the bottom of the fence; it towered above me. I looked at the wall on the other side of the fence and checked to make sure where the particular point was that I intended to climb. The wall was old and cracks ran up it, enough to get hand holds and foot holds that I could use to reach the top.

I went for it, the voices egging me on. I heaved my body weight up towards the razor wire, taking some of the weight on the toes of my boots. It was working, I thought, and began to believe that I'd make it.

Seconds seemed like minutes, time seemed to stand still and the voices egged me on to hurry. Hand after hand, the hooks were used as the screws in my boots took the strain. I reached the top of the fence and the razor wire, and I hurriedly flung the donkey jacket, which I had put over my shoulder in readiness, over the wire and heaved myself on to the wire, the jacket covering a route through.

I did a sort of western roll and rolled over the donkey jacket embedded in the razor wire. I made it. I hung on to the other side of the fence. The savage razor wire bit through my clothes and cut deep gashes into my arms. The wire wrapped itself round my body like a boa constrictor and I fought like a demon, wriggling to get free.

My mind was blank and the voices coaxed me on. I wriggled loose of my clothing, dropped the hooks and plummeted to the ground. For a second, I looked up and saw that most of my clothing was tangled in the wire. All that I was left wearing was a pair of jeans and a white vest, with the money and personal items in my pocket. For a second, I looked at my fellow con on the other side of the fence and triumphantly gave a thumbs up signal to my loyal helper.

Now for the wall, which I attacked with the aggression of a mountain lion. I climbed to the top using the old and worn brickwork to help me. I triumphantly pulled myself to the top and sat on the wall. Confidently, I said farewell to my fellow con and back-flipped over the wall to my freedom.

19
ESCAPE TO THE SOLENT

The tell-tale cuts from the razor wire were on both my forearms; they were deep but had not cut any main veins. I dashed, heading across farmer's fields, into Parkhurst Forest. I was obsessed with getting away as fast as I could.

Vaguely, I thought of the goldfish in the bowl, stood on the tabletop back home in the flat. I had a vision of a fish swimming around and around, going nowhere but back to where it started from. Camp Hill was my goldfish bowl. I'd been doing what a fish does for months, but now I was free, I'd made it out of the bowl, which was the easy part, but I had to now make it to the sea.

The forest was thick and overgrown with brambles and undergrowth. They wrapped round my legs like hands of the damned as I ran, restricting my speed. I reckoned that I had about 20 minutes, tops, before the screws found out I was missing and had escaped.

I sweated profusely due to the adrenaline overload and wiped my forehead, noticing that, although the cuts were deep and needing stitching, they did not bleed. I waded through the forest and time seemed to stretch on forever. My breathing was heavy, my muscles ached and my mind raced at a million miles an hour. I was thankful for the many hours I had spent in the gym.

Five, ten minutes went by and I became nervous as the adrenaline rush started to wear off, thinking what issue the screws would take when they found me missing. My heart was pounding in my ears like a steam hammer, but I had done it, I'd escaped and was on my way to freedom. Fuck them all, nobody knew.

God Almighty and the Devil coaxed me onwards and stated that the edge of the forest was close at hand. The voices told me that they would search for me by air and put screws on the points and docks where there was access to the mainland. The voices also told me that the three prisons on the island would go on lockdown until I was caught or wasn't, whatever the case may be.

My ears pricked up like a hunted fox listening for the hounds. I was alerted to the sound of dogs in the distance. They would be on to my scent, which they would have followed from the scent of my torn clothing.

I'd seen them do it in films when being chased by dogs, so I immediately jumped in the nearby stream that good fortune had put me by. I walked in the cold water to stop the dogs getting my scent. The voices came and urged me on. Time went on and I reached the edge of the forest. I looked out from the cover of the trees and there was nothing but farmer's fields for about quarter of a mile until a country road.

A quarter of a mile of clearing, which may as well have been the width of the Sahara Desert. I looked around. There was, at one place, more trees beside the road. The voices told me I had to move fast because the air search was on its way and I had to cross open ground as quick as I could or I would be spotted from the air.

One quarter of a mile is, in metric terms, about four hundred metres. I believe the world record for a man to cover this distance by use of his legs is about forty-something seconds. At that time, I would have bet any amount of money that I would have beaten the world record at that distance as I sprinted like a tornado across the open farmers' fields.

Everything became a blur. The ground hardly seemed to be beneath my feet as I powered down with my muscular legs. I had safely reached the road and the wooded area. After gathering my composure, I noticed a few hundred yards away down the road a small country shop. I needed some change for the phone, if I could find one.

Quickly, aware that I may be spotted, I headed for the shop. There was only one customer in the place. I bought four cans of Carlsberg Special Brew and changed a £10 note for coins. I was not sure if I was being paranoid as the shop assistant looked at me suspiciously. I left quickly, hoping that the people in the shop would not phone the police.

I speedily went up the road, into the woods and sat down against a tree. Sure enough, as the voices had told me earlier, I heard a helicopter. As it came into view in the distance, it hovered at the edge of the woods where I had made a break for it, across the farmland. I had a gut sensation and the voices came and told me that I was on my way home and that, so far, I had beaten the system and had made it to freedom.

In celebration of having made it this far, I cracked open a can of Carlsberg and drank deeply from the can. Pure nectar. I was pleased with the way things were going. OK, I had covered only two miles, but that was because the thick forest and brambles restricted my route. Like a cat on a hot tin roof, I was edgy and alert. I figured the dogs had lost my scent, as I could no longer hear their pursuit. My wading in the water had paid off.

I decided on a quick five-minute smoke and made a roll-up. There was nothing I could do to mask the smell of smoke, but I reckoned I was safe. As I rolled the cigarette, my hands trembled with uncontrollable nerves, but this was my body going into overdrive, and I was ready for anything. It would take a lot of distance away from the prison to calm my nerves, and as soon as the opportunity came I intended to put as much space as possible between the prison and myself.

I dragged hard on the roll-up, enjoying the bite of the tobacco in my throat, and I swigged from the can as if my life depended on it. I finished the first and opened the second as I watched the helicopter flying in the distance of Parkhurst Forest.

I had made good ground, as the screws would not think that I would be out of the forest yet. I wished and hoped that the voices were right, as they had been in the past; they'd predicted the future and the path fate had taken. I wondered if I was the devil and if the path of fate had really come from the universe at the beginning of time. If this was the case then how could knowing this instantly be something I would live with?

The notions that came to me as I sat in my hiding place were so very important. I felt special, important and that the course I had chosen had been chosen from a higher power. Something outside my body was egging me on and I still found that making a decision came only by notions and statements from God Almighty and the devil.

The second can hardly touched the sides and I opened a third, flicking the butt of the roll-up away. Time passed and the helicopter moved off in the distance, became a speck and then disappeared. My mind began to feel the alcoholic effects of the drink, also fuelled by the exertion. My head swooned as I rushed down the lager. The drunken feeling gave me a false confidence and I prepared to make my move. I did not think it was strange that in the middle of the escape plan I was sat smoking and drinking lager.

I finished my last can of lager and got up to move off. I decided to follow the narrow strip of woodland, until I noticed a public pathway, over a stile on the other side of the road. I decided to take that route, as it once again was going the same way I was heading. I hopped over the stile and was met from the heat of the afternoon sun. As far as I could see, it was farmer's fields, with the public footpath running along the side.

Conscious of being in the open again, I jogged some distance. As I got over the brow of a hill I saw a cricket match going on. There were also a few spectators. Next to the cricket field was an old derelict barn. I ducked in through the broken door; it smelled of horse muck and had not been used for many a year.

I sat down and caught my breath. The jeans I wore were torn and dirty, I would stick out if I were spotted with clothes in that state. In my tobacco tin there was a razor blade. I took the blade out and cut the legs off my jeans above the knees, thinking I would be less suspicious wearing chopped off shorts. I could be a holidaymaker if I was not scrutinised too closely.

I decided to have a roll-up and check out the cricket game, and to see if it would be safe to walk past. I gathered my thoughts and buried the jeans legs underneath some old horse muck; if they found the trail with the dogs the smell of the horseshit would cover my scent.

My eyes were peeled as I walked past the cricket pitch. I wondered if the screws were on to me. I did not think so as I had not heard the air search. I figured they must be searching in the other direction. Again, I followed the footpath past the cricket match and on over the farmer's field. It would be dusk soon and I hurried the darkness of the night up.

I made my way down to the beach, which was sandy, then decided to follow the coastline northwards. The voices came and told me I was nearing the place where I would escape from the island. As it began to get dark I was only a short distance from Newtown, an ancient town on the north-west coast of the island. I came across a holiday park; I took cover at the edge of the shore and watched a few people on the beach beside the holiday chalets and caravans.

After a while the lights in the small holiday village came on. I waited until the night came fully in and headed for the phone boxes (two of them). They were situated beside the resorts social club, which seemed to have just opened. In the phone box, I felt secure as I rang Judith and told her what I'd done.

My woman was angry, not being able to understand why I had done such a serious thing. She asked how I would get across the Solent to the mainland. Not wanting to worry her, I lied and said I had a boat, but really I intended to swim across the Solent and was, above all else, psyching myself up for the effort.

I grew close to tears as the scale of what I intended to do sunk in. It made Judith's words on the phone give me confidence. I was risking my life to be with my family.

The Solent was one the worse stretches of sea in England; the current and tides were atrocious, but it was summer and this time the currents and tides were predictable. However, I did not know this. I picked a spot that I could see from the phone, where I would swim from.

A lone car pulled up in the compound. My heart missed a beat as I saw it to be a police patrol car. They had obviously been keeping tabs on the payphones, so I quickly said goodbye to Judith. I'd ring her later when I was on the mainland and she would have to pick me up.

It was 4 August 1988 and the island was hosting the world-famous round-the-island yacht race from Cowes Harbour, and the place was packed with boats. I was a few miles away from the actual race starting line, and preferred to shy away from drawing any attention to myself.

Quickly I left the cover of the phone. Across the road there was a small outside toilet. I ran in and immediately spotted my life saver – the building had a loft. I climbed on the sink and pulled myself up in to the loft entrance, closing the trap door behind me.

My ears burned as I listened for the enemy. It was pitch-black and the sound of my stifled breathing was the only thing I could hear. It was obvious they were looking for me; I held my breath as the copper quickly looked into the public convenience. It was only at the sound of retreating footsteps that I began to breathe again.

The voices came to me as I waited five minutes for the coast to clear and the police to move on. The voices stated I must take my boots with me as I swam to the mainland. I'd need my footwear when I reached the other side.

Just as I had thought about using an empty container, as I had planned for my never-to-be swim across the Niagara, I knew that I needed something to put my boots in for the swim. I rummaged about at the back of a social club among empty beer crates. There was an empty gallon container that had had cleaning liquid in; I could tie my boots to this and secure it round my chest as a floatation device.

I found a washing line from behind the back of one of the chalets. I tied my boots to the float and then tied the float to myself. I walked down to the edge of the sea. Across the Solent I could see the many shining lights twinkling on the mainland coast; they shone like the stars in the heavens.

For a few seconds, while taking deep breaths, I looked up to the sky. The North Star shone brightly, as if looking down on me alone. The voices told me the danger of losing my life by drowning would not happen, I would make it to the mainland and would make it home. With the complicated Solent tides, I could only pray that I would.

Time came to a standstill. The sound of the surf gently lapping the shore relaxed my mind. The voices would be right; I knew they spoke the truth. Silence was the only thing I heard above the sound of the sea.

Then the surf began to speak as it rolled on to the shore: 'Stephen Moyle, the ruler of the universe.' It was as if the surf was inviting me to my path in life and was welcoming me with open arms. Many ships had perished in these waters, which could throw out erratic waves at the drop of a hat. Not for one moment did I think, to pardon a pun, that it would be plain sailing. I had to show respect for this sea, which I initially did.

Whispers in the surf and in the steady night pricked my ears and made me strain to catch their meaning in the stillness of the early night. I was confident that I would make the task. There had been many times before when I'd swum further, when training to be a lifeguard, but I had never dealt with the strong currents and tides that ruled the Solent ... just many lengths in an Olympic-sized swimming pool.

20
THE GREAT ESCAPE

The voices urged me to go forward into the relative calm of the sea. I tentatively waded out, remembering what had happened when I had done the same in the Niagara, hoping the ground beneath my feet would not suddenly disappear. The cold, waist-deep water chilled my soul.

I took in a mighty breath and stretched out fully. My stroke was strong and, as I swam further from the coastline, the waves grew increasingly large and vicious. I felt that I was wasting my energy battling against the tide and started to reassess my position. I felt a rush of adrenaline kick in and I swam with renewed vigour.

I tried to keep sight of the distant mainland lights, but they kept disappearing and I was vaguely aware that the sea was washing me. I knew this because, as I kept catching sight of the lights on the mainland, they were steadily going sideways. The sea was washing me crosswise and the speed of my strokes pushed me forward, but at a slower pace than the sideways wash. The float that I had tied around my chest was more of a hindrance as it was caught in the tide and floated sideways on the current. It should have been strung out behind me as I swam onwards. This extra effort was making huge demands on my oxygen requirement. I breathed harder and had to avoid intakes of sea water.

The physical effort to battle the tide was starting to tell but I swam harder to keep on going in my intended direction. Here was a battle of wills, me wanting to go one way and the tide trying its hardest to overrule me. I thought of all the effort I applied in the gym; it had come to fruition.

There was a moment that nearly stopped my heart; the voices were laughing and I thought I'd been conned, that the voices had gone to great lengths in setting me up to die by drowning in the sea.

The devil told me this was not true and that the notion I'd just had was God Almighty taking the mickey over my circumstances at that moment. I felt warm in the pit of my stomach as I realised I was being watched over by the voices. I felt comrades with the devil for stopping God Almighty's sense of humour. The devil predicted that, when I made it across the Solent and reached the opposite side, God Almighty would take over the situation and the devil would take a back seat.

God Almighty's power was at its most extreme when an event had been achieved and the devil would lay in wait for the next round. I pressed on and thought that time had slowed down, as if it was making my escape harder and wanted me to strain with all my might to beat the sea and the Solent's currents and tides. I thought for a moment that maybe some other convict had escaped, years ago, and had swum to his freedom like I was doing.

I know people have swum the three-and-a-half mile stretch of the Solent from the Isle of Wight to the mainland for charity, and some just for the hell of it in the Cross Solent Swim, but this was at night, in the dark and without the help of a nearby boat to haul me in to safety. I didn't have the benefit of tidal maps, accompanying swimming mates in near-perfect conditions or the like. I only had my strength of determination and the beckoning lights on the mainland to aim for.

Crosswinds, rolling squall and swell continued to hamper my progress. This was supposed to be a swim to freedom, not a battle of wits. What had happened to the calm and gentle clapping of waves that had originally set me on my way? I was starting to believe that the waves had been sent by the devil, but I continued my strike for the shore, battling not just the devil but also the offshore winds pushing me off course.

How I longed for a rest. I treaded water for a while and recovered some of my strength, but the time I had used in treading water was a victory for the fast-moving tide ... I was losing sight of the lights! But not once did I glance back at 'Hell Island'.

Sometimes a choppy wave would swamp me, and after I rose gasping I would vomit the foul tasting water, wiping the sea from my eyes and nostrils. Then I regained my posture to do battle again with the Solent. Through squinted eyes, I kept a lookout for the mainland through pants and shudders of excitement that were mixed with despair. I saw the faces of the ones I loved and, for a moment, thought my number was up, but then I thrashed with my legs for all I was worth.

I could see the reflection of the moon on the water's surface, tantalisingly teasing me forward. That was my target ... swimming towards the moon and freedom. I could smell the brine and sense the power of the mass I was in; it engulfed me, yet I was at one with it.

I could feel my legs folding and unfolding like powerful scissors, pushing against the very power that was trying to hold me back. I had to maintain control of myself, not allow the sea to intimidate me. If this was a binding exercise then the sea and I would be firm friends, but I couldn't allow it to be my equal. I screamed out aloud, 'I will not be beaten, you bastard!' Then I wondered how many people this sea had claimed as its own, how many were recovered dead and how many survived the hidden brutality?

Although I was in the cold water and my teeth were chattering, I could feel perspiration running down my forehead as visions of failure swam around in my head. Although I was not the first, I felt that I was the first and would celebrate when I'd accomplished my goal. My focus was on reaching the other side of the Solent; dreamily I wondered what I'd feel like when I finally reached my goal. Comparing the swim across the Solent with the many lengths of a pool, I found I could not concentrate hard enough on my mission. As I thought of my family I picked up my stroke, trying to head in a straight course.

Although my swimming stroke became powerful, I wrestled with the waves and I considered that if I were on the same path of the ferry then I'd be sucked under by the boat and be drowned. The sea was insistent in the direction I swam, washed onwards, and there was not a sight or sound of any boats or shipping.

The water seemed to grow colder and it made me gasp for breath from the exertion of the swim. I was not sure how long I had been in the water, but being washed sideways with the current I could see by the lights ahead of me. I was making slow but steady progress towards them.

For some strange reason, I could feel my torso being pulled forwards and downwards. Not only did I have to swim in a forward direction, but I had to finish off my stroke by pushing downwards, a stroke that I christened the Moyle Stroke. My arms felt so heavy and tired, my shoulders were on fire and my mind was gone. What was pulling me down? Was it the devil? My lower back screamed out in pain, my legs were dying and my strict swimming style had come down to me clawing at the water like a drowning spider. I thought to myself, One last push. I could see now how people just gave up and drowned, but my will to survive had not yet died.

As dawn saw the lights of the mainland go out, I swam harder, pulling out all the stops in my swimming repertoire, even using my head to push the water aside. My tired muscles screamed at me to stop, but I took no notice and there, a few hundred yards away, was what I could see was the shoreline – my pace doubled.

I strode from the sea and could hardy stand. This enormous weight around my neck was pulling me down! I looked down at what it was; the damn container was full of sea water! I had been swimming with a gallon weight of sea water weighing me down; no wonder I had found it difficult to stay afloat and swim forwards. I may as well have been swimming with a millstone around my neck!

Involuntarily, I collapsed face down on the beach, gasping for breath. I didn't even have the strength to undo the container. It was pitch-black and the sea washed around my legs as I struggled to catch my breath. It was quiet and the beach where I lay was in darkness. I had achieved my mission and my life with my family was about to become reality again.

For a long time I lay still, the sea washing at my feet as I regained my composure and my senses.

In January 1995 three prisoners, two category 'A' prisoners and a lifer, escaped from Parkhurst Prison on the Isle of Wight. After four days of freedom they were recaptured. My length of freedom far surpassed theirs.

21
FREEDOM

I dragged myself up the beach and lay there in a daze. After a while I gathered some strength and untied the container that had almost become my tombstone, and looked about the place with searching eyes. There were some huts up the beach, towards the road. I made my way to them and managed to gain access to one of them. I took my wet clothes off, threw them over some beams and pulled an old tarpaulin over me and drifted off to sleep – fuck 'em.

I awoke with a mouth as dry as a camel's arse. I needed a drink of water, not sea water either – I'd had a bellyful of that. I picked up my aching body and dressed, it was still dark. My thirst was the issue that I had to deal with and I decided I had to take the chance of finding a pub so that I could use the conveniences to freshen up and get a drink of water to wash the sea salt from my mouth.

I pulled my boots on and slowly walked along the beach until I came across steps leading up to the promenade. There was a scattering of people walking along the beach-side road. The Ship was the name of the first pub I came across. I went in and rubbed my eyes as I saw the time on the clock. It read 10.55pm and the bell for last orders rang out. I had slept for a considerable time.

The place was packed with young men and girls. I grew paranoid as I walked through the noise to the toilet. I felt that all eyes were on me and that they all must have known that I had escaped. The warmth of the pub's interior made me feel calm and I reached the toilet without incident. I gulped the tap water deeply. The taste of the water was sweet as it washed the salt water from my mouth and lips. My cut-off jeans were still damp and my vest was drying on my body. I decided to have a pint.

I watched myself in the toilet mirror as I pulled the plastic money bag, along with my tobacco tin, out of my back pocket. The tobacco and matches were dry; also the folded money was dry. I made my way through the crowd to the bar and ordered a pint of lager. If the cuts on my arms were not seen then I could just be a holidaymaker having a quiet drink.

Just in time, I placed my order before time was called. As I swigged down the refreshing nectar I looked for the phone and saw it in the far corner.

Love was on my mind and tears of relief sprang to my eyes as Judith picked up the phone. I told her where I was and where she should pick me up. She would stop outside the pub, the Ship, in Portsmouth and I would wait on the beach where I could see the front of the road and the pub front.

I knew it would be a few hours before Judith made it to me, so I left the pub and made my way back to the beach, off the promenade. God Almighty's voice came and I listened, intent on getting answers from him. I was an escapee, a fugitive from justice, and that made me a target for evil. God Almighty whispered that I'd be ready for any evil attempts on my fate. I felt important and prayed for my life, and that my family, too, would have a supernatural protector.

Heading home was not a good move. I'd have to find some place safe to stay; God Almighty told me this. The police would go straight to my last known address to search the premises. I considered this and decided to let the police do their worst before it was safe to return to the flat.

I had a piece of paper in my tobacco tin that had two phone numbers: one number was for Nick Glover, the other for Duncan. I decided to ring Nick. I decided I'd ring him the next day to sort out a place to stay.

My heart skipped a beat as the long wait for Judith came to an end. I ran across the road and jumped in her car, where we fell into each others arms, wrapped in a world of love.

My manhood immediately became hard. I wanted, needed, to make love to consolidate this occasion. I told Judith to drive into the next side street, a few hundred yards away. We climbed into the back seat. Judith told me not to come inside her as she was not on the pill.

With lustful abandon, I rammed my tool into her. The feeling was of instant and undying love. We fucked and treasured each intense moment. I wanted her like I never had before. Judith's nipples grew hard as I handled her with aggression. I squeezed her tits, kissing her nipples and neck with desperation. First lovingly, then with intense desire and lust.

Judith wrapped her legs around my waist and ground her groin into my tool. She no longer seemed to care that she was not on the pill; she was totally engrossed in love, sex and the perfect feeling of intimacy. As I felt myself inside her, tears of relief sprang to my eyes. She told me to shoot my load into her, wanting her man to come, and at the same time she reached orgasm.

The orgasm was so intense and powerful. The interior of the car was hot and steamy. I whispered my love for her in her ear so quietly that the words amplified the moment we'd just had, and Judith whispered her undying, unwavering love for me.

We spent the night making love and then slept in the car. We drove back as the morning sun rose. Parked in the car park of the Bull and Bush public house, in the local council estate, Judith went to the phone check if the police had been – they had. I decided that it would be safe to go home to our flat. I was anxious to see the kids.

Donna could not believe I was home. I greeted my daughter with kisses and cuddles as the two dogs ran through my legs and greeted me. Pauline gave me a cuddle and kiss. Baby Michaela was propped in the corner of the living-room sofa and smiled happily. I could not believe how beautiful baby Michaela was. The atmosphere in the flat was brilliant; the meeting of my woman and children was worth the risk.

Within the police force there was a department that dealt with high-profile criminals. Their actions in tracking and capturing these violent men was not documented. This order of special police were called 'D11', and they were accountable only to themselves.

The IRA had a similar group that hunted men down and these were called the 'Black Hand' special men, who worked within the system anonymously. I did not know it yet, but I would be hunted by the D11. It would not take the ordinary CID long to order this manhunt.

Judith also had something she did not know yet. She had conceived in the back of the car the previous night. Life was not easy but it was about to get harder as the twist of the fate unravelled.

The voices told me I'd been blessed without me knowing, and that it would be a time of happiness in the sea of hope. I told Judith, and Pauline listened, that I had not stolen a boat but had swam to freedom.

Nick Glover was happy when I told him what was happening on the phone. He immediately told me he'd pick me up. We arranged to meet outside the Bull and Bush. I said my goodbyes and promised Judith and Donna it was just a temporary arrangement, and that I would phone them later that day; better to be safe than sorry.

Nick Glover and a sidekick pulled into the car park. I ran over and jumped in. We greeted each other, pleased to be in each other's company. Nick introduced his mate. This man was a maniac, a football hooligan who carried an eight-inch knife to the Chelsea matches, his one and only God, beside Nick Glover. I was the biggest of the three. The sidekick was weak and that's why he carried a knife; Nick was wide and stockily built.

Impressed at what I told him about the escape, Nick thought I was mad for swimming the Solent. He immediately showed respect and told me I could sleep on the sofa in his house for as long as I wanted.

I was offered a job by Nick ... laying bricks on a site in East Grinstead and the pay was £90 a day. Nick's hod carrier was Pete Mercer, who looked up to Nick. We met Pete in a pub that was frequented by criminals and villains. Pete was a lucky criminal, not having served time. The voices told me I was able to do business with this young man.

As time and weeks wore on, I introduced myself to a secretary that frequented the pub. I befriended the young blonde, as she was nice to look at. I enquired about the work she did and, as the drinks flowed, she let slip that the firm she worked for had her dealing with the cashflow every day. She worked in a catering firm.

This firm dealt in cash deliveries. The van drivers collected the money as they dropped off the foodstuffs. There were 16 vans that were on the roads everyday. The vans would come back to the yard and pay the cash into the office; these vans would handle between £1,500 and £2,000 cash a day.

As she told me this, my mind went into overdrive as I probed the secretary for information about security; there were two other people who worked in the office, who dealt with computers. One of these two people would take the money when it was tallied up to the bank; it was in a security case that, if not opened correctly, would blow out red dye. I went back to the secretary's house and fucked her hard, turning the conversation between information and sex.

The money case lay open on the office table and the secretary was busy stacking the money into it. A deadly silence came in the office as the three workers jumped with fright as I burst in shouting with all my might. The three workers froze with fear at the sight of the shotgun. I demanded the money and grabbed the case from the table. I ordered the woman who I'd just fucked that evening to put the stacks of bills into the bag. She did not recognise me, not with a balaclava on.

Pete searched me with a curious look as I jumped into the car. I ordered him to drive fast to get away from the job. I pulled a cassette of the band UB40 from my pocket and pushed it in to the car stereo. Immediately, my mood and anticipation went through the roof with the beat of the music.

What we'd just done blew Pete's mind away and the young villain quizzed me about how much I'd stolen. I looked in the carrier bag at the money and, off the top of my head, told Pete we'd got close to £16,000.

My mind was uncontrollable. I kept counting to £2,000 but kept losing track of how much I'd counted. I gave Pete the bag of money and Pete counted the notes into my hands. He made two stacks – one for Pete one for me ... £16,500 in total.

I lit a fag and got out of the car. For a second I viewed the stolen car and then lit a match and flicked it into the car through the open window. We'd be in East Croydon in less than 20 minutes, away from the burning evidence.

The voices came with an extraordinary feeling of pride and reminded me that I had a family waiting at home. They told me it was time to return to the north-east, my hometown.

I gave Pete a grand to drop off for Judith and the kids and said I would phone my family later that night. I got Pete to drop me off at East Croydon train station. I bought a ticket to King's Cross to make my way back to the north-east. I said goodbye to Pete and the train pulled out from the station. One at a time I threw my old clothes out of the moving train's window: footwear and gloves.

I stepped off the train at King's Cross a different-looking man. I could easily have been mistaken for an office worker or businessman, apart from the scar on my face. In fact, I looked a little reminiscent of a young Oliver Reed.

I bought a ticket to Durham City, settling myself in the first-class carriage after buying four cans of Newcastle Brown Ale. With the movement of the train I became drowsy; God Almighty's voice came clear to me. I listened, relaxed, to his praise of what I'd done. I was convinced that what I had achieved was not an act of evil, more so a part of survival for my family and myself.

The voice of God Almighty was soothing and calming as the train took me further away from the offence. I was convinced that I'd got away with the robbery; there was little chance that it could come back to me. A niggling worry was whether the security had recognised me (although I did not think they had). No doubt the police would interview the staff that worked in the office. This was the only way that the job could come back on me. God Almighty whispered his glee and cursed the devil.

When I got off the train I immediately phoned Bob Ashcroft. As he picked me up from Durham train station we shook hands. The pubs were closing so I suggested we go to a nightclub. He did not want to go; there were too many questions he wanted me to answer.

We settled in Bob's house and shared a bottle of whisky, while I recounted what I'd done. Moyley tipped his sports bag and the £8,000 fell on the floor. I gave Bob £200 for himself and his family then gave another £4,000 to put in Bob's bank account until I needed it.

As the days passed, I renewed my association with old friends.

Most of these had been met in the workingmen's club. God Almighty stated that it was unsafe to go to my mother's as, no doubt, word would get round about my escape and one of the places the police would search would be my mother's house.

I made a flying visit to see her anyway, and left her £200. She was worried about me, and my father, Hughie, told me to be careful. I rang Pete Mercer, who told me the police had no idea who was responsible for the robbery and that it was safe for me to return to the south.

I rang Judith and she said that all was quiet and that the police had not been back since they had used their search warrant some two months earlier. I met Bob and an old friend, Tommy Cox, in the Pelton workingmen's club at the top of the town. I decided to have a drink with my two friends before I drove back to Guildford. Tommy Cox was a fully fledged alcoholic. He had a pockmarked complexion and he was unshaven; he was average in height and would drink his weight in lager every day.

All my mates were aware that I had escaped and was on the run. Those that knew me classed me as a legend; a working-class hero that fought the system and would not bow down to his enemies. However, I wondered what my friends would think if I told them about God Almighty's and the devil's voices that had guided me to be present, sitting and drinking in a workingmen's club.

The devil came and told me to show Tommy my new car. Tommy Cox was impressed as he looked over my new toy. I took him for a spin and his complexion changed to death-white as I drove at 100 mph, swinging into a sports field to show him how good the car was. I made sure that Tommy Cox remembered the £50 I had just lent him, because I knew the money would not be paid back.

As I drove the five-hour journey back to Guildford I thought of Judith. I was not sure what I would do without her. In the back of my mind I decided to marry her. I wanted to cement our love. I considered how I would go about proposing to her. I felt sure she'd say yes and I decided to ask her when I got back.

I decided to have some fun and wind up the police. My plan was to go and drink in and around the local pubs; we'd have a pint in as many pubs as possible then, as we supped our pints, one of us would phone the local police and grass me up. We used both cars. Pete Mercer had three mates in his car, and Nick and I used the BMW.

We drove at 100 mph down and through a local village a few miles away. I misjudged a bend and the car slid across the road into a tree. It was a write-off, although Nick and I staggered out of the crash unhurt.

In the pub in town, I made a phone call to Jim Ford and told the villain what had happened to the BMW. Within an hour, the BMW disappeared to the scrap yard, where the vehicle was dismantled and what was left was crushed.

I told Pete to drive me to Judith's flat. I ran in the house and told Judith what she had to do. First she had to insure the BMW, then she had to go to Sainsburys. She should get the shopping then go into the car park and phone the police and report the BMW stolen.

I jumped into Pete Mercer's car and we set off on the mission. All the criminals in the car were on speed. Nick had injected heroin early that morning and was still under the influence.

In my mind I considered which pubs to drink in, and prayed that I would not bump into my enemies: Barrett and Evans. I heard the voice in the car, and the car's occupants fell silent, just like the incident in Lewes jail's gym, where God had let all the cons hear his voice.

God's voice said, 'Stephen Moyle...' – the sound of the engine dictated God's voice. Nick busied himself by building a spliff; the silence lasted a few minutes as we pulled into the Railway public-house car park and the first part of the wind-up went into action.

Brian, the landlord, was pleased to see me. We six criminals drank our pints and Pete phoned the police. After the call we went and sat in our car smoking cannabis. Sure enough, two police cars and a police van pulled up and the police ran into the pub. We drove off to the next pub and then the next, repeating the plan. In each and every pub we visited, I enquired about Barrett and Evans and was told by different people that the pair had gone to ground; they had heard of my escape and were keeping a low profile. I began to curse; surely I must find the slags that had caused my plight.

The police, at first, were confused then, as the phone calls continued, the situation dawned on them; they were being used in a game that made the circumstances more serious. Any ordinary criminal would keep a low profile and watch his back, and keep away from the police. I had taken the game further and it should be down to the police to make the next move. They decided to get the D11 involved. Not only was I a dangerous individual, I was a man that had a dangerous and evil sense of humour that could be only described as psychopathic.

As the police chased round after me, the talk from the locals, and speculation from the criminals, would be described as crazy. It seemed that all the locals were discussing me and the escape. Criminals swapped information on my predicament and were, in some ways, jealous at the way I was dictating events.

It was common knowledge that when I caught up with Barrett and Evans there would probably be murder. I would kill for revenge and the two lowlifes would kill in fear. Something must happen soon.

I could not settle. I was paranoid that the police might come to the flat and search for me. I needed to be in a place of safety so I could propose to Judith. I phoned Charlie and asked him to meet my family and I at the Tillgate pub. The pub was situated in Tillgate Park; there were lakes and trees, countryside that you could blend into. It would be quiet in the park and it was here that I decided to ask Judith for her hand in marriage.

I looked deep into her eyes and popped the question. Judith was overcome with emotion. Her heart skipped a beat as she accepted. I told her that we should get a special licence from the Register Office and get married as soon as possible.

At that time I did not know it, but no one had ever escaped from the prison island and had wed their woman. Policemen would not be expecting me to get married and I decided it was a safe chance to take. Judith and I agree agreed a date of 24 September 1988, at 9.30am, for the wedding to take place.

As Judith went about her everyday routine on the run up to her big day, she sorted out the insurance and the police, telling the different departments that her car had been stolen shortly after she'd bought it. I knew that Alex Blackshaw was being released on Friday, 23 September 1988, and I decided to drive down to the coast and meet the little villain as he got off the ferry at 6.00a.m.

It was the day before the wedding and Judith had an appointment with her doctor. She had missed her period and suspected she was pregnant. The feeling of happiness about the new baby in her womb overcame the concern at our plight. She wanted to tell me so I could share in the joy.

As I stood in the ferry dock, I wore a hat pulled down over my eyes, and there, as big as life, walked Alex Blackshaw. Alex had planned to take the train back to London. I gave him a hug.

The voices whispered in my ear. I was being made aware that there was something going on with my woman. It never entered my mind what the voices were preparing me for. I tried hard to make sense of the psychic discussion going on and it annoyed me. I felt that the voices, God Almighty and the devil, had got me out of the police raid at my pal's house with their timing. The police had just missed me.

I decided I needed to speak to Judith and see my children. I borrowed Pete Mercer's car and sped off. I had arranged for a brand-new Mercedes to pick Judith and the kids up and drive them to the register office the next morning in Riegate.

My gut feeling worried me. There were vibes in my soul that something was amiss with my woman. It was love that made me tick at that moment and I cared that things might not be right, or worse, that Judith might call off the wedding.

I did not have a key for the flat so I knocked quietly and Judith answered. We hugged and kissed each other. The kisses and cuddles, the deep affection and emotions, told me that there was no need for my concern that there may be some other problem upsetting things at that present time.

I felt a twang of guilt in my heart, as in the two months I'd been on the run I'd been unfaithful with three different women, two of which I was seeing and having affairs with at that time.

What I would give to not be a fugitive at large. I would love life if I did not have the police on my back. One day it would happen. I'd be able to kick my shoes off and cuddle up with Judith on the settee with the world locked outside, togetherness being the only thing that mattered.

22
PASSION OVERWHELMS EMOTIONS

The stag party were full of themselves. We had all drank our weight in lager, smoked cannabis until it was coming out of our ears, and all the men, apart from the holidaying Geordies, had at least taken a wrap of whiz. We made it back to the pub where Tennant had a lock-in.

The pub was emptying and only the chosen few were asked to stay back for a late drink. I decided to leave at 1.00am, heading for a house belonging to one of my birds, a ten-minute walk up the road. I was suffering with cold feet and wondering why I was getting married; doubts crept in to my mind, the voices were fuzzy and broken. I wondered what I was doing attending another woman's home; surely I should be with Judith.

I felt horny and wanted to fuck but I was not sure whom I wanted. This girl I was going to see turned me on; she was a good-looking woman with long brown hair and blue eyes, she was slim and was 100% woman. When she went out with me she did not wear knickers and would give me a flash of her uncovered fanny, at times, when no one was looking. No knickers and black stockings turned me on.

She knew I was to be married next day, and she knew about me being on the run from prison; she liked me very much and had had thoughts that something might come of our relationship.

I knew that she had just been widowed; her previous husband had been a heroin junkie and so had she, but since his death from an overdose of the drug she'd stayed off the heroin and the only drug she now touched was cannabis. Her husband had died in the bath and left her with two young children to bring up.

I was cautious when I fucked her. I had feelings that I might be having sex with an AIDS carrier, after her having been on the needle. She told me that she did not want me to get married and that I should live there, in her house, where we could have uninterrupted sex day and night.

I thought of Judith and took strength in myself. I would marry my chosen one and would be, from then on, faithful. These things I decided by talking and listening to that bird that night. My last night of freedom would be the end of my days of seducing women ... I took the woman in my arms and fucked her hard.

I got up to piss and decided not to have early-morning sex. I checked my bell end as I pissed and grew paranoid; there was a small pinprick on the right side of my bell end.

I immediately thought that she had shoved a needle in my cock that was infected with AIDS. But I did away with these notions as I had not been asleep, I would have known if this occurred. I kissed her goodbye and she asked when she'd see me again? I could not answer. I left her house and began the half-hour walk to Nick's house.

The girl faded away to the back of my mind. I was to be married and my thoughts were firmly fixed on Judith and my children. I finished my bath and dressed for the occasion.

The day started without a hitch. I dressed and I watched the clock on the wall. I mentally thought of what was to happen that day. The reception was to be held at Tennant's pub where Tennant had roped off half the pub bar for the private do. The spread I had paid for was being laid on by one of the barmaids: sandwiches and roast chicken drumsticks with other titbits plus a wedding cake, all for £100 and I had, on top of this, left £100 behind the bar so the guests could have a drink.

The eight men in Nick's house fitted in two cars. They left for the wedding. I was suffering from paranoia, but the voices assured me that there would be no police and I would not be arrested. However, I decided to get out of the car at the bottom of the road from the register office and I told my mates to check out the office to see if the coast was clear.

Judith's father was stood in a light-beige suit. I went and spoke to him. He looked out of place. Judith's mother was ill in hospital and could not make the wedding, but the father conveyed her congratulations.

I lit up a spliff and puffed away in front of Judith's father. I was under the impression that the father did not realise I was smoking cannabis. I looked at my watch, Judith was late. I finished the spliff and flicked the butt away, hoping that there were no hold-ups and that the car had not broken down. I needn't have worried as Judith, Donna and baby Michaela were driven into the car park in the Merc, the ribbons on the limo flapping in the wind.

Tennant and his girl drove into the car park behind them; a couple of other girls busied themselves by pinning flowers to our friends' lapels and dresses.

When the registrar asked us if we had been married before, I lied. Judith answered 'no' she had not, and was curious as to why I had lied. The reason for this was I did not want my ex-wife from years ago to have any input into this wedding. I felt bitter that it would mar our celebrations and I did not want us to be associated with the ex-wife's name.

As the Judith and I signed the wedding book, Tina clicked away with the camera. We felt exhilarated as the knot was tied. Donna came forward and kissed her mother and spoke to me. The child was happy because we were happy.

The voices came to me when I lent over Judith as she signed the book. I tried to get as close as I could; Judith smelled fabulous and my heart felt good as it pounded with excitement. I could not wait to get inside Judith's knickers.

The voices in my head swore that this was one of the happiest days of their lives, but Judith was a witch, a very powerful and notorious witch. The voices told me that this was dangerous and that 'forever', despite the oath we had just taken, might not be the case as the times changed.

My mind was devastated. The voices had confirmed my wish to be with my new wife for the rest of my life and hers, and at the same time told me to expect change in our relationship as time went on.

I gripped hold of my thoughts and, with disgust, cursed the voices that immediately changed and praised me. The police, prison, being on the run ... one day would come to an end. I knew the voices were hinting at this.

In the limo, I whispered in Judith's ear what I wanted to do to her. We both felt very sexy and wanted each other. We reached Tennant's pub at 10.00am.

Someone went straight to the disco turntables and started to play music as friends and guests took their seats or went to the bar. Tina was still busy taking photographs.

Judith had brought a change of clothes and told me she would change in the women's toilet. She was gone only a few minutes and I followed her into the bathroom. I was greeted by Judith standing looking in the mirror, in her white stockings. I pulled her into one of the cubicles. My manhood was hard and I needed to feel her legs wrapped around me. I put the lid down on the toilet, manoeuvred my wife in a sitting position so she was facing me, and she lowered herself on to my love shaft.

We came together and still wanted more. Judith felt her stocking tops, they were elasticised, and she asked me what I thought of the patterned nylon on the tops. I loved it and kissed my wife hard.

Among the sexual feelings was the thought of our two children and the unborn baby. We felt good and a part of each other. We were living the moment in each other's eternal love.

As Judith sipped champagne, she felt sad at the thought of her mother lying ill in hospital. She would have liked her to have been present with her father at the wedding. Judith's father, predictably, had not come back to the reception and Judith reckoned if her mother had been there then her dad, with her mam, would have come to the reception for a drink.

We all had a glass of champagne and Bob was called on to give a speech, him being the best man. Quickly, he got through the speech and the friends and guests toasted Judith and I, the wedding couple.

Stood at the bar was Jimmy Charlton. His posture was akin to the Wild Man of Borneo. A strange couple came into the bar and made themselves welcome by sitting in the roped-off wedding area; Jimmy Charlton was having none of it, it made him mad that strangers should take advantage of my good graces. He stormed over, picked up one of the pair's drinks and slung it out of the door, and physically ejected the two freeloaders.

Spanish Joe had brought me a gift, a pair of handcuffs. Lucky for him that I saw the funny side. Judith interpreted the gift differently, like we had been sworn to prison and the police.

As the day wore on, Tennant suggested that the reception should go on a pub crawl. Friends and guests prepared themselves to move on. We tucked into the food to put something on our stomachs, ready for more intake of alcohol. It was about 5.00pm when the celebration split up, the free reception booze completely drunk.

Tina was looking after our kids, and they prepared to leave in the minibus. All the friends and guests decided it was time to take the minibus back, so Judith and I said our goodbyes and thanked everyone for coming to the wedding.

After a few pubs, I told Judith that we should part from the ongoing pub crawl and continue our celebration at the local nightclub, Devincies. I wanted to spend some time alone with my new wife. I rolled a spliff, which I intended to smoke with Judith in the nightclub. The place was packed to the rafters; it took a while for us to get served.

In my heart I was happy; there was no one in the world that I'd rather be with than Judith. However, I felt a pang of guilt as I missed our kids. I did not think it right that they were not included in the moment.

The flat was in darkness as we entered our home. Judith lay on the double bed. The bedside lamp light was on and it gave a romantic glow. All she wore were her black stockings. I got my kit off as Judith asked me to fuck her.

The sound of her voice went to my very soul. There was no foreplay, I was rampant. The amphetamines we had taken earlier on that night played with our feelings. The feel of her stockings on my skin drove me wild as Judith gasped with pleasure.

I withdrew myself from her and kissed my way down her body. I kissed her tits and licked her nipples, which were dark and swollen, all the time feeling her stockings on my skin as I rubbed my hands up and down her legs. Her legs were long, one of Judith's best features. My tongue reached her most intimate part, which was sodden wet with her love juices, and I probed at her clit. We had no concerns when passion overwhelmed our emotions.

Judith knew how to please me; she knew I was very demanding and sexually stimulated. This turned her on; she had a man who was 100% male – the testosterone came off me in waves.

An hour passed. I had already come once, my shaft staying hard with anticipation of our love-making, and I fucked her again. I bent her over doggy style, where the sight of Judith's swollen vulva made me want her even more.

'Fuck me, Moyley. Fuck 'es,' she insisted. I had a bird's eye view of my shaft going in and out of her like a jackhammer. Transfixed by the view and wild with lust, I rammed my wife with all the force I could muster. All that night, we fucked hard.

When we awoke, the next morning, we fucked each other good morning. Afterwards, Judith rang Steve's wife, and made sure the kids were OK. They were, and Judith arranged to pick them up that afternoon.

As we drove to Guildford via country roads, I became horny again as I watched my wife's bare feet on the pedals. I told her to pull in to a turning that led to a farmer's field. She did so and we got in the back seat. We tore each others clothes off, feeling each other. I massaged Judith's tits and, in minutes, the car's windows were steamed up.

I kissed her hard, my tongue deep in her mouth, loving the taste of her desire. We made the best of the confined space in the car and came together. Breathless, we rested in each other's arms. Time went by, love sealed in eternity, and then we drove off.

23
BETWEEN THE DEVIL AND THE DEEP BLUE SEA

One week had passed. I spent my time divided between Judith's flat and Nick's settee. It was Saturday and I phoned the number of Brown that I'd received the previous week from Alex Blackshaw. Brown wanted to see me and we arranged a meeting at Tennant's pub. I asked him how he was standing for cash and he told me he was more or less brassic.

I gave Brown £50. He had wanted to see me because he had information as to where Barrett and Evans were hiding. He told me that he'd spoken to a bloke who had told him where the pair could be found. Barrett and Evans were not drinking locally and probably wouldn't until I was off the scene. I was immediately interested.

I went and saw Pete Mercer, and asked if he still had the sawn-off shotgun we'd used in the robbery. Pete still had the gun stashed and he left to go and retrieve it for me. Steve and Harry came into the bar. It seemed that they could not do without being around me. Nevertheless, I greeted them.

Harry went off to find a drugs dealer; Steve and Harry wanted some speed and used the excuse to have a drink with me. Pete Mercer returned, I told him, along with Nick and his sidekick, what my plan was and why I needed the gun.

We decided to have a drink before we went searching for my enemies. Only time would tell if I would have luck in finding the two men I wanted to kill.

Time would likely mean prison time, for years and years. On the other hand, maybe luck would mean I could not kill the pair because I couldn't find them. It all dictated the future road I would take. How could I be so selfish? I had a beautiful wife and two gorgeous kids, and another baby on the way.

I loved my family, but at the same time I had a strong urge to kill my enemies and put paid to my uncertainties. If I kept searching, possibly, things would work out. The voices had disappeared and, for a moment, I drank deeply from my pint. I wondered if that was bad or good; it would be good if the voices would dictate the future as they had been doing up until then.

We all set off for where my enemies could be found. I would drop Steve and Harry off after I'd sorted the business of Barrett and Evans out. I had the sawn-off shotgun under my sheepskin, holstered in a makeshift pouch.

The two cars pulled into a pub car park and I told Brown to follow me. We went to the boot of Pete's car and I picked up one of the baseball bats and a ski mask. I told the other three to wait in the car until I'd had a look inside.

If there was going to be trouble I would send Brown back to tell them. I held the baseball bat under my armpit, beneath my thick sheepskin. Brown waited at the door and eyeballed the punters through the small glass window in the door. There were about 12 punters in the bar, but the pair I was after were not there. I walked through the pub, clocking the different faces, and made my way to the lounge, which was empty.

I came back in the bar and asked the landlord about the two I wanted to see. He directed me to another bar where I might find Barrett and Evans. I left the pub and told my comrades that I was going to another pub, the Black Bull.

I told Brown to drive while Pete's car followed. I was geared up for trouble and my heart beat fast with anticipation. When we got to the pub, I repeated the same plan as at the previous pub. Again, the pair weren't there and, in frustration, I ordered Brown to drive back to the first pub.

I lost my temper. It seemed that I kept hitting a brick wall when dealing with my enemies. I began to get furious and shouted at my associates what I would do when I eventually caught up with the thugs.

I thought of Judith and the first revenge on Barrett and Evans. I had to finalise this dispute, as it was affecting my thinking. I jumped out of the Princess car, pulling on the ski mask. I pulled out the baseball bat and, in broad daylight, ran along the pub smashing the windows with my weapon.

The landlord ran out and came face to face with me. Without thinking, I smashed the bat over his head. The Guildford criminals could not believe it; they watched the scene going down in amazement. I left the landlord lying on the pavement with blood streaming from a head wound, then jumped in the car and sped off with Pete Mercer following close behind.

Steve and Harry were shocked. Harry called my antics 'out of order' because him and his mate should not have been involved. This pair feared me, they always had, because I was mad and unpredictable with violence.

As I sped along doing a ton, the voices came and I began to regret what I'd just done with the baseball bat. It was madness, as the police were already looking for me over the prison escape. Now I'd have another crime to my name. This was a stupid incident that could have serious consequences. I became angrier with myself and grew agitated. I demanded contact with the voices, and the voices reminded me that any witnesses may have taken number plates of the car, which could have serious repercussions if and when I was recaptured.

The car was not registered in my name, so that was not an issue. The voices told me that I would be grassed. Suspiciously, I mentally went over who the grass might be and came to the conclusion that the most likely candidate would be Steve. How this would happen or when this would happen made me paranoid.

I lent over the back seat and pulled out the sawn-off shotgun, sticking the barrels in Steve's face. Madness and venom threw me into a deep rage. Steve pissed his pants, the hot liquid running down his legs. I threatened him with death if he ever dobbed me in for the day's events, or any other crime.

Judith's mother was close to death and had been released from hospital to die. Mrs Hannaford was on morphine for the tremendous pain she was going through as the cancer ate its way through her lungs. She had been told she had only days left to live and was best off at home where her loved ones would take care of her.

The Hannaford family arranged to have a meal as a way of medication for their mother. She told Judith that she wanted to see me, and felt it important that she spoke to me before she died. The meal was organised at the local pub in a small village called Peas Pottage. I agreed to meet Judith at the Red Lion and would talk to her mother then.

The atmosphere in the pub was nothing less than morbid, although occasionally our children livened it up. Judith's mother looked ill and stoned out of her mind at the same time, but the morphine kept her stable and allowed her to manage.

Judith had a brother called John and a sister called Sue; they were well-to-do. Mr Hannaford came to the bar and stood beside me, buying my mate and I a pint. Shortly afterwards, Mrs Hannaford came to the bar and stood beside me. She wanted to know for what reason I'd married Judith.

I held the steady, painful stare of her mother and told her that

I'd married Judith because I loved her and the kids, and wanted to spend the rest of my life with her. There seemed to be a shift in Mrs Hannaford's steely gaze and her posture relaxed somewhat as she studied my oath. It was probably a dying wish that Mrs Hannaford believed in, as she foresaw that when she was gone her daughter had married a loving man that would take care of her daughter and grandchildren.

The meal went well. The family concerned themselves with the mother, whom they wanted, for the moment, to forget her illness. I was uneasy in this morbid crowd and I wanted to get home with my wife and kids. We left in the Princess. I pulled off the main road and drove down a route that was quickest to get to our flat. There was a line of parked cars on the roadside. A blue Capri pulled out of a side road and, without warning, ran head-on into the Princess. Donna and her sister were flung on to the floor of the car.

I was immediately thrown into a vulnerable situation. Police would come as the traffic was held up behind the Princess, and I could be captured. Quickly, I thought what to do and cursed my bad luck. I pulled Donna and baby Michaela from the Princess. As I looked around, I held my kids and made sure that they and Judith were OK. The driver that had crashed into Judith was lucky; if I had not had the kids with us, then I would have annihilated the guy responsible.

I had to get off the road and told Judith to wait for the police. I took the kids and disappeared into a council estate, and got in a taxi with the kids. I was close to tears with frustration. It seemed like the odds of survival were always stacked against me.

Judith, whilst waiting for the police, managed to drive the car on to the side of the grass verge. The police surveyed the smashed car. They'd connected the Princess to one of the cars used in the Littlehampton criminal damage and GBH case. They'd also hoped to connect and recapture me through this turn of events, and hoped that when the car was collected it would lead them to me.

I telephoned a guy who had a lorry that had a crane on it for collecting scrap or crashed cars. He picked up the crashed Princess and parked it up beside his house just round the corner from where the incident had happened. He decided to scrap the car next morning. For ease, he left the Princess, which was a write-off, overnight on his lorry so he could get off first thing the next day.

The D11 watched as he went about his business. He phoned me and said that the police had raided him, and that they wanted me. Speed, to get out of the flat and back to Guildford, was imperative. Judith would take me straightaway, so we jumped in her car and sped off; the police were too slow again.

24
CRUSHED LIKE AN ANT

Since 5 November I had been home in our family flat on a regular basis. I had shown Donna how to light fireworks in the back yard, while Judith made hot dogs. I had begun to become broody about being away from the family and living out of a suitcase round at Nick's. By this time, Judith's mother had died and I felt that I had to support my wife by being there for her. I did not go to Mrs Hannaford's funeral; I stayed at home and minded Donna and baby Michaela while Judith paid her last respects.

It was Friday, 15 November. I had been staying in Judith's flat and had come and gone wearing a hat, with my coat collar pulled up to disguise myself. Not that my size would have been concealed. I had noticed that over the last three days that council workers were in the flat that looked down on Judith's front door and back yard. I had passed a couple of workers when leaving and returning to the flat. I had pushed my suspicions to one side, but the voices told me to obey my instincts.

I was in the flat while Judith got ready to pick Donna up from school. It was getting dark when she left; baby Michaela was asleep in her chair. Time went by and I became increasingly concerned as it was only a ten-minute walk there and back, yet Judith had been gone for over half an hour.

When Judith had got to the school, Donna had not come out with the other children, so Judith went into the school foyer to look for her. Two detectives from the D-11 arrested Judith and bundled her into the headmistress's office, where Donna was sitting with a policewoman. The police demanded that Judith admit I was in the flat, and said they wanted the front-door key. Judith said nothing. She was heartbroken about her daughter being interrogated and that I was about to be recaptured.

The police insisted she help in re-arresting me. They ushered Judith and Donna into a police car and escorted them to the local police station where they were interrogated. They were separated, mother and daughter, which stressed Judith out as she worried about what they were doing to Donna; she could hear Donna in the corridor asking for her mother. The police again demanded the key to the flat, but Judith claimed she did not have a key and continued to protect me until, reluctantly, she had to hand it over. The police asked her who was in the flat and Judith told them that I was looking after baby Michaela.

I watched the clock. It was dark and I felt there was something wrong. I looked out of the living-room window. The street was deserted when there usually would have been cars parked at the roadside. The worst feeling was the worry that Judith had been in an accident; the phone began to ring and my heart beat with fury.

The D11 got the tip-off that I was staying in Judith's flat through Steve and surveillance. They were desperate to get me back into custody, but they wanted me caught with a gun or drugs, something to get me sent down for many years. They had planned their move from watching Judith and I, so they knew our comings and goings.

The first part of the recapture plan was to nick Judith and Donna. The next, cordon off the two exits to Judith's flat, bring in a communications van and then the armed police. They fixed their telescopic sights on the flat.

They assumed that I had a gun, because the gun that was used in my offence had not been found, and Steve had confirmed that I was tooled up with a double-barrelled, 12-bore shotgun. The police were ecstatic that they had me cornered.

Hesitantly, I picked up the phone and heard the strange voice of a policeman that specialised in siege situations. 'Armed police,' the copper said. I immediately put the phone down and closed the living-room curtains; the police switched the spotlights on to the front door, the glow of which lit up the passageway inside. I felt desperate as armed police spoke through a loudhailer. I was in the dark and looked on at my sleeping baby, worried that the Old Bill might kill her during the arrest. As the minutes ticked by I became more anxious.

The phone rang again. I looked at the phone as if it was to blame, like a virus. The voices came to me and I relaxed a little as they dictated what the future held. I answered the phone. The police told me that they had my wife and child. I threatened the police that, if they were harmed in any way, I would kill those responsible.

The police assured me they were OK and were waiting outside the alleyway to the flat. They asked if I was armed with a gun? I told the police I did not have a gun, but I that had a 4-foot steel bar that I would smash over any copper's head that tried to come through the flat door.

I put the phone down and rang Duncan. Duncan already knew that the police had found me as the police were everywhere in the area. The call to Duncan was listened to by the police communications van as I confirmed to Duncan that I did not have a gun. The police made Judith and Donna stand out at the exit from the flats and wait.

I had not obeyed my instincts. If I'd listened to the voices then I would not have been recaptured. Whilst my enemies, the police, were surprised that I was not armed, the voices told me to take my time before handing myself in.

God Almighty told me it was not the end of the world. I'd laid down my path in life and my road was clear. I'd beaten the system for weeks, even months, and now it would be payback time as the system reaped its revenge. I was going back to jail to face the music.

The devil's voice came and told me to walk out, to give myself up while smoking, as it would make the armed police nervous. I took baby Michaela from her chair and put the little bundle into her cot. I kissed her gently on the forehead and said my goodbyes. I rolled a cigarette and opened the flat door. For a moment I was blinded by the police spotlight; I stood defiant in front of my enemies. Donna saw the whole thing: a five-year-old subjected to this.

Judith sobbed as I passed her and our daughter. I told Judith that baby Michaela was safe, sleeping in her cot, and then I was taken away.

At the local police station I was interrogated. The Chief Constable wanted me back behind bars where I was less of a risk to security, so the D11 did not have long to question me. If they wanted to interview me, they would have to arrange it with the prison.

I denied everything. I was lucky that they had no evidence, only Steve, and he was not enough to prosecute me. The next morning I was escorted in a police convoy with a helicopter overhead to HMP Lewes.

I felt a shiver run up my spine as I was driven through the prison gates. I would be subjected to the utmost of security checks on an ongoing basis. I'd be escorted by screws that would write in a book my comings and goings while in the jail.

As the cell door banged behind me, the screws switched the light out and turned on the red nightlight to observe me while sleeping. And overnight, all of my specially marked, prison-issue clothes had to be deposited on the landing side of the cell door.

Six weeks went by and I had been told by the prison Governor that my escaping offence would be dealt with by Prison Board of

Visitors, and it would up to them to decide how much remission they would take from me for escaping. And when they did eventually decide, they took 180 days from my remission. I'd been on the run for three-and-a-half months, so when the remission added up, by means of being granted 50 per cent remission, I'd lost nearly a year on top of my release date.

I walked into the Governor's office. I'd made the application to see him that morning. There was no way I would say how I had got off the island. It was made clear throughout my return to prison that the system wanted to know how this feat had come about; it meant there was a loophole in their security and I was the only man that knew this.

The men in grey suits and white collars from the Home Office wanted this information so they could close the loophole on the Isle of Wight. I decided to give them a cock-and-bull story of how I escaped from Hell Island. I would not tell the truth because I did not trust the Governor or the system – the slags had just taken 180 days from me. At the moment, the transfer back to the island was top priority for HM Prison Service.

I would do a deal so that I would be imprisoned on the mainland. I spun the Governor a yarn about catching a lift on a boat and that, within the hour, I'd reached the mainland. I gave my word to the Governor and swore that I would not cause any more problems and would serve the rest of my sentence quietly, if allowed a mainland jail.

The Governor did not believe my story and dismissed me. Shortly after this, the PO came to my cell and told me to pack my kit as I was being escorted back to the island after dinner.

On hearing this news, my mind swam in and out of consciousness; the voices came in flashes. The system had again showed it true colours. There would be no give or take from them. They would break me and smash my dreams.

It started: the voices gripped my mind and told me that I had no other choice but to fight my enemies. I had no cannabis and I was strung out as I mentally went over my life's recent events and what to do next. I craved for a joint as the voices moved me into retaliation. I moved the locker, table and chair into a straight line leading from the cell door to the back wall. I pushed my bunk into a position 18 inches from the door, enough room to slip my body in. Thinking I could be there for days in my cell protest, I made sure I could reach a jug of water as I considered how long I may have to stay put. Foolishly, I manoeuvred my body in such a way so that if the screws tried to get through the doors they'd crush me.

The voices told me to play for time, giving the voices sufficient time to manoeuvre these current occurrences. The PO and ten or so ordinary screws came up to my cell and found me wedged behind the doors and refusing to come out. The PO immediately sent word to the Prison Governor and requested to use the hydraulic jack. I could hear the enemies telling me that if I did not give up and come out, they'd hack the door open and that is exactly what they did!

They positioned the hydraulic jack and said, 'Come out now or we'll use the jack.'

As the weight of the door pressed up against me, I screamed in pain, the force of the jack crushing my spine. My screams did not stop. The screws were infuriated that their authority had been denied. In minutes they were climbing over the door. I was frozen with pain, lying on the floor. They dragged me from the cell in absolute agony. I limped as the screws pulled my arms up my back and handcuffed me. I was taken from the prison and into a waiting minibus, and ghosted to another prison.

In the minibus there were six screws. Due to the massive pain in my back, I passed out, hardly able to breathe. It was like an evil nightmare that I had no control over.

25
GHOSTED BACK TO HELL ISLAND

I arrived at HMP Albany, another prison on the Isle of Wight, a top-security dispersal prison, home for the troublemakers doing six years and upwards.

Albany had fences, gates and walls throughout the prison. It held over 400 inmates. There was just one other E-man (escape man) present in the prison and I was exercised with him.

I could not walk properly and limped badly. The pain was unbearable and was no better than when I had arrived at Albany six weeks earlier. I'd been held in the security block since I got there. The doctor eventually prescribed me Voltarol, a medication for pain that had no effect on me.

For the moment, I decided to keep a low profile, which helped to lull the suspicions of the screws. A fellow prisoner wanted a gun and asked me to sort it. I didn't have the contacts but offered to make enquiries. I spoke to the voices and they told me what to do. I went back to see the con and told him he'd have to wait, but that I could make him an incendiary bomb. This consisted of strands from a mop head that had to be new. You'd knot the strands together and they would act as a fuse to the bomb when lit. The bomb end was made of a box of matches and when the mop ends burned slowly down to the matchbox, where the fuse was pushed inside, the matchbox that was halfway open would ignite.

The device was placed in the bottom of a plastic bin that held dirty laundry along with newspapers and, when the fuse burned down and lit the bomb, it would burst into flames; the screws would have to vacate and call the fire brigade.

It was midnight. I had lengthened the fuse so it would go off when we, the prisoners, were all banged up. Within moments, the laundry rooms were in flames. The bomb had been placed in A-wing so as not to give away whom the culprit was. The whole of A-wing was evacuated and the inmates were forced to stand in the exercise yard while the fire brigade dealt with the fire; I looked out over the floodlit exercise yard.

Days passed by and the jail got back to its usual self. I was pleased that the D11 had not been to interview me. I was convinced that I'd got away with my criminal activities while I was on the run. However, life was not any easier. I was only having one visit a month from my family because of travelling difficulties.

The other seven men on my spar (section of the prison) decided to have a drink, so we all pooled together to make four gallons of hooch. It took two weeks for the booze to be ready for consumption. We all went into a cell, which was the farthest away from where the screw sat on the spar landing. The drink was strong and we all agreed it was a success and drank our fill, while rolling and smoking spliffs.

We were all concerned about our treatment from the screws and the system. The drink loosened our tongues and the cannabis delved deeply into our minds.

It was a mousy little villain who finally suggested we barricade ourselves in and finish off the drink and drugs. We began to move the furniture on to the small landing and block the gate at the end of the spar. Within minutes the gate was barricaded with all the furniture from the men's cells.

The screws immediately went into overdrive; they quickly locked prisoners up so to deal with the barricade and mini-riot. They did this to stop the riot spreading throughout the wing. As the prisoners were locked down for the night and while we celebrated with the drink and drugs, more screws from other parts of the jail were drafted in to deal with the riot.

There were close to 30 screws plus the Governor all called to the incident. We laughed and joked at the screws on the other side of the gate. We danced and goaded the screws, waving table legs, torn off our furniture, like clubs.

The screws attacked like worker ants and started to pull at the furniture from the other side of the gate. They armed themselves with riot shields and crash helmets ... truncheons at the ready. Having little to lose, we attacked. Almost all were serving over 16 years. They were subjected to the total despair of serving big prison sentences.

The prison works department arrived on the landing, armed with sledgehammers and hydraulic jacks. Every time the screws made a move to remove the barricade they were forced back by us hanging on to the barricade. The screws then began to smash a hole in my cell wall; the cell was closet to the landing. In moments they had a 4-foot hole in the cell wall, then the screws used the fire hose as I beat them back through the hole.

The water was freezing. We were all saturated, the cold water bringing our senses crashing down. The hole was made big enough for the riot squad to get through. The screws went about their task from behind Perspex shields and crash helmets.

So all in all it had been an eventful party. We'd all drunk and smoked cannabis to our extremes and, to top it all off, fought our enemies to the best of our abilities. The occasion would be remembered for the lesson that the screws gave us cons.

In the cold light of day, we were charged with various breaches of authority. I was charged with barricading and rioting, and all of us had been held in the security block for 58 days, waiting to see the Board of Visitors.

Life was difficult, the screws gave me a bad time by doing the usual antics, no showers and irregular exercise. I'd been in E-man stripes for seven months and had to put up with restrictions. My visits were cut short, which made me furious, and the screws verbally told off my wife when she visited.

They goaded me that the unborn baby was not mine and scoffed that my wife was having an affair. I lost 90 days' remission and had to serve 66 days CC in the block.

The social worker came to see me while I was in the block and informed me that my wife had given birth to a baby boy. We had already decided the name for the baby would be Ben Paul Moyle.

After the social worker left me, I sat down in my cell and thought deeply about how I could be more of a dad under the circumstances. Life had turned. I wanted to be free of my jailers. I sat and decided to write to the *Sun* newspaper, which had covered my escape. The headline in the paper had read: JAILBIRD PRISONER BECOMES A DAD.

I applied to see the Governor whilst in the block and told him that I intended to go to the papers about my treatment and abuse. Two days later, the article was in the *Sun*. I used it as a tool to be transferred. They system relented and agreed that I'd be transferred.

The Governor hated bad publicity and saw that I had some support from the media. They were not prepared to let me become a martyr and thought the easiest way to deal with the control problem was to step back and agree to my demands.

They decided to put me back in mainstream prison and do away with the E-man category. But not in Albany Prison, I was too much trouble for other cons to be tempted by getting involved with me. They decided to lift my section and transfer me to another jail where my crusade and I were less known: HMP Swaleside on the Isle of Sheppey at Sheerness, in Kent.

The prison was brand new and had only been opened recently. I was pissed off. The slags had transferred me from one island to another, although the travelling for Judith and our children was less difficult.

In all, I had lost nine months' remission and dwelled on this. The voices came to me as God Almighty's voice declared that my fight was not over yet; the devil's dwelled on my punishment and present status. I was in ordinary prisoners clothes with ordinary routine.

I kept myself to myself for a few days while I sussed out my neighbours. The voices kicked in and told me that I was imprisoned next door to an ex-police officer. Immediately, I was suspicious and at the same time annoyed that the system had situated me in a cell next to a copper.

I was invited for a drink with the other prisoners on the spar and once again cannabis was used to open our minds, and the hooch relaxed our characters. There was no denying the feeling of hate that was easily detected between the ex-copper and me.

I spoke my mind and deliberately goaded the ex-copper. I was becoming angrier as the drink took hold of my spirit. I borrowed a tin opener and went to my cell for a tin of tuna fish. The ex-copper was in his cell. His door was open and I made my move, deep and vengeful anger hidden beneath my cool composure. I confronted the prisoner, who became defiant and flustered at my confrontation. I saw the punch coming and didn't flinch; the blow caught me square on the jaw.

I reacted automatically, tin opener in hand. The short blade cut the copper across the face and he screamed in pain and frustration that his old occupation had been discovered. The copper ran past me clutching the side of his face. He ran off to the spar and went straight to the screws.

I got rid of the tin opener, throwing it in the empty cell of one of the prisoners on the spar. The screws came to my cell, made sure I was in and banged the door shut. I listened to the voices, which seemed to be excited as to where this event would lead. I hated the incident. I should have been thinking of my family and being released, rather than getting into conflicting situations.

After having dealt with a loss of further remission, I was ghosted to HMP Wandsworth. The system had had enough of my constant re-offending against authority. The Home Office ordered, after hearing of my latest offence, that I be sent back to Hell Island, this time to HMP Parkhurst, the big boys' prison. Wandsworth is the southern equivalent of HMP Durham – the pits.

After a short stay I was ghosted back to Hell Island, to the third of the three prisons on the Isle of Wight. Parkhurst Prison had a reputation as housing the elite of the criminal world, only the best would do. Most prisoners were serving ten years and upwards. It was the cons that ran the jail; Parkhurst screws were there to observe the goings on of the prisoners without getting involved. It was the top prison in Britain and its reputation proceeded itself. Long-term prisoners tried to get to Parkhurst, as the time in that prison could be constructively used.

I was unique, as I was only serving three and a half years, and the other prisoners in Parkhurst were all long term. It was a strange feeling when I walked along the landing looking at the ID cell cards on the doors. They read: life, 25 years; life, 30 years; and then my card read three-and-a-half years.

B-wing, where I was allocated, was different to any other jail I'd been in. The landings and floors of the cells were all wooden floorboards and the stairs were also made of wood. Just outside the wing was a huge boiler house with what seemed to be a 300-foot chimney for the furnace. Every night after lock-up the boiler would be switched on. The noise and vibration actually shook the floors and landings. It was used to stop cons sleeping; the vibrations kept you conscious, no matter how tired you were. The vibrations were so intense that the shaking interfered with the prisoners heartbeats; it made them beat out of time. This would happen every night, without fail.

Cannabis was used to help us cons get some sleep, and the drug was easy to get hold of. Every morning, at 6.00am, the boiler would shut down and the silence was deafening. The prisoners fell into an uneasy sleep shortly after the machinery stopped its vibrations. The early-morning sleep was immediately upset by the screws checking the cells before opening them for slop-out.

Prisoners would compete to be held in the cells on the other side of the building, where a good night's sleep was still possible. No one knew as to the way the screws allocated these cells; whether it was earned through good behaviour or because they were eligible for some other reason.

The screws had stitched me up. The cell I was held in was on the landing, right next to the stairway. The vibrations had made me ill with lack of sleep. The floorboards in my cell ran lengthways, so if you put the bed sideways against the exterior wall the vibrations would be less. But the screws had allocated a cell that had an extra-length bed in and it would only fit the cell lengthways, which made the vibrations more intense.

I became paranoid in my cell. The voices came to me and they told me to search the cell, as there was an alien present in the room. I stood up, paranoid as to what the voices meant and what I would find. Instinct took over, and in one movement I ran my hand along the steel frame of the bunk, at its head. I immediately found a small magnet, like a black penny, stuck on the steel. I examined it, my mind open. I turned it over in my hand and studied it closely. It was a bug, a listening device made to listen to and/or interfere with the workings of the prisoners' minds whilst locked in a prison cell.

I made an application to see the Governor and was granted the interview. I entered the room, closing out the daily sounds of the prison. I shouted and demanded that I be transferred to a mainland jail.

I was told straight that Parkhurst was the only prison that would accept me. I grew angry and told the Governor what I thought and swore revenge when I was released; I was dismissed and the Governor wrote in my file, violent and unpredictable, and recommended for me to stay in an A-category prison.

The screws in Parkhurst, rather than physically dish out law and order, used mental powers to control the prisoners. They rarely got involved apart from in carrying bodies that had been knifed off the wing and over to the hospital wing. One knifing a week was the usual statistic. Mostly it was over a drugs deal gone bad or, if the victim was a nonce or a beast, then he was dealt with and got rid of.

The screws would, for an experiment, every so often allocate a sex case on to an ordinary location to assess the reaction of ordinary prisoners. Whoever, it always came about that the ordinary prisoners would find out who the spies were and would deal with them quickly to get them off the wing and on to protection.

There was a Section 43, which meant that, when on this restriction, the number 43 was written on the cell cards. SECTION 43 GOVERNORS meant that you were restricted in the block for breaches of authority. There were, however, two sections of 43 and this was done so that a nonce or sex case could not be pinpointed, as prisoners could not tell whether it was GOAD (Good Order And Discipline), or a nonce or sex case on protection.

I had several visits on ordinary location, three from my wife and children and two from friends. On some visits I received an ounce of cannabis, in small bits, wrapped in cellophane that I swallowed to get through the security of the visitors room.

I began to associate with an IRA terrorist and his gopher.

Together, with two other prisoners, we would meet in the IRA's cell and drink hooch and smoke cannabis on association.

Why the screw, out of the blue, decided that I should be placed in segregation, I did not know. One dinner-hour lock-up they came to my cell and an SO unlocked my cell door and ordered me to walk to the block. I said nothing. I hated the screw and when I got on to the landing, outside my cell, I found 20 screws lining the walkways down to the block.

The screws weren't taking any chances, knowing my record and violent nature. They were prepared for the worst if I kicked off. I was banged up in the block and, once again, their system had failed.

26
THE SLEEPING DEATH

I'd been in the block a month and the screws still did not give me a reason for it. The prison Governor came to my cell and told me I was being transferred back to Albany Prison on the Isle of Wight, only a short distance away.

I felt the move was done to break my spirit; going back to Albany was like starting my sentence all over again. I was demoralised, as the move once again messed up my visits. The screws deliberately ghosted me about without giving information to my family. I was not receiving letters, as they were constantly posted to prisons I'd already been in and transferred from.

After a month in Albany's security block, I reacted violently. There was no exercise and no showers. Social workers and clergymen, vicars, all ignored my situation. They agreed with the screws and supported the way they abused me.

As I lay in my bed, the night was late and silent, and an evil spirit crept into my cell. The spirit slithered into my bed and began to crush my heart and restrict my breathing. The spirit pampered me and coaxed me to die. With irregular feelings, the evil spirit soothed me and made an attempt to take over my body and kill me. I fought my way back to consciousness and forcefully fought off the evil spirit. I sat bolt upright and made my mind work away from the darkness and into the light.

I stood up and sat on the compressed cardboard chair and rolled a cigarette. Unusually enough, the screws had given me canteen that morning, which I'd been denied for some time. So I had some tobacco and a bottle of orange, fag papers and matches.

I looked out the cell window and saw the devil through the security fences; the apparition, or physical appearance, was massive with wide shoulders and a frame that must have been seven feet tall. The image was all dark and seemed to dwell on its surroundings. The voices came and the devil told me that he was there to collect the evil spirit that had tried to kill me. God's voice told me that it was God Almighty's powers that had pulled me from sleeping death.

My door was unlocked for slopping out and the Governor came to my cell. I was told to pack my kit, I was being transferred. I, again, did not question the system but listened to the voices that told me I was on the last leg of my sentence; that's why the devil had appeared to me – it was an omen.

As I was driven the short distance to Parkhurst, I could not believe my eyes. I was convinced that my visits would stop because, once again, my correspondence was interfered with by the move. I was immediately aware that things were not as they seemed to be. It had obviously been a Home Office decision to transfer me back to Parkhurst, but this time I had been allocated to Parkhurst hospital wing.

I was escorted to a cell on the ground floor and, again denied ordinary furniture. The tables and chairs were made from compressed cardboard, like in the cells in the block.

The voices came as I stared at the cell ceiling. They toyed in good humour with my mind, then they dropped their bombshell – there would be no more transfers and I had to start planning away from the system and on to my release. I was getting a

Parkhurst discharge. My mood immediately lifted as I realised that I only had a few months left before regaining my freedom.

The voices told me that this last transfer had been done to try and nut me off, to get me committed. If I were confirmed as mentally ill, the system would not discharge me, so the voices warned me to gear down and finish the rest of my sentence quietly and not provoke the system.

I stopped eating, but emptied the leftovers of meals in to my piss pot. I was cautious not to let the screws know I was not eating properly, so made sure my steel dinner tray was clean when I put it on the landing to be collected by the cleaners.

I was allowed exercise and, as I came out of the prison wing, I breathed the fresh air deeply. I was first out and on to the path that ran around the area. There was a path that ran across the middle of the area, where there were flowerbeds and neatly cut lawns. Not knowing which direction to walk in, I cut across the middle and walked in between two lilac trees.

I felt a strange power, like an ill omen; something was tracking me. As I turned left, I looked around the exercise area and noticed about 30 prisoners walking in the opposite direction. They stopped all together and stared at me from the far end of the exercise area.

As I turned left again, to walk beside a fence, the wall was behind me. I noticed a thick black cable, partly buried on the other side of the fence. I thought the space was relaxing compared to other exercise yards I'd been in. The force of the electric charge smashed into my mind. It was so strong that it made me stagger the 30 yards along the length of the fence. It was so intense that the voices had to fight to control the charge and stop me collapsing in pain.

There were eight screws situated around the area and they looked on in amazement as I staggered up to the central path and sat down heavily, trying to keep control.

The next morning, the psychiatrist interviewed me. The screws had written a report saying I had been unsteady on my feet and quiet and reserved, and suggested that I was mentally disturbed. I sat quietly and answered the questions with a 'yes' or a 'no'.

These men were trying to destroy me and I acted as if everything was normal, remembering the warning the voices had given me. How I did this was amazing.

I managed to wrangle out of the interview with the psychiatrist by answering correctly and with the correct manner.

Although Judith was writing to me regularly, her letters had changed. I had premonitions that she'd been with another man. She seemed a lot colder in her words. It was a blow to my forthcoming release date, I suspected.

27
CARPET BURNS

My release date came and, at 8.00am on Friday, 9 May 1991, Judith waited outside the prison gates. She'd caught the 6.00am ferry to Parkhurst and had been sitting in the car for over an hour. She was nervous and contemplated how she'd feel when I walked to freedom. She was conscious that the reunion we had been waiting three years for would not go as planned.

She comforted herself by thinking of her children, rather than dwell on her shortcomings. My mother had arrived at Judith's flat the previous day and was minding the kids while Judith picked me up.

At 8.05am, I walked from the prison to where she was waiting. My mind was full of uncertainty for the future. There was no comfort in my mind and in my heart I knew Judith had changed; changed from total devotion to one of harsh reality.

I toyed with what had made Judith stray? In my mind I came up with the affair I'd had with Paula, an affair that had produced a baby! I did not know how close to the mark my explanation was. Judith searched my face as I walked up to her, putting my box of keepsakes on the ground and taking her in my arms and swinging her around.

On the ferry we looked over the side of the ship, watched Hell

Island drift into the distance. We held hands as we watched the source of our pain fade into the background.

My conversation was strained as I tried to ignore my fears over Judith's possible infidelity so I could enjoy the feelings of this long-awaited release.

Arriving home I tried to put aside my suspicions as I greeted my three children and Mrs Moyle, our babysitter. Tears sprang to my eyes as I took in the mood of my kids and mother.

I lent Judith over the bath and shoved my cock in her from behind. I was crestfallen as I saw two carpet burns on the base of her spine.

I fucked her hard. The love drained from me as I dealt with the suspicion that my wife had been with another man. I came quickly as Donna knocked on the bathroom door. I wanted to tell Judith how much I loved her and needed her, wanted her, but the words stuck in my chest. I did not mention the carpet burns, deciding that I did not want to listen to her lies as she tried to explain the marks away. I doubted that she even knew the marks were there, but nothing would surprise me.

We got in the bath together. It was hard for me to speak my mind; it moved backwards and forwards in my head as I thought of how best for my family and I should enjoy the day we'd waited so long to see.

I manoeuvred my wife's legs open wide in the bath and fucked her again. When I came I withdrew, the sperm leaving white strands in the water. I had premonitions as to someone else doing what I had just done to my wife.

Now I was dealing with another sentence, even more painful than being incarcerated in prison. This was one of lies and rejection as I blamed myself for Judith's possible affair. Why this might come about so close to the end of my prison sentence, I just did not know. Donna was nearly seven years old and looked the spitting image of me. I split my affection between my children and spoke to my mother at the same time.

I had been home three days now. My mother had slept on the sofa and she was ready to go home. I decided to take my family on holiday to Scotland, and decided to take Mum home and spend a few days at her house before we left for Scotland.

Donna loved her nana's house and met all her cousins. They played in the alleyway and the street out side the house without a care in the world. Now that her dad was back she loved every minute.

I loved the feeling of being home, back in the north-east and free from jail. The voices came: God Almighty said that I should move back to the north-east with my family permanently. I dwelled on the fact that I was losing Judith. Slowly but surely we were drifting apart. The carpet burns were still fixed in my mind and my heart. I considered that, if we moved up to the north-east, maybe I could rebuild my relationship, as we would be miles away from the affair.

The devil told me I should reject Judith and leave her, and that she'd cheated and was now soiled by another man's seed. I decided to keep up the pretence of happy families until we had finished our holiday.

Blindly, without a map and full of anticipation, we began our journey to Scotland. I had left the two Staffordshire bull terriers with my mum, so it was Judith, the three children and I.

It was a complete character change from Judith that steadily broke my heart. I felt denied and used as I considered the possibility of my wife with another man. Judith knew what she was doing; she was playing games with her witchcraft, causing mental pain to me, her husband. She'd found out about the baby I had fathered to another girl. She'd known this only three weeks and was devastated. It was Duncan's wife that had told her.

She hated what I'd done. For three years she'd been lied to and felt abused, and her trust was in shreds. In her own mind, Judith had decided to leave me once we had returned home from Scotland.

We spent time travelling around and drove through Inverness to admire the scenery; the hills and mountains were infectious. Judith was drunk and I was left to drive. We came to the coast. The beach was sandy and full of holidaymakers enjoying the summer sun.

I woke Judith up and the family piled out of the car. We bought sandwiches, crisps and soft drinks, along with a bottle of whisky from the bar we'd just visited.

Unbeknown to us, the Scottish landlady of the place we'd just left had phoned the local police and reported Judith and I for drink-driving, and explained to the police that we also had children in the car. The cow had told the police the colour and make of the car, and the number plate and what direction we had headed off in.

It was teatime and my family had all been happy playing on the seaside; the tide was out as Donna played at the waterside.

Judith now took the wheel. She was drunk and still swigging from the whisky bottle with me. The hotel in the middle of the countryside was called the Nags Head. They had no rooms available so I decided to get the family some drinks from the bar. The bar was empty but for a few locals. I ordered two double whiskies, two double vodkas and orange, and soft drinks for the kids.

A plain-clothes police officer followed me into the car park and stopped me when I got to the car. The police officer confronted me, having received information earlier that day about me, my family and the drink-driving. I ignored the officer and the copper jumped on my back. The drinks spilled and I was in a fight. Within minutes, a police car had arrived with reinforcements.

Judith got out of the car, screaming and shouting until she, too, was restrained. The kids started crying at the sight of the police arresting their mam and dad. After a struggle I was bundled into the back of the police car.

They took the three children into care. Judith and I were dealt with in court the next day. The police removed my cuffs and I was charged with assault on the police, breach of the peace and being drunk in charge of children. Judith's charges were the same, except she was also charged with drunk driving.

We were to appear in Thorpe Sheriff's court that morning and were escorted to face the Sheriff. We were bailed to appear four months hence to answer the charges against us. Social Services were in court and noted that we were not drunk, and were a caring family, but we would have to appear that afternoon in front of a panel that would decide whether Judith and I were fit to get our kids back from care.

28
SMASHING MY WORLD TO SMITHEREENS

The social worker gave us an address and a time to appear in front of the panel. Judith had repercussions as to what would happen if her children were taken away permanently. I assured Judith that this would not happen. I fished a lump of cannabis from a pair of dirty underpants in the car and skinned up a spliff, pleased that the police search had missed it.

I entered the interview room stoned out of my mind. There was a panel of six people sat around a large table. These people were social workers and care workers that would decide if we were fit to be responsible parents and have the children back. The mood of the room was as if the panel members were the enemy and were there solely to split up the family.

We were questioned as to why we had been drunk with our kids in tow. I told the panel that I'd recently been released from prison and was celebrating my freedom by being with my family and getting drunk. I apologised and told the panel I was ashamed and that the events that had led up to that point would not happen again.

I told the panel that it had been I that had bought the drink and insisted that my wife drink with me. Right on cue, Judith started to sob into a tissue.

They decided that the children should be handed back to us the next day. We went and found a hotel room, the address of which was forwarded to the social workers by phone so they knew where the meeting place would be to return our children.

We did not have to wait long and were excited and happy, relieved to get the kids back. Donna ran to us, happy to see us. The baby and toddler were handed to Judith, who mothered them.

The mood was solemn as we set off home via my mother's to pick up our two dogs. Judith planned her move as we set off home with the dogs. We got home at 10.00pm. The kids were tired and we put them to bed.

Judith opened here legs wide. She lay on the settee naked. I shoved my cock in her sweet fanny and fucked.

Once in bed, I reached over in search of Judith but she was not there, and there was a deadly silence in the house. I cocked my ear and listened to the silence. There was no wife rattling about in the kitchen and no kids playing. I got up, aware that all was not well. The house was empty and I wondered where my family was. The car was not parked out front and I thought, maybe, Judith had taken the kids to the shop.

As I read a note that had been left on the mantelpiece my world was smashed to smithereens. Judith had left me, and the one line that said it all was: 'You are not the man I married and I do not love you any more.'

I thought the worst and tried to deal with the pain in my heart and soul. She'd left me, taken our kids. For four days I searched. I'd walked the two Staffordshire bull terriers while looking for my family. All our friends had been searched and none of them had seen Judith and the kids; they had disappeared and I became more anxious.

It was 11.00pm and I walked back from the local pub, the Johnson. I was pissed and torn apart by the events. I stopped at the garden gate and surveyed the car that had just pulled up at the roadside.

Judith got out and I was stuck for words. In my chest, deep in my heart, I played with the worst thoughts of what could be happening with my family. Judith needed clothes for the kids and herself. She'd also ran out of money; as our account was joint she needed my signature as well as her own to make a withdrawal. The family had been staying in a hotel in Honley, and Judith's circumstances had led her to return home.

She made it clear that she was going to divorce me and that I would not see the children ever again. The kids were asleep and I felt compelled to check up on them. It was strange, my two daughters tucked up in bunk beds and Ben asleep in his cot in the other room.

God Almighty's and the devil's voices trickled through my mind as I looked at my children. I was angry and God Almighty told me to be wary; the devil told me that there was an answer to my pain, and foretold that I would be locked up again soon and that there was nothing I could do about it.

I confronted Judith, who was in the kitchen making a cup of tea. She ignored my questions and answered me with grunts. I grew angry and asked if she had been with someone else.

She blanked my demands for information. I acted with aggression. She was deliberately winding me up by not answering. I spun Judith away from the cup of tea she was making and slapped her around the face. Judith was shocked, this act of violence shaking her reality. Previously I had never laid a finger on her.

She clawed my face with her nails. I wiped the blood from my face and punched her in the head, not wanting to mark her face. I forced my will on her and demanded the name of the man I thought she'd been with over the last four days. Judith insisted she had been in a hotel.

The conflict subsided and she went to the bedroom, and decided to get away from me by changing into her clean nightie. As she tried to put her nightie on I slapped her again. All she had on were her knickers and bra. I was stimulated at the sight of her in her bra and panties as she ran into the bathroom and locked the door. I went back into the living room, sat down on the settee and pondered the disaster of my life.

As I heard the front door open, I quickly jumped up and ran into the hallway. I saw Judith in her knickers and bra run up the garden path and on to the main road. The two Staffordshire bull terriers ran after her. Driven by fear and loss, I also chased after her.

She ran into a garden and banged on the door. There was no answer. I was devastated that Judith had involved some outsider in our argument. I took hold of her by the hair and dragged her from the garden. The two bull terriers jumped about excitedly, thinking we were playing. They jumped upon Judith as I dragged her on to the road by the hair.

The bull terrier bit Judith's arm and locked its jaws. I was dragging Judith and the dog at the same time. The skin on Judith's left arm tore into shreds like paper. She screamed for help but there was no one around.

As I got Judith into the light of the passageway I saw the deep wounds caused by the dog that refused to let go. I was choked at the wounds the dog had caused and kicked it off her. Quickly I ran a bath and carried Judith to the bathroom, gently putting her in the tub.

There was a knock on the door. It was the police. One of the neighbours had reported the disturbance. I eyed the two coppers and casually said there was nothing wrong. I called to Judith and asked her to reassure the police that all was well. She shouted she was OK and I slammed the door on the coppers.

I went back to the bathroom and closely examined my wife's wounds. I knew Judith would have to go to the hospital. I helped her from the bath, gave her a towel and handed her a dressing gown. Her left arm hung limp at her side as she struggled to get her other arm through the sleeve of the dressing gown.

The hospital was quiet and reception was not busy. The receptionist looked at Judith and pointed her towards a wheelchair, and told us which way to go for casualty. I told Judith to tell the nurses that she'd been in a motorbike accident that had involved barbed wire.

I wheeled her into an emergency room that had a reclining bed, and lifted her from the wheelchair on to the bed. Two nurses examined her injuries. Judith whispered in the nurse's ear and told her that I had been responsible for her condition. She said that she feared for her life and wanted the police to arrest me. The nurse immediately phoned the police.

I could not wait any more. I would have to leave and get home to see to the kids, worried that they may have woken up and found they were all alone. I came out of the hospital and walked straight into a waiting police car, but they only watched me drive out of the hospital and that is when they went to interview Judith.

They took a statement from Judith regarding the assault, and Judith asked that her father be notified of the events leading up to the hospital. The local police seemed not to be surprised that I had walked straight into a GBH charge, this time against my own family.

I checked the kids and made sure they were all safe and sound. The knock on the door screamed police, and the memory of the voices telling me I would be locked up again sprang to my mind.

Eventually I opened the front door where I was arrested for GBH. Judith's father stood beside the police and, as I was cuffed, Mr Hannaford came into the house to mind our kids until Judith returned home the next day.

29
NUTTED OFF

The voices of God Almighty and the devil sent me a present; alone in a dingy-smelling police cell I was awarded Three Queens Spiritual. One apparition was from my past, the second was for the assault on my wife, and the other was for strength to face the future and rebuild my faith.

The voices assured me I was in the right and had acted accordingly and correctly towards the woman I loved. It was the loss of my children that began to concern me. Although my marriage was over with, I still loved and needed me children.

A relationship with my kids 'would happen' said the voices, but it would be many years to come before my kids and me would meet and build a relationship. My wife would be the one to try and stop a relationship with my kids and I had to be aware of this.

Three Queens for three episodes did not end the pain inside me. I was on my way back to jail. I'd been released only three months earlier and now I was back behind bars in HMP Lewes.

Judith and the kids moved house and did not inform me of the address. She was awarded a house because of the offence and because she did not want me to know where she lived in case I attacked her and the kids.

They say a boy's best friend is his mother – well ... my mother travelled the 300 miles to visit me, bringing me clean clothes and food.

My body and face bore the scars of my love for Judith, and it had all been for nothing. The past love we had shared was shattered. My application for bail was turned down as my case was passed on to the Crown Court. The system that would not let the escape saga pass over had got their revenge; I was going to prison for a very long time.

There was one place in prison that was worse than the punishment block and that was the hospital wing, where nutters and nonces resided. They screws reported my behaviour as being strange and said that I was unaware of my surroundings. They escorted me to see the psychiatrist in the hospital wing. I was then committed to the hospital wing, and there was nothing I could do about it.

I was situated on the two's landing. The screws refused me a bed and just gave me a mattress on the floor. I lost a lot of weight as the food was shit, although it was not like it had been in Parkhurst. Despair set in as I received my divorce papers. The legal letter made me think of how much I had loved my wife and how unbelievably sad I was at the loss of my children.

As the date of my trial grew closer, God Almighty and the devil's voices came to me and advised me on my case. They did not go in to detail about how much time I would get, only that it would be a very long time.

Simon Scamell Solicitors, whose reputation for winning court cases I already knew of, visited me in Lewes's hospital wing and informed me that the prosecution was going to ask the judge that I should receive a hospital sentence, rather than send me to prison for a long time.

I sat in front of Judge Crocker. I had decided to plead guilty on the strength that my sentence would be less. Judith sat in the public gallery with her family. Her brother and sister kept Judith calm and Mr Hannaford contemplated what the prosecution was saying. The prison psychiatrist was called as a witness and was questioned about my mental condition.

I listened and eyed the judge, not at all happy to be in front of the same judge that had sentenced me previously. The woman psychiatrist spoke clearly to the prosecution's line of questioning. She then did a strange thing as she was being questioned on her thoughts about my mental illness. She kicked her leg out and asked, 'Have I got shit on my foot?' The whole court heard her make the statement and looked at the judge to see what he thought. Then the psychiatrist started her bombshell, quoting from a report in front of her, which read that I had told officers that I did not want to go to an RSU (Regional Secure Unit), and would escape as soon as I could.

I was angry and shouted from the dock that this declaration was not the case and I'd never said that. Simon Scamell had organised an independent doctor to examine me, as he expressed concerns about my mental condition. He had stated that I was suffering from schizophrenia. The judge told me to be silent.

The prison had investigated my incarceration and planned for me to go to Broadmoor by making certain I was a security risk. My mother sat in the public gallery; she shed a few tears as she foresaw me being sentenced.

Scamell's barrister made it clear that I was not mentally ill and did not warrant being diagnosed as a paranoid schizophrenic. He asked the judge to sentence me to prison, and by pleading guilty I had admitted my guilt and involvement. I regretted what had happened and apologised to my ex-wife.

The judge was not swayed by the attempt at mitigation and decided to sentence me on the strength of reports from the prison's hospital wing. The atmosphere in the court was expectant; the clerks, secretaries and legal teams all watched the judge do his summing up. The judge had agreed that I was mentally ill and had not been responsible for my actions.

In the bus the voice of God came to me, the devil did not. The voice warmed my heart with admiration. Then the devil's voice came to me and reminded me that I would be able to have a smoke as soon as I got back to the jail. I had obeyed the no-smoking laws in the court and the cells. The screws made sure of this by confiscating the cigarettes and tobacco – the game had just begun.

I was escorted to the hospital wing where my own clothes were confiscated and I was issued with prison clothes. It was around 5.00pm and we were opened up for tea. I walked out from the cell I was in, down a set of stairs. The glass booth for visiting stood at the foot of the stairs. Both God Almighty and the devil entered my soul as I manoeuvred down the stairs. I'd lost my family and had received a life sentence. Dwelling on these things, I went into overdrive.

I ran down the last few steps and charged the glass booth with my head bowed. The window shattered as I hit the glass. I wanted to hurt myself badly. Locked doors, bars, walls and razor-wire fences – I had nothing to live for. As the glass bit in to my head and neck, I hoped I'd die.

EPILOGUE

Injected with massive amounts of anti-psychotic drugs, I was restrained in the padded cell, my face and neck held together by crude stitches. The following morning I was shipped out to Broadmoor Special Hospital ... sectioned off as a psychopath!

I was labelled 'criminally insane'. The voices came to me, and God Almighty and the devil assured me I would have my day in court to settle this matter, although I was not clear how I'd achieve this ... but I would. I would have my day in court.

Herein, the story of my sanity ends, but then there's the story about the insane times I spent with all the infamous madmen in Broadmoor, and how a law named after me, 'Moyle's Law', came about, but that's another story. Stay sane, Stephen Moyle ... a decent sort of psychopath.

Other titles by Stephen Richards
available from John Blake Publishing

Insanity: My Mad Life
Charles Bronson with Stephen Richards
ISBN: 1844540308

The Krays and Me
Charles Bronson with Stephen Richards
ISBN: 1844540421

The Good Prison Guide
Charles Bronson with Stephen Richards
ISBN: 1844540227

The Lost Girl
Caroline Roberts with Stephen Richards
ISBN: 1843581485

It's Criminal
James Crosbie with Stephen Richards
ISBN: 1844540596

Street Warrior
Malcolm Price with Stephen Richards
ISBN: 1904034632

Lost in Care
Jimmy Holland with Stephen Richards
ISBN: 1844541614

Crash'n'Carry
Stephen Richards
ISBN: 1844541061

The Taxman
Brian Cockerill with Stephen Richard
ISBN: 1844541347

Viv Graham, Britain's Most Feared Gangster
Stephen Richards
ISBN: 1844541274

Hailey's Story
Hailey Giblin with Stephen Richards
ISBN: 1844541916

Scottish Hard Bastards
Jimmy Holland and Stephen Richards
ISBN: 1844542424

Fight to the Death: Viv Graham and Lee Duffy –
Too Hard to Live, Too Young to Die
Stephen Richards
ISBN: 1844542459

Born To Fight
Richy Horsley with Stephen Richards
ISBN: 1844540960